C000235884

COLD WAR INTERCEPTOR

COLD WAR
INTERCEPTOR
The RAF's F.155T/O.R. 329 Fighter Projects

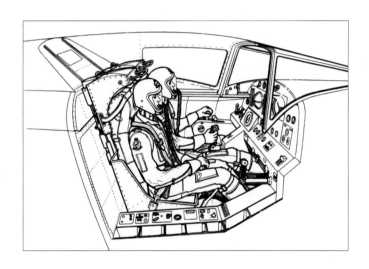

Dan Sharp

TEMPEST
BOOKS

First published 2017
This edition 2019

ISBN: 978-1-911658-03-0

All rights reserved. No part of this
publication may be reproduced or
transmitted in any form or by any
means, electronic or mechanical,
including photocopying, recording,
or any information storage retrieval
system without prior permission in
writing from the publisher.

© Dan Sharp 2019

Tempest Books
Mortons Media Group
Media Centre
Morton Way
Horncastle
Lincolnshire LN9 6JR
Tel. 01507 529529
www.mortonsbooks.co.uk

FRONT COVER:
Fairey Large two-seat fighter by
Daniel Uhr.

To Tony Wilson, whose
unfailing support made
this book possible.

Contents

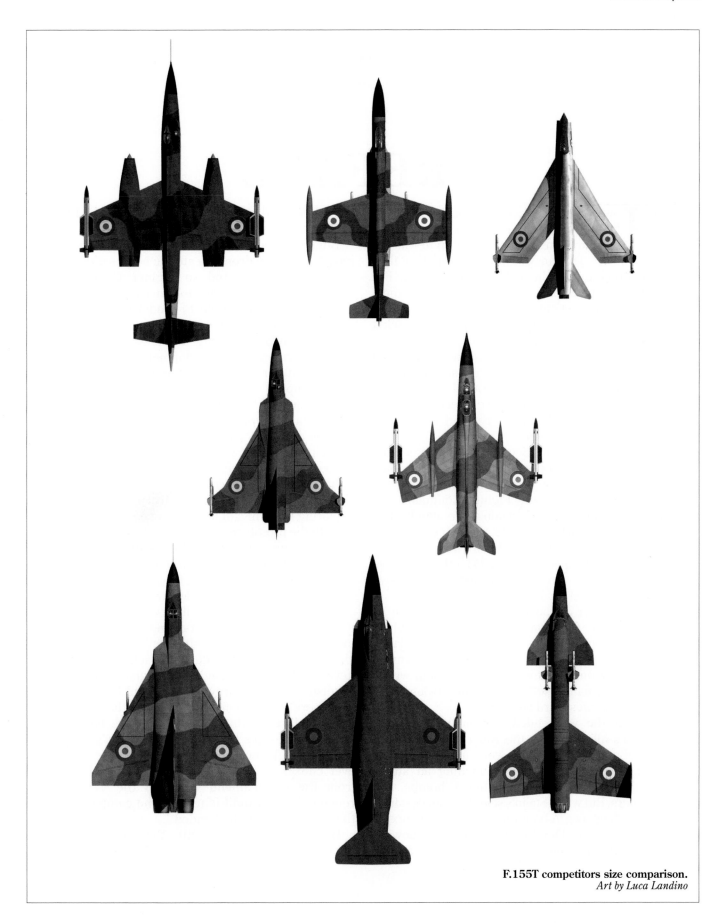

F.155T competitors size comparison.
Art by Luca Landino

1

PREFACE

How do you stop a wave of Soviet bombers flying straight for Britain armed with nuclear bombs at speeds of up to Mach 2 at 60,000ft? The answer is you launch a fleet of interceptors at them, flying even faster. For that sort of performance you'll need the most powerful turbojet engines in the world – and even then you'll need to add some advanced rocket motors for extra grunt.

And you'll need the very latest passive infrared or active radar-guided air-to-air missiles to ensure a solid kill during that final, critical attack. If the interception fails there won't be a second chance, and just that one bomber's payload will wipe a British city off the map.

But it's 1954 – the Second World War ended less than 10 years ago and the RAF's only just retired its last Spitfires. Throughout the darkest days of the war, Fighter Command had been Britain's bulwark against air attack. The organisation, formed in 1936, was an aerial shield during the Battle of Britain before being split into two parts during November 1943 – the defensive Air Defence of Great Britain and the offensive Second Tactical Air Force.

The former organisation, soon to return to the Fighter Command name, fielded fighter aircraft to protect the British Isles. The latter organisation flew fighters against the Germans on the Continent before setting up camp within (West) Germany itself to deter the Soviets from any further westward advances.

When the war ended, the new shield was Britain's alliance with the Americans and their atom bomb. The Soviets were unlikely to risk their own annihilation by launching an attack on the West using conventional bombs and bombers. But when Stalin's scientists successfully tested their own A-bomb in 1949, the balance of power shifted. The Korean War the following year then demonstrated how, without a one-sided nuclear threat, the 'cold war' could quickly become a 'hot war'.

But if the Soviets did attack Britain, they would have to do so by dropping atomic bombs directly over the country. And so Fighter Command became the nation's protector once again.

There was a scramble to modernise Fighter Command's aircraft and equipment, which had become outdated during the austerity years. New programmes of development commenced and existing programmes were, where possible, speeded up.

The injection of cash that made this possible sparked a new golden age of aviation for Britain, and the country's famous aircraft manufacturers participated in a succession of competitions for lucrative contracts to build powerful new fighters. Exotic experimental aircraft appeared, showcasing Britain's technological prowess while exploring the limits of performance.

Both the prototypes and the production aircraft were, in many cases, as well known then as they are today. But they weren't the whole story. The thing about 'secret' aviation projects is that most people are not supposed to know about them.

While the RAF and the civil servants supporting it wrestled with the ever-changing and often unclear nature of the threat posed by the Soviet Union's air force – that fleet of Mach 2 bombers never really materialised – companies such as English Electric, Fairey, Hawker and Saunders-Roe were busy designing aircraft that could defy that threat. A huge amount of work was put into these designs by some of the nation's most talented engineers but only a select few were ever chosen to receive a development contract from the Government. Many of the 'rejects' remained secret until long after the competition that spawned them had ended.

Having grown up with the concept of Supermarine Spitfires fighting Messerschmitts during the Second World War, and the regular stand-off between English Electric Lightnings and various types of probing Soviet bombers during the Cold War, I felt as though I was familiar with British fighter aircraft.

The Lightnings disappeared, to be replaced by Tornados, and still it simply did not occur to me that for every fighter I knew of, every aircraft design that reached production, there were others that never made it. In the late 1990s, my eyes were opened to the concept when a friend pointed out luft46.com, a website showcasing the weird, wild and sometimes wilfully obscure aviation rejects produced by Nazi Germany.

It seemed somehow appropriate that the 'bad guys' should have come up with so many failures while the mighty British Spitfire went from strength to strength, each new mark giving it an ever-increasing lead over the enemy's machines. Then updates to the website ceased and I decided to carry out a little research on these curious aircraft designs for myself – using original wartime documents rather than other people's books for information, these often being full of confusing and contradictory information.

A few years later, I happened upon a book called British Secret Projects: Jet Fighters Since 1950 by Tony Buttler. This proved to be full of British jet fighters which never left the drawing board – some good, some bad, some beautiful and some downright ugly. Buttler's book differed from German 'projects' volumes in being very coherent and well set out. There was a logical progression of projects and some historical background to indicate why they arose and why they failed. I resolved to broaden the scope of my own primary source research to include British cold war designs.

The fighters that interested and intrigued me most in Buttler's original book were those designed shortly before it was decided that Fighter Command should, once again, be divested of its position as the nation's aerial safeguard in favour of the V bomber deterrent and guided weapons that had yet to be fully developed.

Each of the huge interceptors designed to meet that deadly wave of Mach 2 Soviet bombers was, in its own way, a technological wonder. Any of them could have been built – providing the RAF with an advanced fighter that would no doubt have become a legend in its own time. The fact that none of the competitors reached the finishing line before the race was prematurely ended is undeniable and unfortunate, yet I cannot help but wonder what a squadron of Fairey interceptors might have looked like flying overhead...

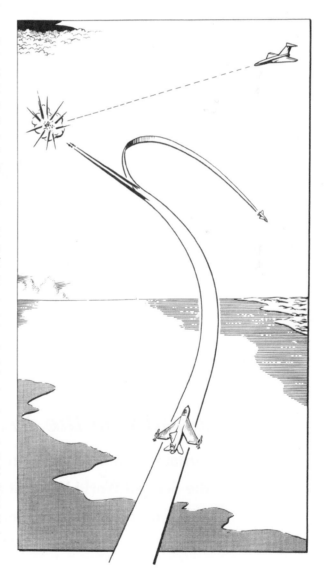

2

INTRODUCTION

Rebuilding the RAF: 1950 to 1955

Britain spent five years stripping back the RAF after
the Second World War but all that changed when the
Soviet Union revealed the terrifying extent of its postwar
technological progress...

When the Korean War began on June 25, 1950, 10 of RAF Fighter Command's 44 squadrons were still equipped with Supermarine Spitfires while another six were flying de Havilland Mosquitos and four more the piston-engined de Havilland Hornet.

Most of the remaining 24 squadrons were flying outdated early marks of Gloster Meteor or de Havilland Vampire jet fighters. Just six had the latest Meteor – the F.8. None of the aircraft were equipped with air-to-air missiles, relying instead on Hispano 20mm cannon, and only the night fighters carried radar.

And 13 days before the outbreak of war, the Chief of Air Staff Sir John Slessor held a meeting where it was agreed that the size of Fighter Command should be reduced to just 28 squadrons – 15 for day fighters, 10 for night/all-weather fighters and three for long-range/intruder fighters.

At the end of the Second World War, Britain was heavily in debt to the United States and the Labour government, under Clement Attlee, made establishment of the welfare state its priority. Funding was stripped away from the armed forces and the RAF in particular suffered severe cuts. It had been expected there would be no further major conflict for a decade and hence no need for new fighter aircraft until 1957.

Defence spending plummeted from 52% of GDP in 1945 to just 6% in 1950 as the nation's resources were diverted elsewhere. Research budgets for new developments in aviation were squeezed hard, resulting in the abandonment of promising projects such as the Miles M.52 supersonic research aircraft.

The parlous state of the RAF's equipment at this point was alleviated only a little by the prospect of the de Havilland Venom on the horizon – still two years away from entering service – and the more distant F.3/48 (the Hawker Hunter, entering service in 1954) and F.4/48 (the Gloster Javelin, entering service in 1956).

However, Attlee had little choice but to significantly increase defence spending when the threat posed by the Soviets began to take on a whole new dimension; it was revealed in September 1949 that the Soviets had successfully tested their own atomic weapon. And the Korean War showcased completely unforeseen developments in Soviet technology – specifically the Mikoyan-Gurevich MiG-15 jet fighter.

It had been thought that the Soviets were years away from developing the A-bomb and during the war years, Soviet aircraft was derided as basic, simplistic and inferior. Now it was clear that Stalin's forces had taken huge steps towards closing the perceived technological gap between East and West.

No RAF fighter units were sent to fight in Korea, but the Australian RAAF's 77 Squadron operated Meteor F.8s against Soviet MiG-15s and found themselves entirely outmatched. The best British fighters had, at last, been comprehensively surpassed by those of the enemy and for a nation which had prided itself on its world class aerial prowess just five years earlier, this knowledge came as a deeply unpleasant surprise.

When the Korean War began in June 1950, nearly a quarter of Fighter Command's squadrons were still equipped with Spitfire Mk.16s, Mk.21s and Mk.22s. PK312 was the first production model F.Mk.22. *Author's collection*

Ordered shortly after the beginning of the Korean War, the Supermarine Swift was meant to complement the Hunter but it was rushed into production before its inherent early design flaws had been ironed out. This example is seen in November 1954 undergoing engine tests at Vickers-Armstrongs' South Marston facility. *Author's collection*

Three months after the beginning of the Korean War, in September 1950, the Supermarine Swift was also ordered into production (entering service in 1954). This followed test flights of the company's experimental Type 535 – a development of the Royal Navy's Supermarine Attacker. For 1951 as a whole, the total spent on defence rose to 9.86% of GDP and after Sir Winston Churchill won the General Election in October it continued to rise, peaking at 11.17% in 1952.

In addition, over in the US, President Harry S Truman had signed the Mutual Defense Assistance Act on October 6, 1949 – the first US military foreign aid spending since the Second World War. This made additional funding available to the British government which could be spent on buying new aircraft from British manufacturers.

This abrupt injection of fresh resources coming hot on the heels of a five-year wind down would have a dramatic effect on those parts of the government charged with commissioning, ordering and purchasing equipment for the RAF and Royal Navy.

It was the job of the senior RAF officers at the Air Ministry, the Air Staff, to work out exactly what sort of aircraft and equipment their front line units were likely to need, based on the sort of operations they would be expected to carry out in the event of a conflict, and come up with an Operational Requirement (OR) outlining them.

The Ministry of Supply's technical specialists would then act as a buffer between the 'end user' RAF and Britain's aircraft manufacturing companies by drawing up detailed Specifications for particular aircraft or items of equipment, based on the OR. The Specification would then be presented to those companies chosen to tender for the job of developing and making the desired kit.

Once an agreement had been reached with one or more companies to supply a particular design, a decision on whether to proceed would be taken by the Minister of Defence. Assuming he agreed to go ahead with the procurement, and assuming the Treasury agreed that the necessary finances were available, the company would be presented with a development contract. This was

The appearance of the Mikoyan-Gurevich MiG-15 during the Korean War stunned the West and prompted a surge in funding for the RAF. *Planes of Fame*

The Gloster Meteor F.3 became obsolete in 1945 when it was superseded by the F.4, but was in service with RAF auxiliary squadrons during 1950. *Author's collection*

the formal process, but in practice there was usually a great deal of debate, delay and then departure from it in one way or another.

While work on the Hunter, Swift and Javelin continued, as an interim measure the Government signed a deal to purchase 430 Canadair CL-13 Sabre Mk.4s – a licence-built version of the North American F-86 Sabre, the only fighter capable of facing the MiG-15 on anything like equal terms – so 370 of them could be stationed in West Germany as part of a 4000-strong fighter force intended to deter Soviet aggression. The remaining 60 would be allocated to Fighter Command in the UK. The deal, part-funded by US military, was agreed in early 1953.

Britain's aircraft manufacturers had not been idle during the five-year funding drought, however. English Electric first submitted a brochure for its proposed transonic fighter, the P.1, in November 1948, leading to the construction of a mock-up in April 1949, the drafting of a new requirement based on it in May 1949 (OR.268), and finally the issuing of a full specification for it (F.23/49) in April 1950.

The prototype Hawker Hunter, WB188. The Hunter was the RAF's first truly postwar fighter yet it did not arrive in service until nine years after the war ended. *BAE Systems*

When the extra money became available, though, rather than simply ordering the P.1 into production or cancelling it, an Experimental Requirement (ER) was issued for a one-off aircraft that would provide research data for the P.1 project. In practice, ER.100 was issued on October 28, 1950, and resulted in the Short S.B.5. When it finally flew in 1952 it essentially just proved that the design of the P.1 was sound – something English Electric had been saying all along.

Meanwhile, Fairey too had submitted a proposal for an experimental high-speed design, in September 1948. This evolved into a series of delta wing designs by April 1949, and in May 1950 these saw off competition from Armstrong Whitworth. A contract to build two prototypes was finally placed in October 1950. A new specification was written around the Fairey design, ER.103, and it would ultimately be built as the World Record-breaking Fairey Delta 2.

Guided weapons

Another key area of aviation and aerial weaponry research which

The Gloster Javelin was the RAF's new all-weather fighter but did not enter service until 1956, when it was arguably already obsolete. Efforts to develop the design would be overtaken by events. *BAE Systems*

received additional funding after the beginning of the Korean War was missiles and rocket propulsion.

When the Allies defeated Germany and ended the Second World War in Europe, Britain and America gathered up as much information about advanced German missile and rocket technology as they could find. The British in particular were more interested in missiles and rockets than they were in German work on aerodynamic innovations such as swept wings and area rule.

Thousands of technical drawings were gathered showing every component of missiles including the V-2, Messerschmitt's Enzian surface-to-air missile, the Ruhrstahl X-4 air-to-air missile, Rheinmetall-Borsig's Rheintochter surface-to-surface missile and many more.

The capture of Dr Hellmuth Walter and his Walter Werke facility at Kiel in May 1945 also provided a wealth of information about high-

test peroxide (HTP) fuelled rocket powerplants such as the HWK 109-500 rocket-assisted take-off engine, the Messerschmitt Me 163 B's HWK 109-509A and the Me 263's dual-chamber HWK 109-509C.

Germany saw liquid-fuelled rockets as the perfect propulsion system for point defence interceptors, the incredible speed and rate of climb they provided more than outweighing their primary drawback – very poor endurance. The Me 163 B, for example, burned through its entire fuel supply in just seven and a half minutes at continuous maximum thrust.

Less than a year after thewar's end, the Royal Aircraft Establishment (RAE) at Farnborough set up a Controlled Weapons Department. In April 1946, the Rocket Propulsion Establishment (RPE) was formed at Westcott, Buckinghamshire – staffed by British and German

rocket scientists working together. The former was soon renamed the RAE Guided Weapons Department and the latter eventually also became a division of the RAE.

While funding was being sapped from the rest of the military research programme, spending on guided weapons research increased steadily during the 1945-1950 period and most of the major aircraft manufacturers – notably de Havilland, Bristol, English Electric and Fairey – established guided weapons divisions to take advantage of this additional source of revenue.

Prior to the Korean War, the Fairey-developed radar-guided solid fuel rocket-propelled Red Hawk missile had appeared to be the most promising air-to-air guided missile project. However, it was believed that this would not become available until 1957 so a more basic version guided by a radio wave beam was prepared, called Blue Sky.

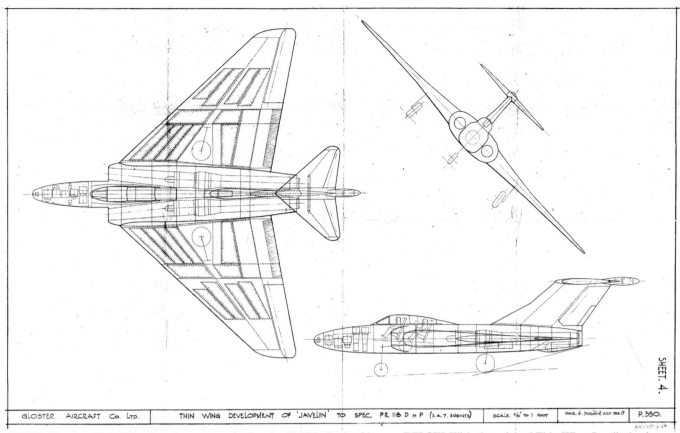

GLOSTER AIRCRAFT Co. LTD. | THIN WING DEVELOPMENT OF 'JAVELIN' TO SPEC. PR 118 D & P (S.A.7. ENGINES) | SCALE: 1/6' TO 1 FOOT | ISSUE. 4. (REDRAWN) JULY 1953. LB | P.350.

SHEET. 4.

ABOVE: The first Thin Wing Javelin, as seen in drawing P.350. *Jet Age Museum* **BELOW: With the original Thin Wing Javelin having been designed for reconnaissance, a second version was drawn to show the aircraft as an all-weather missile platform.** *Jet Age Museum*

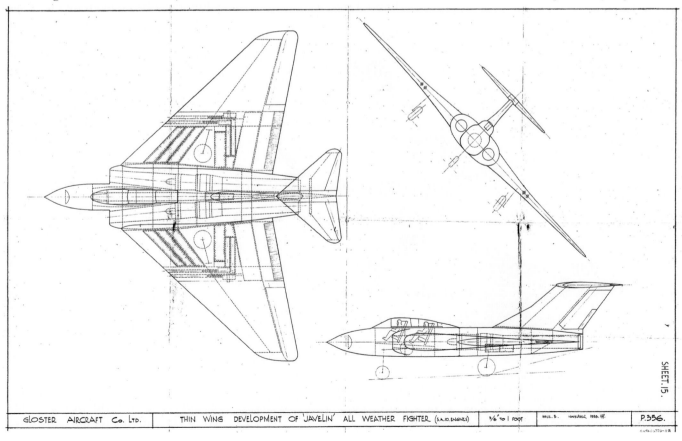

GLOSTER AIRCRAFT Co. LTD. | THIN WING DEVELOPMENT OF 'JAVELIN' ALL WEATHER FIGHTER (S.A.10. ENGINES) | 1/6' TO 1 FOOT | ISSUE. 5. NOVEMBER 1953. LC | P.356.

SHEET. 15.

Another strand of guided weapons research had begun with OR.203 of September 1945. This had called for a long-range expendable bomber, effectively a heavier British equivalent of the wartime V-1, capable of carrying a 10,000lb nuclear weapon for 1500 miles at 40,000ft. Developing the guidance system for such a weapon was, however, some way beyond the state of the art at that time. Nevertheless, the idea of unmanned aircraft carrying out the dangerous missions that had proven so costly during the Second World War was an attractive one and efforts in this direction continued to gain traction into the 1950s.

Rocket fighters

When the funding surge took effect, a huge range of additional guided missile projects began, most of which fall beyond the scope of this publication, and earlier experimental work on rocket engines for aircraft could also finally reach fruition.

Both Armstrong Siddeley and de Havilland had been designing and building rocket motors since 1946, the Snarler and Sprite respectively. The former received its first flight test in November 1950, the latter in May 1951. This development was viewed with particular interest, given the sudden need for interceptors capable of tackling incoming Soviet bombers laden with atomic weapons.

Now Armstrong Siddeley and de Havilland set to work on far more powerful versions of their earlier engines – the Screamer and the Spectre. The Air Staff meanwhile set out their need for a jet interceptor with supplementary rocket propulsion – mixed propulsion – in OR.301 of August 22, 1951, with competing firms required to submit their tenders by April 30, 1952. At a conference to discuss the submitted designs, two were chosen to proceed – the Avro 720, given the specification F.137D, and Saunders-Roe's SR.53, given the specification F.138D.

In 1955, work began on the next generation of mixed propulsion aircraft, with Saunders-Roe being contracted to develop a new interceptor based on the lessons learned from the SR.53 for both the RAF and the Admiralty. This design, the P.177 or SR.177, is discussed in more detail elsewhere.

Light fighters

The charismatic designer behind the English Electric P.1 and the Canberra jet bomber, William Edward Willoughby 'Teddy' Petter, left English Electric to join Folland Aircraft in October 1950 after a disagreement over responsibility for production of the Canberra. Once more demonstrating his genius for identifying a need before anyone else was even aware it existed, Petter foresaw that the next generation of fighters would become ever larger and more complex – making it prohibitively expensive to build them in large numbers.

If the Soviets were likely to launch a bomber offensive en masse, large numbers of interceptors would be needed to stop them all. Petter's concept involved building an aerodynamically advanced airframe around one of several small but powerful new turbojets then in development. The aircraft would also carry advanced armament – a large number of Microcell rockets or two 30mm Aden cannon, which were also under development at this time.

Rather than seeking to create a 'Volksjäger' for austerity Britain, something like Nazi Germany's Heinkel He 162 which deliberately sacrificed high-end performance to facilitate mass production, Petter wanted to make an aircraft that could, if necessary, go toe-to-toe with the Soviet's best fighters thanks to careful design and use of the very latest technology.

Petter's concept rapidly gained support from the Air Ministry and a new Operational Requirement was

The British government became so concerned about the shortcomings of the RAF's equipment that it agreed, with USAF aid, to buy 430 Canadair CL-13 Sabres for the RAF in West Germany during 1953. They had all been replaced with Hunters by June 1956, the remaining ex-RAF machines going to Italy (180) and Yugoslavia (121). Many were also returned to the USAF. *Author's collection*

The revolutionary English Electric P.1 took years to develop into the Lightning – thanks in part to the rigorous testing it had to go through. *BAE Systems*

issued in July 1951 – OR.303. This called for a light fighter capable of intercepting incoming bombers at an altitude of between 25,000-30,000ft. Several other designs and ideas were put forward by competing firms but a development contract was awarded to Folland by the Ministry of Supply in October 1951 without the usual competitive tendering process.

The design put forward by Folland at that point was powered by a pair of engines developed by Rolls-Royce for use in missiles – the RB.93 Soar – which the company then decided not to build. Folland's Light Fighter project was put on hold until Bristol offered a suitable alternative in the form of the BE.22 Saturn. The project continued into 1953 but government funding was not forthcoming, prompting Petter to build a technology demonstrator, the Fo.139 Midge, powered by an Armstrong Siddeley Viper 101 engine. This made its first flight on August 11, 1954, and following

tests at the Aircraft and Armament Evaluation Establishment (A&AEE) Boscombe Down an order was placed for half a dozen examples of the developed version of the Midge – the Fo.141 Gnat.

Night fighters

With the Gloster Javelin under development as the RAF's new

night and bad-weather fighter, thoughts turned to ways of developing the type to its full potential. The RAE had spent some time examining design alterations by which this could be achieved and changes to both its wings and its T-tail appeared to be the way forward, along with more powerful engines.

While day fighters, all-weather fighters and mixed propulsion fighters were under development, there were some who believed that a smaller, simpler design was the way forward. The result was the Folland Midge, a low-powered technology demonstrator for the Folland Gnat fighter. *BAE Systems*

The Fairey Delta 2 was a contemporary of the English Electric P.1 with a highly advanced aerodynamic form, yet its full potential as the basis for a fighter was never realised. *Author's collection*

In 1953, the RAF decided that it wanted a thin-wing version of the Javelin specifically for photo-reconnaissance operations but it was also keen to see an advanced Javelin capable of carrying heavier armament. The reconnaissance specification was PR.118D&P and Gloster duly obliged by drawing up the first Thin Wing Javelin development to meet it, shown in drawing P.350 Issue 4 of July 1953.

An armed version was drafted as drawing P.356 in November 1953 and in March 1954, a prototype of the Thin Wing Javelin was ordered. A new Specification was drawn up around it later that year – F.153D – though this was not issued until March 1955.

It was thought that the Thin Wing Javelin would be capable of supersonic speeds in a shallow dive and able to carry a combination of Red Dean and Blue Jay missiles plus a pair of Aden cannon. Red Dean, originally conceived by Folland but under development by Vickers, was a huge weapon with a radar homing tip. The de Havilland Blue Jay used infrared to find its target, making it a heat-seeker. With the original Javelin not yet in service, work on the Thin Wing Javelin progressed in parallel until the structure of the F.153D had changed so much that it became a completely new aircraft.

Naval and other types

While this range of new fighters was being developed for the RAF, the Admiralty ordered a second range of new fighters to better suit its own requirements – the de Havilland DH.110 Sea Vixen and the Supermarine Scimitar, plus a naval version of the Saunders-Roe P.177. Even the turboprop-powered Westland Wyvern carrier-based strike aircraft was still under development during the Korean War, only entering service in 1953. A new requirement issued in 1952, NA.39, would result in yet another new naval strike fighter – the Blackburn Buccaneer.

Vickers, Handley Page and Avro were heavily involved in developing the Valiant, Victor and Vulcan bombers respectively during the early 1950s, while Fairey was struggling with the design of its Jet Gyrodyne and Rotodyne helicopters. Bristol was working on its Sycamore and Type 173/Belvedere helicopters, plus its Britannia turboprop airliner and the Superfreighter transport; Saunders-Roe had its Skeeter helicopter in development, as well as the enormous Princess flying boat airliner.

Rocket engines that had been under development since the Second World War came to the fore during the early 1950s. Saunders-Roe's mixed propulsion jet and rocket-engined SR.53 appeared to show how fighters would be made in the future. Prototype XD145 is shown here undergoing testing at Boscombe Down on May 16, 1957. *Author's collection*

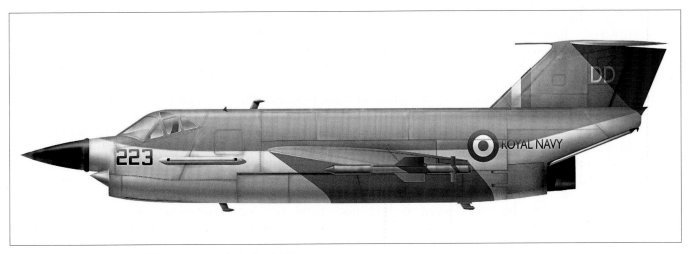

Saunders-Roe P.177, Royal Navy version. *Art by Daniel Uhr*

In short, Britain's aviation industry was working flat out on a large number of highly advanced projects – civilian as well as military – which taxed its capabilities to the limit. Resources were thinly spread, but the Government felt obligated to keep companies afloat to ensure there was no loss of technical capability and production capacity overall.

The sudden increase in funding during 1950 resulted in numerous new projects running in parallel and was creating an aviation industry bubble.

Mutually assured destruction
The sudden realisation, in September 1949, that the Soviet Union had its own nuclear weapons, coupled with the Korean War in 1950, created an impression that if a Third World War came, it would involve waves of Soviet bombers sweeping across Europe towards Britain.

But the situation abruptly changed again in 1953. During 1948, English Electric hired wartime radar specialist Leslie H Bedford to lead its new guided weapons division, known as the Navigational Project Division for secrecy's sake. During March 1952, Bedford's team began to assess the potential of a surface-to-surface guided missile, fitted with a nuclear warhead, that

was capable of hitting targets 2000-3000 miles away.

On January 16, 1953, Geoffrey William Tuttle, Assistant Chief of the Air Staff (Operational Requirements), sent a memo headed 'The Long Range Surface-to-Surface Weapon' to Deputy Director of Operational Requirements Group Captain Colin Scragg, which read: "It is quite clear to me that the deterrent to aggression which will be offered by a front line of Valiants, Victors and Vulcans will not be a deterrent nor a successful Hot War weapon for ever.

"It is therefore important that we consider now the best way of replacing them. At present our short term policy will be to have the low level bomber with an inertia controlled propelled atom bomb and the thin winged Javelin, with a smaller atom bomb flight refuelled. I do not believe that either of these or both will last very long, nor do I believe that they are a real deterrent. We must, therefore, think of something else."

He said that a surface-to-surface missile capable of carrying an atomic warhead was needed – rather than a winged expendable bomber – which could be developed within 10 years if work began on it immediately.

OR.203 (Issue 2) was circulated on August 14, calling for a supersonic

nuclear missile with a range of 2500 nautical miles. Just over a month later, on September 17, Scragg invited the Air Staff to a presentation by Bedford and his team. He wrote: "The visit is designed to introduce a new concept in which we are likely to become more closely involved in the future and which will have many most difficult and unusual problems. The presentation will be unofficial and without prejudice to any decisions on our part or the further work which the firm may be undertaking."

A copy of Bedford's report was attached to each invitation. It read: "Our investigation leaves us in no doubt that the long range weapon is not in the pipe-dream category but is a practical possibility. This being so, it is quite certain that the potential enemy would not fail to fully exploit our geographical disadvantage by the use of such a weapon against us. Certain forms of the weapon such as the ballistic rocket are virtually immune from defensive counter-measures of any kind. In this case, the only possible defence is therefore attack. From a military point of view our ability to launch such an attack, clearly advertised and substantiated, is probably the only useful war deterrent."

He said that such a missile would be unstoppable: "A weapon of this type reaches a speed of 17,000ft per second approx. and can probably be considered invulnerable to defensive countermeasures for all time. It is therefore probably the ultimate form of weapon and the circumstances appear to us to justify the bold step of proceeding straight to the ultimate solution without going through intermediate and subsequently obsolete techniques."

In April 1954, the US approached the UK with a proposal of cooperation on the development of ballistic missiles armed with nuclear warheads. This resulted in the Wilson-Sandys Agreement of August 1954, where the US would work on a long range missile and the UK would develop one for the medium range.

By August 8, 1955, Bedford's report had resulted in OR.1139, which called for a medium range ballistic missile system for the military. This would become de Havilland Propellers' Blue Streak.

The future of fighters

Bedford's report effectively sounded the death knell for Fighter Command – the home defence organisation which, during the Second World War, had fought so hard to keep British skies clear of intruding enemy aircraft. With an effective ballistic missile nuclear deterrent, there would be no need for a fighter defence force. From a political perspective the appalling concept of mutually assured destruction was a hugely attractive prospect, since abolishing Fighter Command would result in vast savings for the public purse.

But the missiles were a long way from being ready. And the Russians did not have them yet either. It was against this backdrop that planning continued for an RAF interceptor force to defend against ever faster and higher-flying Russian bombers.

In March 1956, the Ministry of Supply's Controller of Aircraft, Air Chief Marshal Sir John Baker, set out the situation that the British

aircraft industry found itself in during the mid-1950s: "Despite their increasing complexity, the industry is handling as many aircraft projects today as at the peak of the war effort mainly for three reasons – the emergence of the Russian threat after the 1950 crisis, the urge to catch up after the postwar recess and the competitive standards set by the advancing state of the art.

"All this happened in a period when it had also been decided to embark on a full-scale guided weapon programme and when the country's expanding economy, with all its inflationary tendencies, put a premium on the nation's technical manpower and resources.

"Whatever the effect of these wider influences, it was the foregoing three factors which largely explain why we are now developing concurrently 10 different types of fighter, three variants of the V bombers and many different marks of each aircraft with all their attendant complexities.

"To take the fighter range as an example. The Swift and Hunter were competitive for the new Avon axial-engines. The P.1 promised higher performance still. So does the P.177 with its mixed power plant. The Navy claimed its own 'all-weather' fighter and selected the DH.110 which was being developed in competition with the Javelin. To parallel the Hunter/Swift development the Navy also called for the N.113 (Supermarine Scimitar).

"At the same time, the 'Gnat' was started as a 'light' fighter in an attempt to overcome the complexity problem. Meanwhile, the need to maintain and enlarge the RAF night fighter force resulted in the development of the Venom for the all-weather role at one end of the scale and the thin-wing Javelin at the other.

"As to the various marks in each project, these are derived from variants of new weapon and

propulsion systems, promising improved performance and fighting qualities, or of differing roles and duties required to be undertaken by the same basic aircraft.

"The result was the planning of seven marks of Swift, six marks of Hunter and eight marks of Javelin before any aircraft was delivered to the Service. There are also nine marks of Canberra embracing the straightforward bomber, the interdictor and the high-altitude photo-recce roles, while the V bombers themselves are planned for high and low altitude and alternative PR versions.

"Alongside each type, there is normally a trainer version required to be specially developed with a whole range of synthetic devices and flight simulators to cover every phase of the aircraft's operation and maintenance on the ground. Altogether, and including the more important of the marks, there are some 45 military projects under active development with

While the next generation of RAF interceptors were being developed, guided weapons technology was steadily improving. In 1953, it was realised that the threat of mutually assured destruction posed by ballistic missiles with nuclear warheads might render both manned interceptors and surface-to-air missiles unnecessary. Britain's nuclear deterrent was to be de Havilland's Blue Streak, seen here being test-fired at Woomera in Australia as a space launch vehicle during the 1960s. *Author's collection*

differing roles or weapon systems, as well as 17 civilian transports or communication aircraft and 13 helicopters.

"There is yet another factor to put into the account. We are developing in almost every case new weapons, new controlling and navigation equipment and new engines, in fact virtually the whole 'weapon system' in conjunction with the new airframe vehicle itself. The systems include the new British AI equipment for the fighters and the NBS for the bombers. From the 'Aden' gun to 'Red Dean', new weapons are being planned for new aircraft in a programme which has allowed no time or experience in their associated development before both are required for front line service.

"In the equipment field crash programmes and orders 'off the drawing board' are coming to be regarded as the normal rather than the exception, to almost the same extent as in the earlier aircraft programme, with all the consequences of extra cost and retrospective modifications from which the primary projects have suffered in recent months.

"It is entirely reasonable to base a well-conceived programme on making the major advances in those fields which scientific research and development in techniques show to be feasible and then to develop the projects to their limit by short step advancements. The Spitfire was itself so far in advance at its inception that we were able to develop it year by year throughout the war.

"But we failed to appreciate after the war the need for continuing these long step advancements in appropriate sequence, and the extent to which the hurried introduction later of more modern and complex systems in such numbers and variety would so quickly saturate the technical resources available. Thus there was no coherent planning to keep research, development and production in balance and the main incentive on the firms after 1950 was to scramble for a place on the production band-wagon where there seemed to be room for all and sundry whatever their size and quality.

"It is small wonder that the industry is overstretched or that their own estimates of their capacity and ours of their future prospects are difficult to analyse while all these earlier practices and phases are evolving out of past decisions and policies."

Sir John's solution was remarkably prescient: "In planning our future programme, therefore, our aim should be to encourage associations, if not amalgamations among the firms so as to concentrate our resources more effectively in support of those projects which it is essential to retain or introduce into the programme."

This was for the future, however. Back in 1952, before the prospect of intercontinental ballistic missiles, there was cash in the pot and a pressing need to provide an effective defence against Soviet bombers…

ROYAL AIRCRAFT ESTABLISHMENT

The design having engines in the fuselage

June 1952

Artwork by Luca Landino

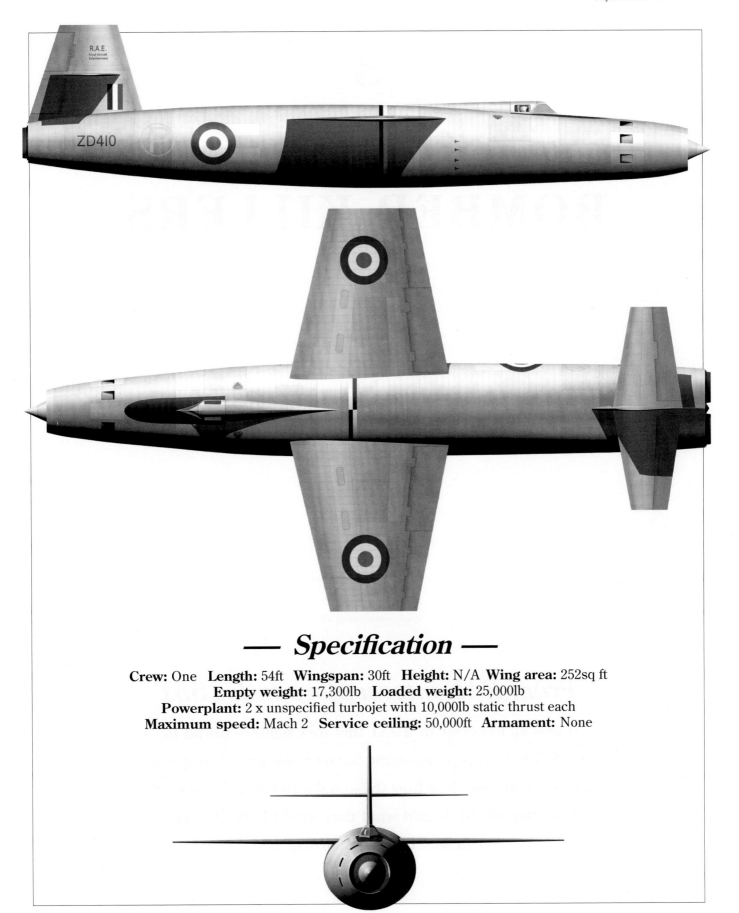

— *Specification* —

Crew: One **Length:** 54ft **Wingspan:** 30ft **Height:** N/A **Wing area:** 252sq ft
Empty weight: 17,300lb **Loaded weight:** 25,000lb
Powerplant: 2 x unspecified turbojet with 10,000lb static thrust each
Maximum speed: Mach 2 **Service ceiling:** 50,000ft **Armament:** None

3

BOMBER KILLERS

From RAE interceptors to F.155T

It was all too clear by 1951 that new fighters would be needed to intercept incoming Soviet bombers – but it was a great deal less clear how these fighters would be armed, how they would fly and what they would look like. The debate began in earnest...

With the Korean War stalemated and with the development of Britain's new wave of jet fighters – the Hunter, Swift and Javelin – proceeding steadily, thoughts began to turn to what might replace them.

During a conference on further Hunter and Swift developments in December 1951, a discussion took place among Air Staff officers on what sort of performance the next generation of fighters might have. Little scientific research had been carried out on what might be feasible, given the engine developments then in progress, but it was agreed that Mach 1.8 ought to be achievable.

The following month, a new Air Staff Requirement was drafted for a supersonic day fighter. Its wording was vague and when copies were circulated, feedback suggested it would be very difficult to work out what form the fighter should take without knowing more about what the next generation of Soviet bombers was likely to be capable of.

At the same time, the Royal Aircraft Establishment's (RAE) structures department began a six-month study to work out what sort of configuration a Mach 2 aircraft might have.

The draft requirement was revised in February 1952 under the title The Future Interceptor Fighter. A second version of this, The Future Requirement for a New Generation of Fighters to Succeed F.3 and F.4, was printed in April 1952 and given a slightly wider circulation – across the Air Ministry, Fighter Command and the 2nd Tactical Air Force – along with a formal request for comments.

Two months later the RAE's report, entitled An Investigation into an Aircraft to Fly at a Mach Number of 2, Aero.2462, was published. Its three authors, C H E Warren, J Poole and D C Appleyard, stated: "An investigation has been made into the possibility of designing an aircraft to fly at a Mach number of 2, to have an operationally useful endurance, and to be capable of landing and taking off conventionally. The work covers the performance and the stability and control characteristics. The aircraft is envisaged as a research aircraft capable of development into a fighter. No assessment has been made of the tactical use to which the aircraft could be put."

They reported that Mach 2 ought to be "readily attainable in a design based on existing knowledge, and that no new engine is essential" but some of their conclusions, seen with the benefit of hindsight, seem surprising.

They wrote: "Aircraft designed to fly at moderate supersonic speeds (Mach numbers from, say, 1.2 to 1.6) are normally characterised by highly swept-back wings of moderate thickness, having engines in the fuselage with simple forward-facing (pitot-type) intakes in either the nose or wing roots.

"At some Mach number higher than 1.6 it is envisaged that the optimum form of aircraft will undergo a profound change, so that at Mach numbers higher than, say, 1.8, unswept wings, admittedly of extreme thinness, come into their own, engines in nacelles again become a possibility, and the oblique-shock type of intake offers potential advantages."

The authors came up with what they called "the basic design" – a single-seat aircraft with unswept wings powered by two turbojets in under-wing nacelles that was capable of conventional take-off and climb at high subsonic speed to 45,000ft, followed by 10 minutes level flight accelerating up to Mach 2. An operationally useful load of 1500lb could be carried and all-up weight would be 25,000lb.

The reason given for using very thin unswept wings was primarily to provide greater lift at low speeds for landing. The wing was so thin, it was argued, that above Mach 2 it made little difference whether the wing was swept or unswept. Putting the engines in nacelles under the wings was fine because "on an unswept aircraft… there is no priori reason why housing the engines in nacelles should lead to a high interference drag, although there appears to be no evidence on this point. There are, however, other reasons in favour of housing the engines in nacelles.

"With the thin wings that will be required it will be impossible to carry any fuel in the wings, so that one is forced to store all the fuel in the fuselage. Since the fuel must be balanced with respect to the centre of gravity, it must clearly be carried more or less alongside the engines, which, because of their great weight, determine to a large extent the position of the centre of gravity.

"This will lead to a stubby fuselage of small fineness ratio (length/diameter) and hence of high drag. In fact, calculations indicate that a design having engines in the fuselage has a greater drag than a design having engines in nacelles.

"A more important factor in favour of a nacelle design, however, is its greater simplicity and flexibility. The housing of the engines in the fuselage obviously presents numerous problems in the layout of the engines, intake ducts, and jet pipes, and the enclosing of them in a low drag shape, which do not arise when they are housed in nacelles."

Having the engines in nacelles would also make it easier to install variable centrebody intakes too. However, their report later points out that the additional weight of the nacelles themselves would negate some of the advantages the type might otherwise have over their alternative design, which they simply called 'engines in the fuselage'.

While much of the report concerns the importance of returning to a layout not too dissimilar to that of the Gloster Meteor, the authors also looked at aerodynamic heating at high speeds and the use of other powerplants. Ramjets were dismissed because they would not work well with an unswept-wing aircraft but "the possibility of using rockets, on the other hand, is more promising. Their use, however, will be governed by the operational role that the aircraft is expected to fulfil, but a good case can be made for a short endurance rocket-propelled aircraft".

The first draft

Although its impact was not felt immediately, Warren, Poole and Appleyard's report would prove to be highly influential. A month after its publication, comments on the 'New Generation of Fighters' requirement were gathered and examined. They seemed to mostly fall within three broad categories of disagreement – whether the new fighters should be designed purely for intercepting bombers or purely for tackling enemy fighters; whether they should be designed to operate at low to medium altitude or high altitude only; and whether they should be pure day fighters or able to operate at night and in all weathers.

These points were discussed by the RAF Aircraft Research Committee, a sub-committee of the Aeronautical Research Council (ARC) during its final meeting in October 1952, but no decisions were made. Three months later, an experimental specification for a Mach 2 research aircraft – ER.134T – was issued based on the Warren, Poole and Appleyard report. This called for an aircraft capable of reaching Mach 2 and sustaining it for 10 minutes. Armstrong Whitworth, Boulton Paul, Bristol, English Electric, Hawker, Saunders-Roe and Vickers-Armstrongs all tendered designs, and although Armstrong Whitworth was initially selected the firm proved unable to follow through owing to other work and Bristol's Type 188 was chosen instead – the contract being placed in December 1953.

Meanwhile, in January 1953, the process of drawing up a draft Air Staff Requirement for a supersonic interceptor, circulating it for comment, and gathering in the comments for further discussion began again. In April, it was decided that a working party ought to be set up with a mandate to explore all options for the future air defence requirements of Britain. However, this proved to be easier said than done and the working party's terms of reference alone took months to agree.

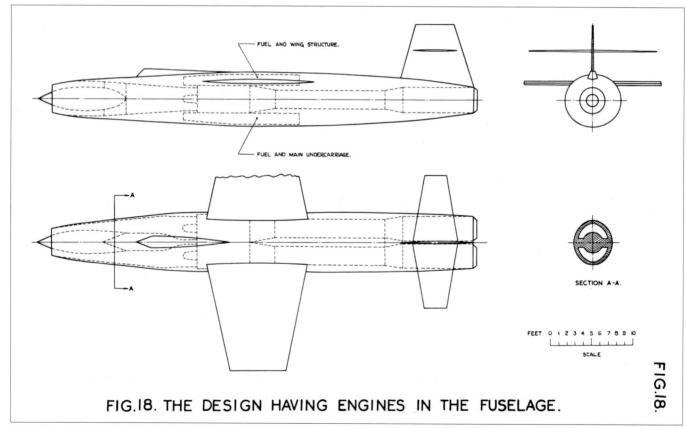

FUEL AND WING STRUCTURE.

FUEL AND MAIN UNDERCARRIAGE.

SECTION A-A.

FEET 0 1 2 3 4 5 6 7 8 9 10
SCALE

FIG.18.

FIG.18. THE DESIGN HAVING ENGINES IN THE FUSELAGE.

The RAE's alternative to its 'basic design' was the 'engines in fuselage' design. This was generally dismissed as inferior due to the difficulty involved in getting to its engines for maintenance and the way in which they filled up fuselage space which might otherwise have been used for fuel. *BMGC*

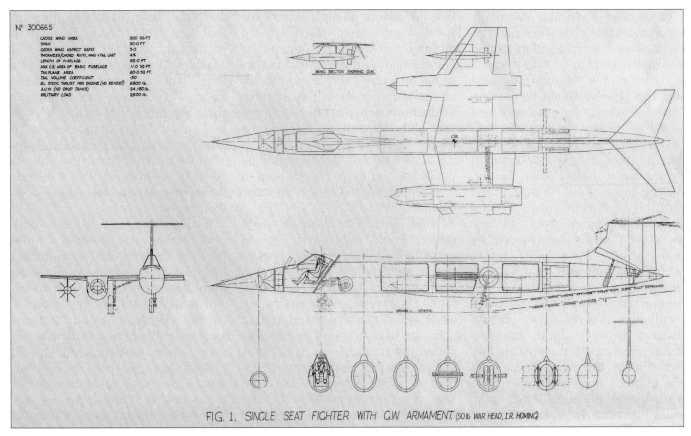

FIG. 1. SINGLE SEAT FIGHTER WITH G.W. ARMAMENT. (50lb WAR HEAD, I.R. HOMING)

When a joint RAE/Radar Research Establishment team investigated the potential for a Mach 2 interceptor during the early months of 1954 they built upon the earlier 1952 research of Warren, Poole and Appleyard. The 'basic design' was used as the basis for this – the first of four sample interceptor designs. *BMGC*

After the second round of re-drafting and comments, a new version of the draft interceptor requirement was printed and circulated on October 31, 1953. The introduction to this one read: "Experience has shown that it is essential to the proper defence of this country that new and improved types of fighter aircraft should reach the service at regular intervals. Otherwise our fighter defences must inevitably lag behind the offensive potential of our probable enemies and so lack the performance and technical superiority necessary for successful action.

"The manned fighter is, of course, only part of the air defence system, in which AA guns, ground-launched guided missiles and the air counter-offensive all play their part, but progress in these other fields, though considerable, has not yet reached the point where the fighter is no longer required. Current technical information indicates that the manned fighter will be essential for many years to come, while the threat of atomic bombing adds weight to the need to have the most efficient fighter force possible.

"Owing to the complexity of modern aircraft and their equipment it takes six to seven years from the moment of its inception before a fighter can take its place in operational squadrons. Thus new fighter aircraft planned now could not arrive in service before about 1960. By this time the Hunter, Swift and Javelin will have been in service for some six years, and, although it is hoped to extend the operational usefulness of these aircraft by introducing various improvements, the limit of their effective operational life should then be approaching.

"Beyond the Hunter, Swift and Javelin the only new fighter aircraft now being developed are the F.23 [Lightning] and the Rocket Interceptor. Both of these might come into service in 1957/58, but the latter is a project of very limited application, while the former, as our first supersonic fighter, may well suffer from the disabilities which frequently attend first comers in a new field. In any event, these two projects cannot be regarded as in any way lessening our need for a new generation of fighter aircraft early in the 1960s.

"Accordingly, the Air Staff consider that the time has come when it should state a requirement for a new generation of fighters to take over from those now building and under development."

Since the RAF's future manned fighter force would have to cover all altitudes from sea level to

70,000ft, and given the seemingly insurmountable difficulties likely to be involved in building a fighter that was just as good at 100ft as it was at 70,000ft, the Air Staff decided that two fighters would be needed, "one designed for the greatest possible ceiling and for best performance above about 40,000ft, and the other designed for optimum performance below that height. As the low altitude fighter would probably be effective up to 55,000ft the height band from 40,000ft to 55,000ft would be covered by both aircraft.

"It is felt, however, that there is no need to sub-divide the future fighter task beyond the two types mentioned above. The design division between high and low altitude also marks the dividing line between the two main divisions of the fighter's approach to its task, while the development of automatic blind approach aids, and the fact that the advent of high supersonic speeds and air-launched guided missiles with effective ranges far greater than gun armament makes some form of radar essential for all fighters, makes the present distinction between day fighters and night/all-weather fighters no longer applicable."

The low altitude fighter would be the larger and more complicated of the two but beyond this, no further detail of it is given.

The high altitude fighter, a single seater, would only carry guided weapons and would employ a pursuit course attack above the weather so sophisticated airborne intercept radar (AI) would not be necessary – just a pilot-operated search radar.

Rocket motors would supplement conventional turbojet engines, but overall the aircraft was to be kept as small, simple, cheap and easy to service as possible. Ceiling would be "not lower than 70,000ft" and "the time from the moment that the pilot presses the button to start the engines to the aircraft reaching 70,000ft is not to be more than five minutes". Top speed above 40,000ft was "not to be less than Mach 2.5, if possible it is to be Mach 3.0". Endurance was to be about an hour and manoeuvrability was to be the "best possible at 60,000ft". Armament would be four de Havilland Blue Jay missiles "or their replacement".

A large section of the draft requirement was devoted to the pilot's comfort and equipment including automatic air-conditioning in a pressurised cabin, pressure suit with oxygen supply, standby cockpit lighting, good forward view, extending cockpit for a better view while landing, jettisonable canopy and survival pack. With regard to servicing, the aircraft had to be easy to refuel and rearm for a complete turnaround within 10

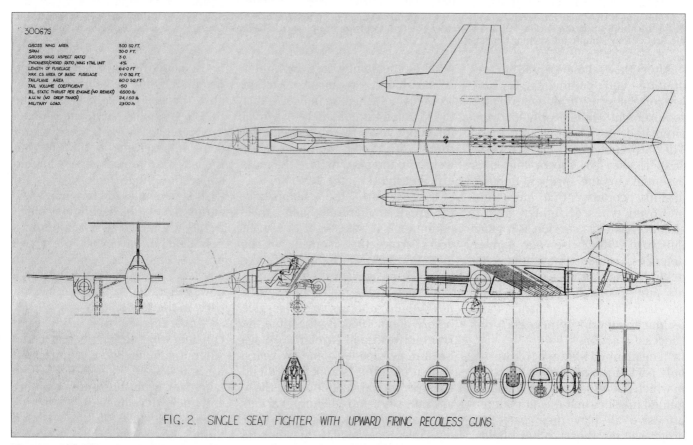

FIG. 2. SINGLE SEAT FIGHTER WITH UPWARD FIRING RECOILESS GUNS.

The second RAE sample design had a battery of upwards-firing recoilless guns in place of the first design's guided weapons. *BMGC*

minutes. Target in-service date was January 1961.

This all read a little bit like a pilot's wish list – which, given the way it had been pieced together from RAF officers' comments, it was. At this point, the Air Ministry's Director of Operational Requirements (Air) (DOR[A]) Air Commodore Wallace Hart Kyle stepped in to tighten up the requirement and give it more focus on the performance a new interceptor would actually need, rather than the performance it would be nice to have.

The threat

A second draft, following his intervention, was produced in November 1953 which kept the same introduction, but added a new section marked 'the threat'. This stated: "Although it is not possible to assess the air threat to this country in the early- and mid-1960s with any degree of precision, it is reasonable to assume that our only probable enemy – Russia – has a technical potential similar to our own. This does not mean, however, that he must necessarily develop the same kind of offensive weapons. The Russian has an advantage over us in that in attacking major targets in the UK and Western Europe he is not faced with a range problem, as we are, amounting to some 1500-2000nm: His range requirement is no more than 400-500nm.

"On the other hand, his major potential enemy is not the UK but the USA for which the range requirements are even greater than our own against Russia. It seems reasonable to suppose, therefore, that the Russian bomber development programme will be concentrated mainly on developing long-range aircraft capable of attacking the USA and that the bomber threat to this country will consist mainly of such of these aircraft as could be diverted from their primary target plus any

shorter-range bomber aircraft which the Russians may develop as an aid to continental operations generally.

"In addition, we must also expect the Russians to develop weapons of the V2 type, but as these could not be countered by any fighter they are outside the scope of our present considerations. On this basis, we must expect that by the early 1960s the Russians will have long-range bombers of the improved V Bomber Class. Because of the reduced range requirement when operating against this country, we must expect these aircraft to be capable of attacking us at all heights from sea level up to 60,000ft and possibly 65,000ft at high sub-sonic speeds of the order of Mach 0.95.

"Fairly early in the 1960s improved versions of these aircraft might have the capability of making short supersonic bursts at speeds up to about Mach 1.3 at heights between 30,000ft and 55,000ft. However, because of the very large range requirement involved in any Russian attack of the USA the Russians are unlikely to develop a long-range bomber capable of sustained supersonic flight before about 1967/68, which is not within the operational life of the new generation of fighters, which are the subject of this requirement.

"In regard to the shorter-range aircraft that might be used against us, it must be remembered that while these are not likely to be given the top place in the Russian bomber development programme it is equally improbable that they will be ignored. The Russian mind thinks in terms of large armies, and the army interests, which are powerful politically, will insist that adequate air support is available to them. Moreover, we must not forget that the Russians might well apply certain features – such as sustained supersonic flight – to comparatively short-range bombers, mainly as an essential development stage before

applying them to larger longer-range aircraft."

The actual threat, in fact, "other than V2 type weapons" was likely to be long-range bombers flying at between 60,000-65,000ft, mainly at Mach 0.9-0.95, but capable of short sprints up to Mach 1.3 between 30,000-55,000ft, and short-range light bombers flying at Mach 1.8-2.0 above 30,000ft.

Under 'technical considerations' the second draft states that a manned fighter is unlikely to be effective below about 3000ft and "some other means of air defence at low altitude is required". This was being investigated and was likely to be a guided weapon capable of operating up to altitudes significantly higher than 3000ft – so the new RAF interceptor would need to cover only the high altitude region. It would also need blind flying aids and AI, which meant "the present division between day and night/all-weather fighters is ceasing to be valid, and that one type of high-altitude fighter should meet the future needs of the Royal Air Force."

The upshot of all this was a top speed reduced from Mach 3.0 to Mach 2.5 and a ceiling reduced from 70,000ft to 65,000ft. And "while the aircraft is to be designed primarily as a guided weapon carrier it will also be required to accept guns as secondary armament. This is necessary in order to provide against enemy countermeasures in the guided weapon field". The guns would be a pair of 30mm Adens with 150 rounds each. The four Blue Jays became "at least two and, if possible, four Blue Jays". The interceptor was still a single-seater, but the survival pack was deleted.

A third draft in January 1954 added a radar operator, making the interceptor a two-seater, and deleted the guided weapons for low-altitude defence, stating instead that "the performance of the Developed Javelin indicates that it should be capable of dealing with the enemy

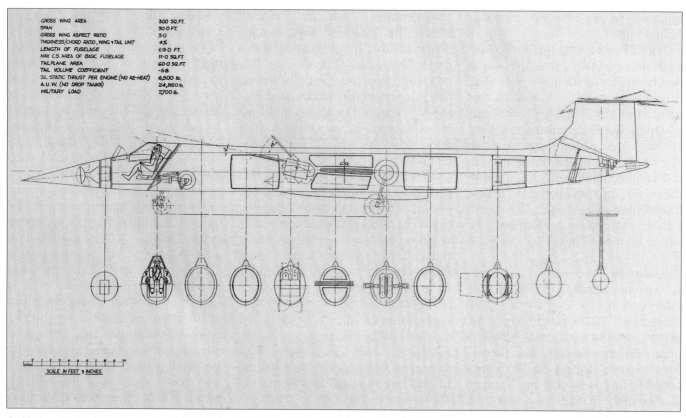

GROSS WING AREA	300 SQ.FT.
SPAN	30·0 FT.
GROSS WING ASPECT RATIO	3·0
THICKNESS/CHORD RATIO, WING & TAIL UNIT	4%
LENGTH OF FUSELAGE	69·0 FT.
MAX C.S. AREA OF BASIC FUSELAGE	11·0 SQ.FT.
TAILPLANE AREA	60·0 SQ.FT.
TAIL VOLUME COEFFICIENT	·58
S.L. STATIC THRUST PER ENGINE (NO RE-HEAT)	6,500 lb.
A.U.W. (NO DROP TANKS)	24,850 lb.
MILITARY LOAD	2700 lb.

SCALE IN FEET & INCHES.

A third armament option for the RAE interceptor was to fit it with a pair of retractable Aden cannon in its upper fuselage. *BMGC*

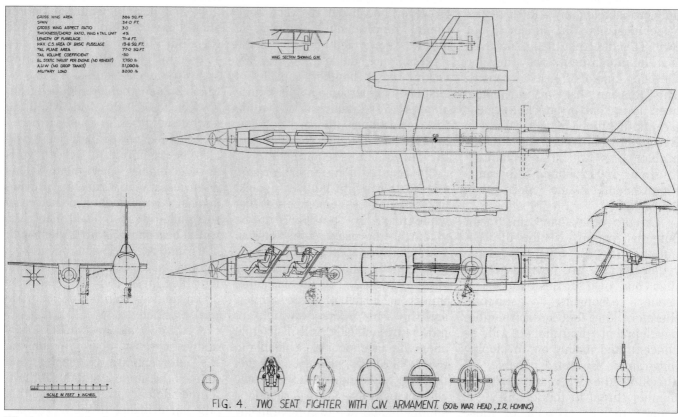

GROSS WING AREA	386 SQ.FT.
SPAN	34·0 FT.
GROSS WING ASPECT RATIO	3·0
THICKNESS/CHORD RATIO, WING & TAIL UNIT	4%
LENGTH OF FUSELAGE	71·4 FT.
MAX C.S. AREA OF BASIC FUSELAGE	13·6 SQ.FT.
TAIL PLANE AREA	77·0 SQ.FT.
TAIL VOLUME COEFFICIENT	·50
S.L. STATIC THRUST PER ENGINE (NO REHEAT)	7,750 lb
A.U.W. (NO DROP TANKS)	31,200 lb
MILITARY LOAD	3200 lb

WING SECTION SHOWING C.W.

SCALE IN FEET & INCHES.

FIG. 4. TWO SEAT FIGHTER WITH C.W. ARMAMENT. (50lb WAR HEAD, I.R. HOMING)

Whether or not the future interceptor should have a second crewman was a hugely contentious point. This sample RAE design shows a two-seater but the overall report concluded that a second crewman was unnecessary. It was a point which divided the Air Staff and resulted in months, if not years, of arguing. *BMGC*

bomber threat during the early 1960s, from 1000ft above ground level to 45,000ft". Under 'climb', the altitude was reduced to 65,000ft, but a blank space was left for the number of minutes it should take to get there as this was still under review.

The introduction became: "Current development indicates that manned interceptors will form an essential part of the air defence system for many years to come. By 1960, ground-to-air guided weapons will be in service, and ultimately the margin of performance over the threat will only be obtained from these weapons. However, by 1960 guided weapons will be very much in the development stage, and the disappearance of the manned interceptor from the field must inevitably be gradual, as the guided weapons improve in performance and reliability."

Bringing the firms in

While this version of the requirement was being assessed, the composition and terms of reference of the Air Defence Committee Working Party were finally approved by the Chiefs of Staff – nine months after the initial decision to set it up. The working party was to be led by RAE director Sir Arnold Hall, and his team quickly set about investigating all aspects of how to design a Mach 2 fighter for defence against Soviet bombers.

The fourth draft produced in February 1954, saw the introduction changed again to: "Current technical development indicates that, while the surface to air-guided weapon is probably the ultimate solution to our air defence problem, the manned interceptor will be necessary for many years yet to come, and the changeover from fighter to guided weapon defence is likely to be gradual."

The time-to-climb requirement was also altered: from an undetermined number of minutes to

65,000ft, to three minutes to 60,000ft.

Finally, with the fifth draft in March 1954, the operational requirement was given a number – OR.329. Now the introduction read: "It is accepted that the ultimate solution to the air defence of the UK must depend on the development of surface-to-air guided weapons. However, weapons currently being developed are limited in range and cannot by themselves fulfil the task. They are moreover untried and, even assuming their satisfactory development, are unlikely to be available in operational numbers before 1960. Increased range, together with a solution to the mid-course guidance problem which this implies, must be provided before the manned interceptor aircraft can be dispensed with entirely.

"Even allowing for the optimistic rate of development of surface-to-air guided weapons it is unlikely that a system and weapon stockpile capable of fulfilling the entire air defence task could be available before 1965.

"By about 1962 it is possible for Russia, operating from European bases, to threaten the UK with high-speed/high-altitude bombers which could not be dealt with by fighters currently being developed. The Air Staff therefore require a high-altitude interceptor fighter to be developed as a weapon system to the following requirements."

Two Blue Jays were specified as the main armament but the option to fit a gun "and/or rocket armament as an alternative to guided weapons" was to be investigated, the interceptor was now firmly a two-seater, it was also firmly accepted that rocket power "may be employed" in conjunction with turbojets, time to climb remained the same at three minutes to 60,000ft, but endurance now needed to be one hour, 17 minutes. A note further down states that external fuel tanks would be acceptable to achieve this.

Top speed was lower than previously: "The maximum level speed at 60,000ft is to be not less than Mach 2." Aspirations for a Mach 3 or even Mach 2.5 interceptor had evidently been abandoned as impractical.

Many other details remained the same but now the projected in-service date was given as January 1962 – a year later than before. Comments on the fifth draft were requested by April 10, but on March 17, 1954, Kyle wrote a letter stating: "You will remember that when I showed you our study of the background to a new fighter requirement I said that an OR emerging from it would shortly be available. Here it is. But I must warn you now that it is being studied by the Ministry of Supply etc. and has not been formally accepted. I cannot therefore guarantee that the final specification will conform completely with this requirement. However, I shall be surprised if it varies a great deal from it.

"My object in sending you this now is to save time and to give you something on which to base your thinking, if you intend to put in design studies when these are called for. Forgive me mentioning the security aspect, but I would be grateful if you would be personally responsible for the safe custody of the document."

The recipients of this first numbered version of OR.329 were Sir Sydney Camm at Hawker, Joe Smith at Vickers-Armstrongs, Richard W Walker at Gloster Aircraft, Stuart 'Dave' Davies at Avro, Freddie Page at English Electric, Ronald Bishop at de Havilland, Albert G Elliott at Rolls-Royce, Major Frank B Halford at de Havilland Engine Co, William Lindsey at Armstrong Siddeley Motors, and Maurice Brennan at Saunders-Roe. Archibald Russell of Bristol Aeroplane also appeared on the original list, his name being crossed off, but it does appear as though he was sent the OR accompanied by a lengthy personal letter from Kyle on March 18.

All these 11 firms were given a preview of OR.329 yet others are noticeable by their absence – Fairey Aviation and Armstrong Whitworth in particular.

While this was going on, the Ministry of Supply had finally been brought into the debate, though its initial reaction seems to have been hampered by confusion arising from the overlapping responsibilities of its senior personnel. On March 19, the Ministry of Supply's Director-General of Technical Development (Air), George W H Gardner, wrote to Geoffrey Tuttle, Assistant Chief of the Air Staff (Operational Requirements), telling him that a date would be set to discuss OR.329 and its sibling OR.330 – for a supersonic reconnaissance/bomber aircraft.

Also invited was Sir Arnold Hall, whose team at the RAE had been working flat out to prepare their paper – Defence Against High Altitude Bombers by Mach 2 Fighters, Aero 2513. Gardner wrote to Tuttle: "I trust that you personally will be able to attend, and I have also invited Hall to come and have warned him that we will lean heavily on his advice in view of the profound studies which have been in progress in his Establishment."

However, Tuttle had already arranged for the Deputy Chief of the Air Staff, Sir Thomas Pike, to discuss the requirements with the Ministry of Supply's Controller of Aircraft, Sir John Baker, on March 8, 11 days earlier. At this meeting, Baker promised to deliver the MoS's comments within three weeks. On March 29, Tuttle wrote back to Gardner saying that three weeks had now passed and Baker's comments had not arrived, that he would like to sit down with Gardner and Hall to discuss the requirements, and that he was uncertain how this sat with regard to the seemingly separate meeting with Baker.

On March 29, 1954, the Ministry of Supply's Principal Director of Research and Development (Aircraft) Arthur Edgar Woodward-Nutt wrote a memo headed 'Interceptor Fighter', saying: "More details are required of the thinking underlying the definition of the threat to be met. This draft requirement appears to assume an enemy bomber flying at Mach 1.3 at 50,000ft in 1962. The Draft Supersonic Bomber Requirement [for OR.330] assumes a cruising speed greater than Mach 2 at 60,000ft, the capability of reaching 70,000ft, and the aircraft is to be in service in 1963. Are these, in fact, more consistent than they appear to be on the surface?

"Details of the equipment are required before we can go very far in exploring this requirement. For example, the main armament of the fighter is described as a guided weapon 'of the same weight and dimensions as Blue Jay'. No indication is given of the kind of weapon, or of the kind of services, sighting, radar etc. which it may require. Is the fighter intended to operate under close control? Is a pursuit course attack, or rather only a pursuit course attack envisaged? Is the performance required consistent with the proposed date of availability in service of January 1962? If not, which should be given preference?

"Is the LCN number quoted practicable for a supersonic fighter with thin wings? If not practicable with normal wheels and types, would unconventional landing arrangements be acceptable? These might, of course, imply unconventional launching arrangements as well."

LCN was 'load classification number' or the strength of runway required to operate the aircraft. The OR.329 aircraft was likely to be extremely heavy and there was understandable concern about its ability to operate from runways, which had not been upgraded since they were built during the Second World War.

On March 31, Kyle finally wrote to Armstrong Whitworth chief designer Henry Watson to offer him a copy of OR.329 for information, though there was still nothing for Fairey.

The Hall report

After three months of intensive work, the report produced by Hall's working party was published at the beginning of April 1954. The foreword said: "This report contains ideas on the design and use of an air defence system employing a supersonic fighter aircraft; it deals with some of the considerations which apply in the design of the aircraft, its equipment, and the ground control system under which it operates.

"It is not meant to be an exhaustive treatise; it is intended rather as a contribution to thought, and if it forms a useful addition to the many points of view which must be put on these matters, it will have served its purpose. Contributions to this paper have come from specialist staff at both the Royal Aircraft Establishment and the Radar Research Establishment.

"The broad conclusion of the study is that 'all-weather' aircraft capable of a top performance of the order Mach 2.5 are practicable at a reasonable all-up weight and that they can, with the normal 200 miles range of early warning, form a component of a good defensive system against bombers of the 'V' type, and against later developments with speeds up to Mach 1.3.

"I wish to draw attention to this limitation on the upper speed against which fighter defence is likely to be really effective, since it is one which is not immediately evident; the report shows the reasons which lead to this conclusion and indicate what might be done to extend the limit a little."

He said it was essential to set up a fighter system that could later be swapped for a guided weapon system with a minimum of difficulty and cost. Practical aircraft forms had been studied but "this is not to say that these particular forms are the only possible forms, or are necessarily the best forms; there is much room for variation at the instinct of the designer".

The summary on the following page stated: "The concept of the supersonic fighter defence system is not very different from the ground-to-air missile defence system at present being studied by RAE. For this reason, a number of the main components, particularly the ground radar equipment, are common to both systems.

"It is believed, therefore, that the supersonic fighter will fill an important gap in our defence systems until such time as the true worth and effectiveness of ground-to-air missiles has been experienced. In the interim period, both fighters and missiles can be used together under certain raid conditions."

Under 'the discussion group' it is noted that the starting point was, unsurprisingly, Warren, Poole and Appleyard's An Investigation into an Aircraft to Fly at a Mach Number of 2 – which explains why the same 'basic design' of a Meteor type layout appears once again in Hall's report, albeit with much more detailed features.

Four components necessary for a supersonic interceptor defence are set out: an early warning radar with a range of 200 miles; a ground-

controlled interception radar "to give a range of about 160 miles on the bomber and to be capable of a high degree of precision in the plan position of the aircraft with moderate height accuracy. It is expected that each sector will be able to control 20 fighters simultaneously. The number of sectors must therefore be planned to match the expected raid density"; a communication link between the ground and the fighter, capable of controlling and even flying the fighter remotely ("the link has a high degree of security against jamming"), and finally the supersonic fighter itself.

The report argued that there were only really three fuselage options and two wing options available – a fuselage with engines completely inside it, in nacelles alongside it, or nacelles out on the wings, and wings

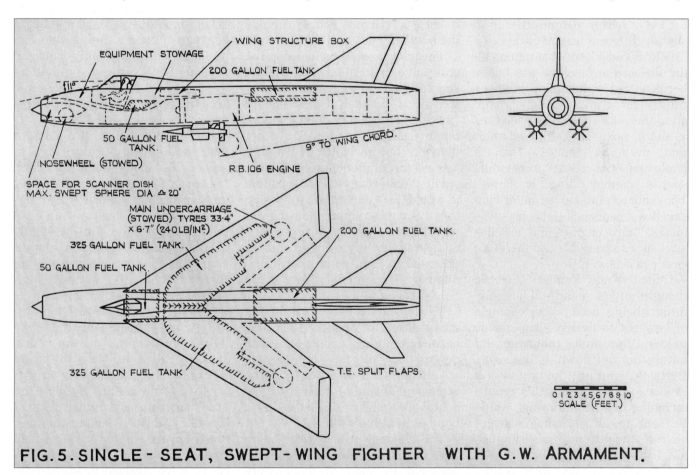

FIG. 5. SINGLE-SEAT, SWEPT-WING FIGHTER WITH G.W. ARMAMENT.

The fifth and final aircraft design showcased in the RAE's 1954 report was this depiction of a single-seat, swept-wing fighter with guided weapon armament. It bears an uncanny resemblance to English Electric's P.6 and was used as an example of how not to design a Mach 2 fighter. *BMGC*

with little or no sweepback or wings with a large angle of sweepback.

The fighter ought to have two engines rather than one because, it was reasoned, two small engines were usually lighter than one large one for the same thrust. And it was preferred that these should be mounted outside the fuselage because then "the fuselage space is available for the stowage of bulky items of load, e.g. elevated guns, moderate-pressure undercarriage wheels, inertia navigator, large radar scanner, auxiliary rocket motor, air brake mechanism, and mechanism for tailplane actuation. A comparison between Figs. 1 and 5 makes this point clear."

Fig. 1 showed a single-seat fighter looking very similar to the Bristol Type 188, while Fig. 5 showed English Electric's P.6/1, drafted by the company 11 months earlier for ER.134T, barely disguised with a slightly different fin and cockpit. The RAE considered that putting all the fuel in the fuselage was better because it would allow thinner wings; "for a given canopy frontal area, the pilot's view is better over a sharp nose as compared with that over an intake. This is important, since at supersonic speeds canopy drag is large". The shorter intake of underwing nacelles reduced jet pressure losses, and engines in nacelles were more accessible and therefore easier to replace.

Quite what English Electric thought of its 'nearly-a-Lightning' design being used as an example of how not to design a supersonic fighter, the first prototype P.1 having not yet flown, is unknown. Certainly, during the course of events to come, the RAE's report, including the P.6 drawing, would be sent to all of Britain's major aircraft manufacturers – English Electric's competitors.

According to the RAE report, the slender-fuselage, straight-wing interceptor would need to reach an altitude of 50,000ft and a speed of Mach 2 within five minutes of take-off. It would have a ceiling of almost 65,000ft and would be able to cruise at Mach 2 for 10 minutes. Total endurance was one hour. All-up weight would be 25,000lb, carrying a single airborne-intercept radar, "upward firing guns or guided weapon armament" and communication/navigation equipment.

In terms of the mission itself, "early in the discussions it became apparent that, with the large turning circles associated with high-altitude high-speed flying, the chances of freelance combat, even with a complicated AI were not a practical proposition unless the raid was of extremely high density. The system proposed, therefore, is that the fighter shall fly, or even be flown, under ground control to bring it into a pursuit course behind the bomber".

The pilot would then take control, at a range of 10 miles, and use the simple AI and his weapons to destroy the target bomber. Unfortunately, "the chance of intercepting, before bomb release, a bomber other than the one to which the fighter was vectored after take-off, will be small. We therefore considered that it would be economical to design the system so that each fighter would have a very high probability of destroying the particular bomber allocated to it, at some cost in the number of fighters which could be controlled.

"Since it is of paramount importance to reduce the time between fighter take-off and destruction of the bomber to a minimum, it follows that the armament should be such as to give a high probability of destroying a bomber in a single attack".

The chances of a bomber being able to shoot down the fighter assigned to shoot it down were "likely to be small" so the fighter would not need any passive defence equipment. Based on the idea of the fighter being flown from the ground during approach, "we do not think… that there is any compelling reason for putting a second man in the aircraft".

In terms of guided weaponry, "since tail attack only is proposed, infrared homing is a promising guidance system, and our earliest choice of weapon is a natural development of the present Blue Jay. If a direct-hitting missile proves feasible, an infrared homing missile would weigh about 180lb; but this would go up to 270lb for a near-miss type. Our second choice is an active radar homing missile, which would weigh about 430lb, and could if necessary be further developed for all-round attack.

"These missiles are powered by solid-fuel rockets and they can be used at altitudes up to 60,000ft. When the fighter's Mach number is between 1.5 and 2 the missiles can be launched at any range between 2000 and 4000 yards at angles of up to 15 degrees off the bomber's tail; accurate aiming of the aircraft is not, of course, essential."

But the RAE team also thought that some form of alternative to guided weapons was prudent: "Keeping the speed of the fighter up during the combat stage has a number of advantages and we therefore consider it to be highly desirable that the armament chosen should have a high chance of a kill (greater than 70%) at such high overtaking speeds.

"This is not possible with forward firing guns or rockets, because the fighter must break off the attack at long range in order to avoid collision. Thus, if the two aircraft are to pass one another by 100ft, the break-off range of a fighter flying at Mach 2 against a Mach 0.9 bomber must be 1000 yards giving a kill chance of about 25%. If the fighter speed were reduced to Mach 1.45, the pass distance for a 70% chance of a kill would be only 100ft.

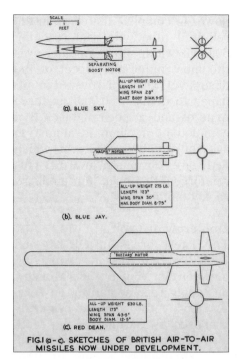

FIG.1 (a-c). SKETCHES OF BRITISH AIR-TO-AIR MISSILES NOW UNDER DEVELOPMENT.

Guided weaponry in development at the time when OR.329 was being drawn up. None of these was regarded as suitable for Britain's future interceptor in its then-current form, but Blue Jay was generally regarded as the most promising. *BMGC*

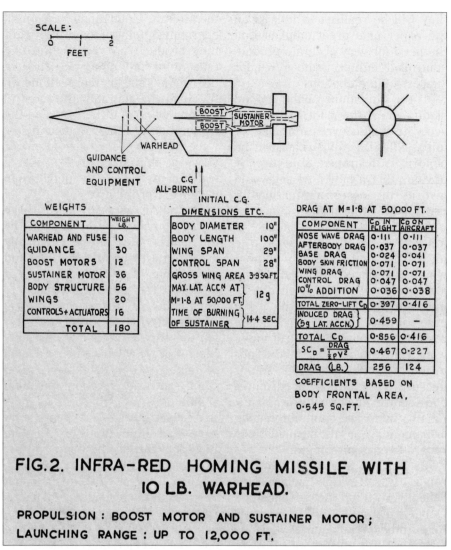

FIG.2. INFRA-RED HOMING MISSILE WITH 10 LB. WARHEAD.

PROPULSION : BOOST MOTOR AND SUSTAINER MOTOR ;
LAUNCHING RANGE : UP TO 12,000 FT.

An RAE sample infrared homing missile design from the 1954 report. Its compact size was derived from its relatively tiny warhead – which would have required a direct hit to knock out a Soviet bomber. *BMGC*

"We therefore propose a new armament system in which, at high overtaking speeds, the pass distance is considerably greater for a given kill chance. The armament consists of 16 to 25 recoilless guns elevated at 30 degrees to 45 degrees. The fighter flies on the path of the bomber, but about 200ft below it, and the guns fire in salvo at the appropriate point. The line of sight is provided by the gunsight and is visual in day and infrared at night. The system is essentially a single pass system but the lethality is high.

"With the high overtaking speed and the small radar cross section of the fighter aircraft, it is fairly certain that insufficient warning of the fighter's approach will be available in the bomber for counter activity to be taken. The chances of fighter-on-fighter combat at these high speeds are also extremely remote."

Air Ministry vs RAE
Kyle asked Group Captain Harold Peter Broad, the Air Ministry's Deputy Director of Operational Requirements 1, to assess the RAE paper and, reporting back on April 8, he wrote: "The weakness of the paper is that it is limited by its assumptions. These assumptions, which emerge in the course of the discussion and are not fully stated at the start, confine the authors to consideration of a single-seat fighter on the lines of an improved F.23 [Lightning], and although the possibilities of a two-seater and of collision course weapons are touched on, their theme is not developed.

"There is nothing new in the paper. So far as it goes it is entirely in accord with our present thinking and it confirms that our policy for the F.23 is on the right lines. However… it is doubtful if the aircraft proposed is really suitable to succeed the F.23, in fact there are several statements in the paper which go to show that our concept of a two-seater with full AI is the better solution.

"For example, it is stated that relatively simple pilot-operated search radar is feasible because of improvements that can be made to ground-controlled interception control. This is a very bold assumption since, although these improvements are planned, it is impossible to say at this stage when they will be realised in full. Again the paper puts great emphasis on the need for very accurate ground-controlled fighter manoeuvres for successful interceptions.

"If the limitations of the ground station or of the pilot make such accurate manoeuvres difficult or impossible, the whole basis of the concept is destroyed. It is patently obvious that a better AI set would give us the necessary margin for error in the other fields."

Among his "other points of interest", Broad mentions the idea that an enemy bomber which sacrificed extreme high-altitude flight for a measure of manoeuvrability would be the "worst case for the fighter" and that the report had stressed that "a straight-wing, twin-engine layout on the lines of the Meteor is preferred. This is because it simplified installational and centre of gravity problems. Finally, there are some interesting armament proposals, particularly in regard to pass-pursuit guns".

Also asked to review the RAE report was Group Captain Neil Wheeler, the Air Ministry's Deputy Director of Operational Requirements 2 (soon to become DDOR 1 in place of Broad). Wheeler had headed his own committee during the previous year which produced its own report in December 1953. He wrote that while his team had started with the operational problem, then recommended the sort of interceptor that might solve it, the RAE had started by recommending the sort of interceptor that might reach Mach 2 "then set about examining how to fit such an aircraft into the defence system. I submit that, whatever the merits of our conclusions, our method of tackling the problem was more logical".

On this basis, he wrote, "the case for a single-seater is extremely weak… on page 8 of the report RAE state that there is no compelling reason for putting a second man in

the aircraft. Unfortunately, from an operational point of view, thereafter they produce no very compelling reason for not doing so. Indeed, the whole tone of the sections on AI, instruments and the control system is one of difficulties and the exploration of relatively new fields. I see no reason for us to alter our views at this stage unless – as I stated in my paper – the penalties in design are prohibitive".

The RAE appeared to have underestimated the threat posed by the Soviets: "RAE's report is mainly based on a threat of Mach 0.9 and throughout they do not appear to attach the same importance to 'time to height' that we do. I remain convinced that in order to cater for the worse threat (i.e. possibly Mach 1.3) we will have to use a form of mixed power to achieve rapid climb and acceleration potential at altitude.

Wheeler also appears to have had little time for English Electric: "During the course of my examination before Christmas, English Electric were keen to put over what they termed the 'dynamic approach'. This consists of climbing to about 45,000 to 50,000ft, levelling out and accelerating to Mach 2, and then taking advantage of the considerable kinetic energy for gaining height rapidly.

"English Electric were obviously influenced by the fact that the acceptance of such tactics would greatly add to the capabilities of the F.23. RAE also appear to be strong advocates of this theory and even suggest that an extreme case can be made for 'zooming' to 70,000ft, which is above the true ceiling of the aircraft. Whilst zooming appears to be an admirable method of attempting an interception above one's ceiling it seems wrong in principle to plan for an aircraft carrying out such tactics as a normal practice simply because it lacks acceleration potential at the greater height or has insufficient

power to complete the climb in the required time." He said reaching 60,000ft within three minutes was the most important aspect of the design yet "as we discovered in our paper, to demand 60,000ft in three minutes and a speed of Mach 2 at completion of climb is almost to ask for the impossible; of which RAE are obviously aware". This reinforced the need for auxiliary rocket motors.

One crew or two?

The latest drafts of OR.329 and OR.330 were discussed at a meeting between Air Ministry and Ministry of Supply representatives on April 21, 1954 – the meeting originally proposed by Gardner of the MoS, involving himself, Tuttle and Hall. The atmosphere seems to have been confrontational, with Hall saying that "he was very doubtful whether the aircraft envisaged by the Air Staff would be capable of performing the task and said there was a marked difference between Air Staff and RAE thinking". However, Lewis 'Nick' Nicholson, the RAE's head of aerodynamics, said the RAE's study had been linked to a pursuit course weapon and "if a collision course weapon were used then there was some promise of defending against bombers of up to Mach 2 with a manned fighter, the changeover from a pursuit to a collision course weapon making a difference of about 0.5 Mach".

The discussion then boiled down to whether the aircraft needed one crewman and a simple radar or two crewmen and a large complex one. In summary, Baker as chairman, asked the RAE and RRE to carry out a further study, which Hall said he would be pleased to do. Tuttle was asked for more information as to why two crewmen were necessary and he replied that he was "unable to justify the need scientifically. [He] believed that the enemy will never do the expected and in such circumstances two brains would be better than one".

Afterwards, Tuttle felt aggrieved with the RAE's interjections during the meeting and wrote to Gardner on April 26: "Whilst I agree that RAE's comments will be invaluable, we would of course like them submitted to us as those of the Ministry of Supply as we do not send draft requirements officially to RAE. Perhaps, therefore, you would be good enough to ensure that the Ministry of Supply comments incorporating those of RAE and other establishments as necessary are forwarded here as soon as possible.

"I can go as far as to say that the issue of the next draft of the requirement which will form the subject of the Operational Requirements Committee meeting is now held up until we receive them. The sooner we get your comments the sooner we can have the ORC meeting and the sooner we can get industry started. Perhaps, therefore, you will be good enough to hurry the whole thing up."

On May 3, Colonel Cuthbert L Moseley Jr, of the USAF, sent over his team's brief comments on OR.329, which amounted to asking for the results of airframe de-icing tests and alternative armaments investigations mentioned in it, and stating that: "On the basis of technological data available to this office, this requirement is within the state of the art for the 1960 time period.

"It is recommended that the following be incorporated in the requirement: 'The range, endurance, and weapon lethality must be such that each interceptor can attack more than one target on each sortie, with a high probability of kill per attack'."

On the same day, Air Vice-Marshal Leslie William Clement Bower, Senior Air Staff Officer of Fighter Command, whose men would be flying the new interceptor, sent over

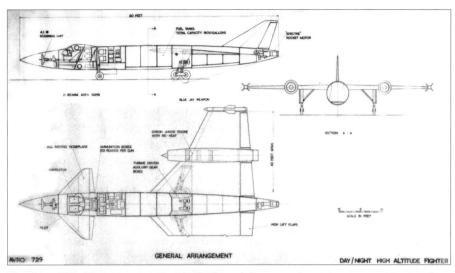

The Avro 729. Eleven companies, including engine manufacturers, were sent an early copy of OR.329 'for information' in March 1954. Avro, like Hawker, seems to have got stuck straight in and designed the 729 to fit the requirement. Yet when the list of companies being invited to tender was eventually drawn up, Avro was relegated to the 'B-list'. Exactly why this should have happened is unclear, but it may have been down to Avro's perceived workload. *Avro Heritage Museum*

his comments too. Unlike many of his Air Staff colleagues, he was in favour of a minimum performance search radar in the aircraft and a maximum performance control radar on the ground. He also wanted a single-seater with good all-round visibility "since its only defence when returning to base is by evasion". Collision-course guided weapons were needed as well as a gun or rockets "to achieve the necessary degree of lethality" and anti-jamming equipment.

Kyle received a letter from Captain Duncan Lewin, Director of Naval Air Warfare with the Naval Staff, on May 11, saying he had been made aware of OR.329 and "as you know I hope to produce a parallel requirement with a view to one basic aeroplane doing us both. It would be a great help if you could send me a copy of your draft at this stage so that we can begin with the spade work. I have no intention of trying to 'jump the gun' and get in first with our requirement. It would suit me better not to produce my formal requirement until after you do".

On June 2, Kyle received a letter from Roy Ewans at Avro, deputy

to chief designer 'Dave' Davies, regarding the preview of OR.329 sent in March. Ewans wrote: "Dear Digger, [Kyle was Australian] may I refer to your letter of March 17 to Dave on the new fighter. We have gone quite a way on this aeroplane but before we can say that what we have done will meet performance we have to get a pretty firm picture of the weight of equipment that will be carried.

"The major part of the unknown equipment is that covered by your addendums 1-5. I don't know that we particularly want to have all of these but I would like to be able to get from you or someone else some idea of what is likely to be involved.

"On the radar side we have installed a Mk. 18 with a 30in diameter dish and a 40.5in swept diameter. The total weight is 800lb. For the guided weapon we have assumed standard Blue Jay and I expect you will want to have a developed version of this. Apart from the above we have found the aircraft fairly plain sailing."

Kyle wrote back on the 4th saying he was encouraged to hear this and would like to visit Avro during the week commencing July

5 if possible and "if this could be linked with my long-promised flight in the Vulcan so much the better". As a P.S. he wrote: "I am taking this opportunity of returning the receipt for the brochure on the 727. I am sorry not to have done this before. As you know it is very difficult for me to give official encouragement on this project. Nevertheless it is very interesting to us." The 727 was Avro's submission for a NATO tactical fighter programme. Avro's design to OR.329 was the 729.

Tuttle sent Gardner another not-so-subtle reminder on June 15 that the Ministry of Supply's comments on OR.329 were urgently needed and Wheeler, who had asked the Central Fighter Establishment for a view on whether the fighter should have one seat or two, received a fairly non-committal answer on June 21.

From behind or head-on?

The 51st Operational Requirements Committee Meeting (ORC) was planned to take place on July 13 at the Air Ministry with Sir Thomas Pike as chairman, but on July 5 Pike consulted Sir Dermot Boyle for his views and on July 7, Tuttle sat down with Pike and Boyle to work out their collective stance before the ORC meeting. They agreed there was no need for Aden cannon or rocket armament, that the crew should be two, that the AI radar need not be "the maximum possible", and that the aircraft "should be designed to carry drop tanks for extra fuel which it would use when on a standing patrol at subsonic speeds".

At the ORC itself, the chief area of discussion was whether the interceptor should use a pursuit or collision course attack – coming at the enemy bomber from behind or in front. Opinion now appeared to sway towards the latter, provided it was technically possible to house a radar dish big enough to allow for a collision course attack.

In addition, thought was now being given to which companies would be invited to tender for OR.329 when the time came. A memo written by the Air Ministry's AD/TD Plans, W H Curtis, dated July 21, 1954, entitled 'The supersonic family of aircraft – invitations to tender for', gives the position at that point: "The prime contracts to be awarded within the next 18 months or so comprise: the supersonic high-altitude reconnaissance aircraft, OR.330; the supersonic bomber and the day/night high-altitude supersonic fighter, OR.329. It seems not unlikely that contracts for the first and last of these three will be let at about the same time, roughly late 1955; the contract for the bomber rather later, say during the second quarter of 1956.

"The low-altitude bomber, OR.324, appears temporarily to have been 'shelved' and, it is thought, cannot be put out to contract till well after the three aircraft referred to above. Should this thought be wrong and the tender-invitation stage be reached at about the same time as the bomber referred above, then invitations should be sent to those firms listed hereunder for the bomber.

"I have therefore reviewed carefully the forecast loading, at the relevant times, of all firms in the industry, with a view to determining which, on these grounds, should be invited to tender for the three aircraft referred to in the first paragraph.

"In short, I now feel that, in due course, the following firms should be so invited: Reconnaissance OR 330 – Blackburn & General; de Havilland; English Electric; Handley Page; Hawker; A V Roe; Saunders-Roe; Short and Harland; and Vickers-Armstrong.

"Bomber [unnumbered OR, split from OR.330] – Blackburn & General; de Havilland; English Electric; Handley Page; A V Roe; Saunders-Roe; Short and Harland; and Vickers-Armstrong.

"Fighter, OR.329 – Armstrong-Whitworth, Bristol, de Havilland, English Electric, Gloster, Hawker, A V Roe, Saunders-Roe, Vickers-Armstrong."

Four of the firms listed by Curtis were underlined – Blackburn & General, Short and Harland, Armstrong-Whitworth and Hawker.

He continued: "Of the above, the four firms underlined – together with Fairey, Percival and Westland – are in the process of tendering for the naval two-seat strike aircraft, NA.39. If one of the four succeed, it should be struck out of the above lists since it will not, it is thought, have sufficient capacity available to accept more than one of these four jobs."

Regarding Hawker, Curtis states: "Hawker has been included in the reconnaissance list purely because, there being no development potential in the Hunter, they will be in a parlous state unless they 'land' something; they are an obvious choice to tender for the fighter."

Blackburn was successful in NA.39 with the design that would eventually become the Buccaneer and was therefore removed from the OR.330 lists.

During August 1954 a new version of OR.329, the sixth draft, was worked on, with Fighter Command and the Ministry of Supply arguing over the need for the interceptor to reach 60,000ft in three minutes. Fighter Command stated this was essential, while the MoS, with the backing of the RAE, wanted to change the design requirement to read "take-off and climb to reach Mach 2 at 60,000ft in seven minutes at the attacking position".

Now OR.329 was coming together it had to be put before the highly influential Defence Research Policy Committee (DRPC) to gain approval. The DRPC's backing was essential to gain full Government support for the project. A paper prepared

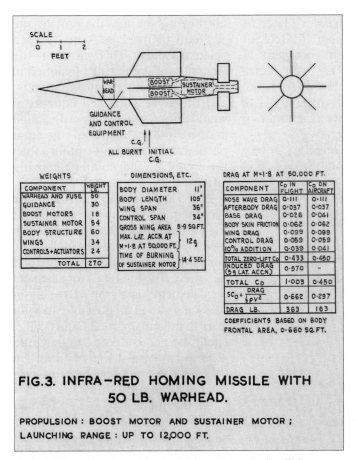

FIG.3. INFRA-RED HOMING MISSILE WITH 50 LB. WARHEAD.

PROPULSION: BOOST MOTOR AND SUSTAINER MOTOR;
LAUNCHING RANGE: UP TO 12,000 FT.

WEIGHTS

COMPONENT	WEIGHT LB.
WARHEAD AND FUSE	50
GUIDANCE	30
BOOST MOTORS	18
SUSTAINER MOTOR	54
BODY STRUCTURE	60
WINGS	34
CONTROLS + ACTUATORS	24
TOTAL	270

DIMENSIONS, ETC.

BODY DIAMETER	11"
BODY LENGTH	105"
WING SPAN	36"
CONTROL SPAN	34"
GROSS WING AREA	5.9 SQ.FT.
MAX. LAT. ACCN. AT M=1.8 AT 50,000 FT.	12g
TIME OF BURNING OF SUSTAINER MOTOR	14.4 SEC.

DRAG AT M=1.8 AT 50,000 FT.

COMPONENT	C_D IN FLIGHT	C_D ON AIRCRAFT
NOSE WAVE DRAG	0.111	0.111
AFTERBODY DRAG	0.037	0.037
BASE DRAG	0.026	0.041
BODY SKIN FRICTION	0.062	0.062
WING DRAG	0.099	0.099
CONTROL DRAG	0.059	0.059
10% ADDITION	0.039	0.041
TOTAL ZERO-LIFT C_D	0.433	0.450
INDUCED DRAG (5g LAT. ACCN.)	0.570	-
TOTAL C_D	1.003	0.450
$SC_D = \dfrac{DRAG}{\frac{1}{2}\rho v^2}$	0.662	0.297
DRAG LB.	363	163

COEFFICIENTS BASED ON BODY FRONTAL AREA, 0.660 SQ.FT.

A second version of the sample RAE homing missile. This one has a much larger warhead, meaning that a direct hit was not essential, but the overall size and weight of the weapon was significantly increased, as was the drag it produced. *BMGC*

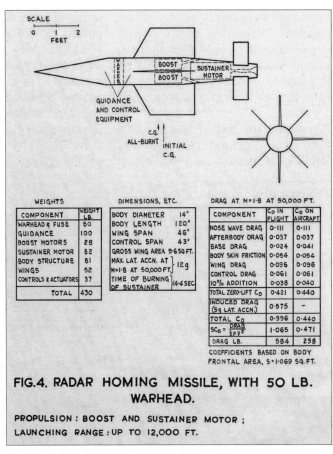

FIG.4. RADAR HOMING MISSILE, WITH 50 LB. WARHEAD.

PROPULSION: BOOST AND SUSTAINER MOTOR;
LAUNCHING RANGE: UP TO 12,000 FT.

WEIGHTS

COMPONENT	WEIGHT LB.
WARHEAD & FUSE	50
GUIDANCE	100
BOOST MOTORS	28
SUSTAINER MOTOR	82
BODY STRUCTURE	81
WINGS	52
CONTROLS & ACTUATORS	37
TOTAL	430

DIMENSIONS, ETC.

BODY DIAMETER	14"
BODY LENGTH	120"
WING SPAN	46"
CONTROL SPAN	43"
GROSS WING AREA	9.65 SQ.FT.
MAX. LAT. ACCN. AT M=1.8 AT 50,000 FT.	12g
TIME OF BURNING OF SUSTAINER	14.4 SEC

DRAG AT M=1.8 AT 50,000 FT.

COMPONENT	C_D IN FLIGHT	C_D ON AIRCRAFT
NOSE WAVE DRAG	0.111	0.111
AFTERBODY DRAG	0.037	0.037
BASE DRAG	0.024	0.041
BODY SKIN FRICTION	0.054	0.054
WING DRAG	0.096	0.096
CONTROL DRAG	0.061	0.061
10% ADDITION	0.038	0.040
TOTAL ZERO-LIFT C_D	0.421	0.440
INDUCED DRAG (5g LAT. ACCN.)	0.575	-
TOTAL C_D	0.996	0.440
$SC_D = \dfrac{DRAG}{\frac{1}{2}\rho v^2}$	1.065	0.471
DRAG LB.	584	258

COEFFICIENTS BASED ON BODY FRONTAL AREA, S=1.069 SQ.FT.

RAE sample radar-guided missile design. These weapons were particularly unappealing to aircraft designers, despite their ability to operate in all weathers without penalty, because of their massive size and the associated drag they produced. Carrying them would either mean a loss of performance or a larger aircraft design. *BMGC*

for Pike to submit to the DRPC read: "In about 1958 the F.23 and the developed Javelin should be in service, and capable of meeting the threat from bombers comparable to our own 'V' Class. The rocket fighter could also be in service if it is decided to develop it beyond the research stage. These aircraft, with development, might be expected to carry the defence to about 1963.

"Although no intelligence information is available on the threat at this time, it is reasonable to assume that by the early Sixties the Russians will have developed a supersonic bomber capable of at least Mach 1.3 and able to operate at heights in the region of 60,000ft. The proper weapon to meet such a threat against the UK is a guided missile, but although weapons of the Red Shoes [English Electric Thunderbird]/Red Duster [Bristol Bloodhound] family should be in limited service, it is virtually certain that the longer range area defence weapon will not be available. In these circumstances the reliance must still be placed on manned fighters.

"A detailed tactical study of the problem a high-altitude threat of this nature would pose has been carried out, and it does not appear that the F.23, even in its most advanced form, would be capable of reaching the height in the required time.

It is a fundamental feature of the turbojet that it suffers from a loss of power at high altitudes, and the only means of attaining the necessary acceleration potential at height is by the use of a rocket motor.

"The problem of installing a rocket motor in the F.23 is a matter for detailed design study. Preliminary studies indicate that this can be done, and an improvement in the high-level performance of the F.23 could undoubtedly be gained in this way. The effect on the handling characteristics and performance has not yet been fully investigated.

"However, neither the F.23 nor the rocket interceptor can meet the full all-weather requirement. At best, their equipment can only be improved towards this end. Moreover, both are single-seater fighters and the new Air Staff Requirement is essentially for a two-seater aircraft.

"It is, therefore, concluded that before the area defence guided weapon becomes available, a new two-seater supersonic fighter will be required, employing mixed power, capable of reaching 60,000ft in three minutes and accelerating rapidly up to a speed of Mach 2. It would be armed solely with guided weapons."

Finalising the list

Kyle signed off on the sixth draft of OR.329 on August 11, 1954, which

outlined the interceptor just as put to the DRPC, and in October 1954 this new draft was sent to 11 aircraft firms for still more advance information. At the same time, the Ministry of Supply completed its first draft of Specification F.155T.

It began by introducing a way of designing aircraft which had

not been given any thought by the Air Staff themselves – the 'weapon system' concept. This was where the aircraft was specifically designed to use certain weapons and equipment, and those weapons and equipment would be specifically designed and tailored for use by that particular aircraft – rather than the weapons and equipment being 'off-the-shelf' items.

The introduction read: "The Air Staff requires a day/night high-altitude fighter. The speedy development of the aeroplane is considered extremely important – the Air Staff operational requirement asks for it to be in service as soon as possible and not later than January 1962. This project shall be considered under the weapon system concept whereby the aircraft and its systems are treated as a single entity."

Furthermore: "There is no intention that the aircraft designer shall of necessity be responsible for the design of specialist operational equipment. He is however encouraged to study, by collaboration with its designers, its purpose and features with a view to influencing not only its configuration to suit his particular aircraft design, but also its function in order to achieve the best integration of the aircraft and its equipment from all points of view (e.g.) operational, functional, servicing, accessibility, reliability, power supply. He will furthermore be responsible for its installation in the aircraft.

"The designer shall include in his brochure a heat balance statement for the entire aircraft, but with particular attention to the provision of cooling the cabin and equipment, for typical cases in the flight plan proposed for his aircraft. An RAE report No. Aero 2513, GW20 has been prepared; this contains a wealth of ideas on the use of a supersonic fighter. It gives an analysis of the problem which though not similar in all respects to

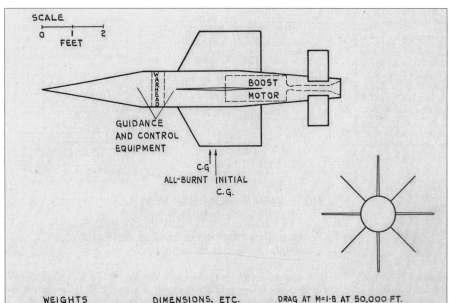

Using only a boost motor in a radar homing missile would mean its size could be reduced slightly, but it was still a very difficult weapon to wrap an aircraft around. *BMGC*

that presented in this specification suggests possible solutions."

The remainder of the spec stuck closely to OR.329 and otherwise followed the standard form of Ministry of Supply aircraft specifications with regard to methodology and process. F.155T was amended in November with the section concerning the RAE's report removed from the introduction and moved to the back of the spec.

On January 5, 1955, the list of firms to be invited to tender an aircraft to Specification F.155T to meet OR.329 was: Armstrong Whitworth, de Havilland, English Electric, Gloster, Hawker, Saunders-Roe, Vickers (Supermarine), and Westland.

The following day, Fairey was added to the list and Westland was deleted "because of their poor showing in the NA.39 competition", according to the Ministry of Supply's newly appointed F.155T development project officer Ian Otto Hockmeyer. Copies of the specification would be sent to Blackburn, Bristol, Handley Page, A V Roe and Short and Harland for information – the 'B list'. Quite why Avro had been relegated to the 'B' list when just six months earlier it had reported finding the OR.329 fighter design such "plain sailing", and had been identified as a natural contender for OR.329 less than five months earlier, is unclear. Certainly, Avro was also a contender for OR.330, but then English Electric had no problem tendering for both.

The Ministry of Supply's Woodward-Nutt wrote on January 11, 1955: "I think we should consider transferring Glosters to List B in view of their pre-occupation with the Javelin and the F.153."

On January 14, 1955, the Under-Secretary of State for Air, George Ward, sent a letter to Gardner which read: "Unless the technical reasons for excluding Shorts from the list of those invited to tender are very strong, they should I think be included on this list.

"For social and political reasons connected with the provision of employment in Northern Ireland I think we might be held to be at fault if we did not give Northern Ireland an opportunity to compete for work for which they might be found to be suitable."

Shortly thereafter, Gloster was dropped and Short and Harland was promoted to the 'A list'. Hockmeyer was also required to supply reasons for the exclusion of the other "design-approved" companies from the F.155T lists – Boulton Paul, Folland, Handley Page, Heston, Martin Baker, M L Aviation, Percival and Westland.

The Aircraft Specification No. F.155T Day/Night High Altitude Fighter document itself was finalised on January 15 and the final list of eight firms that would be invited to tender – Armstrong Whitworth, de Havilland, English Electric, Fairey, Hawker, Saunders-Roe, Short and Harland and Vickers (Supermarine) – was approved on January 24, 1955.

Tenders were to be returned by 10am on August 9, 1955. According to a letter from Glynn Silyn Roberts, the Director of Military Aircraft Research & Development (DMARD) (RAF), dated February 2, 1955, "it is suggested that firms should be asked their estimates of selling price for orders of 250 to 750 aircraft".

The F.155T competition begins
The invitations to tender went out on February 17 and Hockmeyer set out to personally visit each company in turn to discuss the requirement. He visited Short and Harland on February 24, English Electric on the 25th, Vickers-Armstrongs on the 28th, Saunders-Roe on March 1, Armstrong Whitworth on March 2, and Fairey on March 4.

There was no visit to Hawker owing to a "considerable reluctance to accept a visit from the project officer", according to Hockmeyer himself. He does not appear to have

visited de Havilland either, but the reason for this is unknown.

During his visit to Shorts in Belfast, chief designer David Keith-Lucas requested a copy of Defence Against High Altitude Bombers by Mach 2 Fighters, since the company did not have one, and this was duly sent over on March 14. Vickers-Armstrongs requested information on the handling of HTP rocket fuel, which Hockmeyer sent over on March 17.

Other firms requested more information on the missiles to be carried and the radar systems to be used. At the same time, Fighter Command was calling for a change to the requirement which emphasised the need to climb to 60,000ft in three minutes, giving at least five minutes' flying time at that altitude – in fact, they wanted 12 minutes at 60,000ft. Back in July of 1954, the requirement had been changed to require that the aircraft should be in "an attacking position at 60,000ft… in seven minutes", giving just one minute of flying time operational altitude.

On March 4, Tuttle's replacement as Assistant Chief of the Air Staff (Operational Requirements) at the Air Ministry, Air Vice-Marshal Harold Vivian 'Harry' Satterly, wrote to Pike, saying: "In short, Fighter Command believe that the OR as it stands calls for an aircraft with insufficient operational flexibility which would be incapable of utilising to the maximum extent the effective ground control cover."

However, Satterly pointed out that Fighter Command's demands would have unfortunate consequences for the aircraft designers: "I have been advised that to meet Fighter Command's case in full, which would mean a combat endurance of 12 minutes and the ability to reach 60,000ft in three minutes in the same sortie, would add some 40% to the weight of the aircraft to meet OR.329 as it stands. The general view that I have had from the Ministry of Supply and industry is that the aircraft will in any case be of the order of 40,000-50,000lb. I therefore instructed my staff to make a very careful examination of the Fighter Command proposals in order to see if a compromise were acceptable."

The compromise he suggested involved the aircraft having to reach 60,000ft in six minutes, at which point it would need to be 70 miles from base and travelling at "a speed not less than Mach 2". It would have to allow four minutes' combat at Mach 2 – with the guided weapon being released at the end of the four minutes – and including landing time would need to be able to spend a total of 45 minutes in the air.

Throughout the course of the OR.329/F.155T process, Fighter Command seems to have continually objected to anything short of an aircraft which could reach an altitude of 60,000ft within three minutes of the aircraft's engines being started. The process went on regardless.

Short and Harland sent a letter to the Air Ministry on March 16, 1955, stating that owing to its other commitments the company had decided not to submit a tender to specification F.155T. This left seven competing firms.

The April 5 meeting, chaired by Roberts, took place at the Air Ministry. Present were some of the British aviation industry's very best and brightest – Armstrong Whitworth sent chief designer E D 'Dixie' Keen and project designer H F Butler; English Electric sent chief designer Freddie Page and chief engineer Ray Creasey; Fairey sent technical director Robert Lickley; for de Havilland there was chief designer Ronald Eric Bishop, and Phil Smith and Geoffrey Trevelyan, both designers; for Hawker, chief designer Sir Sydney Camm and designer Vivian Stanbury; Saunders-Roe sent chief designer Maurice

Brennan and Richard Stanton-Jones; and Vickers-Armstrongs sent chief designer Joe Smith and designer George Henson.

There were also two representatives from each of the weapons firms – de Havilland Propellors and Vickers-Armstrongs – 10 Air Ministry representatives, 22 from the Ministry of Supply, two from the Radar Research Establishment, 11 from the RAE and Hockmeyer as secretary – a total of 65 men.

Roberts opened by introducing the topic and "said he regretted that there had been considerable uncertainty both regarding the operational requirements and equipment possibilities". As a result, the in-service date set at January 1962 might have to be pushed back. He also stressed the importance of the weapon system concept.

Herbert James 'Jimmy' Kirkpatrick, Kyle's recent replacement as Director of Operational Requirements (Air), then set out the Air Staff position. He said that "in the introduction to OR.329, the fighter was placed in its strategic setting as being something which would be needed in the early years of the introduction of guided missile defence. A recent study of future air defence had made it clear that, even with a fully deployed guided-weapon defence system, a manned fighter would continue to be needed, if only for the object of interrogation".

He told the designers that "the Air Staff realised that the project was an ambitious one, but it bore comparison with what the Americans were attempting to do with an earlier target date". The Air Staff were "very ready to compromise where they could do so without giving up vital requirements. There were, however, certain things on which they could not compromise. They very definitely wanted a crew of two. They believed that,

almost irrespective of the degree of automaticity, the interception was going to call for extremely accurate flying and, in the presence of jamming, the carriage of a radar operator would certainly increase the chances of making each attempted interception a success. This was of the utmost importance against a nuclear threat".

And secondly, "they regarded it as most important to be able to carry either collision course or pursuit course weapons, if possible a mixed load of two of each kind. Here again they realised the difficulties. If it were really impractical to carry two of each type of weapon simultaneously, then they were prepared to consider the carrying of alternative loads, either two collision-course or two pursuit-course weapons. There would, however, have to be provision for very quick changeover between the two types".

When the general discussion of operational and technical queries was opened, Hawker chief designer Camm jumped straight in. He said "that what was asked for in the specification was quite impracticable by 1962, in any case he felt the Air Staff assumptions were based on an over-pessimistic view of the threat". Brennan, of Saunders-Roe, said he thought the specification could be met.

Weight was a big problem. The interceptor's weaponry and related equipment was likely to weigh 10,000lb and therefore, it was argued, the aircraft would need to be some eight to 10 times that. Fairey's Lickley said all equipment would need to be designed with the lowest possible weight in mind – which would take time.

Pressed further on how they might be prepared to compromise, Air Staff representatives were reluctant to discuss any specifics except accepting two weapons of one sort, rather than a mixed load of four.

The Radar Research Establishment team, supported by the RAE, said they thought a collision course weapon would be best, but the Air Staff was similarly reluctant to accept this. Lickley pointed out that reducing the load to two weapons meant more fuel could be carried; sticking to one type of weapon would allow further gains since only one set of services would be needed for those weapons.

Page, of English Electric, "suggested that the divergence between what was wanted and what seemed possible, led to the need for two parallel studies, one of collision course with a degraded performance and one on the pursuit-course case".

At this point Gardner weighed in, saying that if Page's idea was combined with the Air Staff's likely concession on weapons, a way forward might be found; "he advised the firms to put the Air Staff flight plan on one side and to design a system to meet the ultimate objective". The conclusion of the debate "was, therefore, that the onus rested upon the firms concerned to study all the interrelated factors".

A letter sent by Hockmeyer shortly after the meeting states: "On April 5 a meeting was held between the chief designers of the competing firms, Air Staff and Ministry of Supply, at which the difficulties of meeting the specification were discussed. As a consequence of this meeting it was agreed to treat the two types of weapon as alternative loads. Issue 2 of the specification embodying OR.329 revised on these lines was issued in July."

Specification F.155T Issue 2 was published on July 5, 1955 – the final version before submission of tenders, for which a new date of October 5, 1955 was now set. Issue 2 retained most of the features of Issue 1, such as the January 1962 in-service date, the weapon-system concept, the need to destroy "very high-altitude supersonic enemy raiders" at 60,000ft and Mach 1.3 and two crew. The difference from Issue 1 was, as Hockmeyer pointed out, in the weapons. Two radar-guided missiles were preferred, but two passive infrared homing missiles were permissible – as opposed to both sorts having to be carried at the same time.

In performance terms, the "normal warning time" sortie was as follows: "(i) Start take-off and climb to reach 60,000ft 70 miles from base in six minutes at a speed of not less than Mach 2. (ii) Four minutes' combat at Mach 2 (at the end of this four minutes the aircraft is at the weapon release point). (iii) Return towards base at economical cruising speed (15 minutes). (iv) Descent and approach (15 minutes). The fuel allowance for

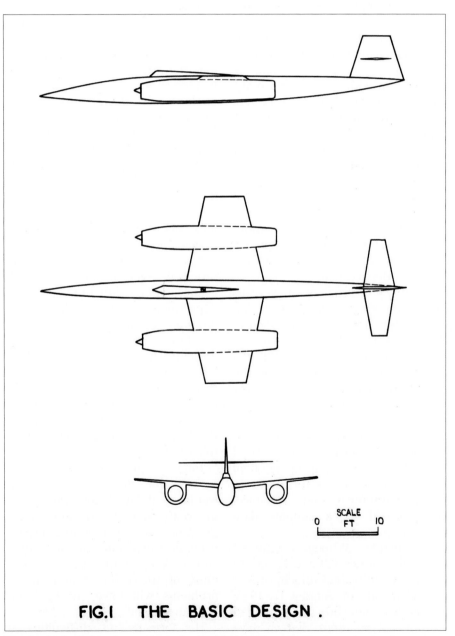

FIG.I THE BASIC DESIGN .

The 'basic design' as it was shown in the 1952 RAE report 'An Investigation into an Aircraft to Fly at a Mach Number of 2, Aero.2462', by C H E Warren, J Poole and D C Appleyard. It would prove to be hugely influential on British experimental aircraft designs for years to come. *BMGC*

the descent and approach phase should be based on GCA conditions. (v) Baulked landing, followed by a second circuit, and landing (5 minutes). Total time approximately 45 minutes."

Regarding the pattern of approach used by the interceptor: "A choice between collision- and pursuit-course tactics involves consideration of many conflicting characteristics, the chief of which are interception time, AI size and range, closing speed and missile size, range and lethality. The Air Staff believe that the use of all round collision course tactics will provide the system with greater capability, but regard an alternative system using an attack from the rear cone and incorporating passive homing as necessary to be complementary to such a system."

During June 1955, the RAE and RRE agreed to form a new joint Supersonic Fighter Study Group to continue working on OR.329, under the leadership of William Stephens, the head of the RAE's guided weapons department.

On July 25, 1955, Hockmeyer was still attempting to arrange a visit to Hawker. His letter, addressed to "The Resident Technical Officer, Hawker Aircraft", states: "Will you please draw the attention of the firm to the fact that I shall be on my summer leave from the fortnight commencing the 27th August, and if the firm therefore are likely to require me to pay them a visit round about that time to clear up any final points before they settle down to the preparation of their brochure, they should fix a suitable date fairly soon."

Meanwhile, Wheeler arranged for copies of OR.329 and F.155T to be sent to John McCulloch, of A V Roe (Canada), on August 17, 1955, to see whether his company had "any ideas" on them. Sixteen days earlier, on August 1, 1955, it had been announced that the Canadian government intended to place a pre-production order for Avro CF-105 fighters.

The RAE's Supersonic Fighter Study Group held its first meeting that month and ran into problems immediately.

Hockmeyer had been made a member of the group at Roberts' insistence and on August 22, 1955, Roberts wrote to RAE deputy director Francis Edgar 'Frankie' Jones: "I understand from Hockmeyer that at the first meeting of the Supersonic Fighter Study Group you decided that one of your main objectives would be to provide material which would assist us at headquarters in our examination of the tender design brochures of the aircraft to Specification F.155T. I also gather that you did not expect to be able to report until the end of the year. I am a little puzzled about the phasing of the timescale because it is quite obvious that we shall not be able to put the brochures into cold storage until your report is available.

"You will also of course be required, even if not as a study group, but certainly in your normal departmental responsibilities, to do quite a lot of work on these brochures and I foresee serious difficulty in trying to tackle both jobs simultaneously. It is less than two months between now and the date when the brochures should be in your hands, and I would very much like to receive your view on this problem."

Jones replied on August 26 to say that although the report would be delayed until the end of the year "there is no doubt that a great deal of information is rapidly becoming available on the subject and certainly by the end of October most of the difficult and thorny problems will have surfaced and been discussed".

He foresaw no difficulties in being able to produce the report and pass judgement on the firms' designs simultaneously.

Commenting on this in a handwritten note dated September 13, 1955, Hockmeyer wrote that this was "not really okay, but a completely satisfactory answer was not to be expected". Much of the rest of the month was taken up with finalising procedures for quickly assessing the firms' brochures – which duly arrived during the first two weeks of October 1955. It should be noted that although they were always referred to merely as 'brochures', the documents in question were not the sort of publicity tools full of overestimations, glaring omissions and thinly veiled spin that we understand today. These were hefty technical statements of intent and they were classified secret. Their publication and distribution was tightly controlled and their contents carefully dissected in minute detail by Britain's top specialists in aeronautical design and engineering.

INTERCEPTOR TIMELINE

December 1951
At a conference to decide the future development of the Hawker Hunter and Supermarine Swift, a discussion takes place on the type of fighter needed to succeed them – and replace the Gloster Javelin, too. It is considered that the next generation of fighters should be able to fly at around Mach 1.8.

January 1952
A draft Air Staff Requirement for a supersonic day fighter, unnumbered at this stage, is drawn up and circulated throughout the operational requirements branch. However, it is decided that more information about the potential threat posed by the enemy, and what would be required to meet it, is needed.

February 1952
Draft paper 'The Future Interceptor Fighter' is prepared.

April 1952
A second draft paper, 'The Future Requirement for a new Generation of Fighters to Succeed F.3 and F.4' is prepared and circulated throughout the Air Ministry, Fighter Command and the 2nd Tactical Air Force for comment.

June 1952
RAE publishes 'An Investigation into an Aircraft to Fly at a Mach Number of 2', outlining what it believes will be the best high-speed aerodynamic forms.

June-July 1952
Comments on the second draft paper are collated and points of disagreement include whether the fighter should be designed to destroy only enemy bombers or enemy fighters, whether it should be able to operate at high or low altitude, and whether it should be able to operate at night and in all weathers.

October 1952
Meeting of RAF Aircraft Research Committee to discuss the paper on Future Fighters. No definite conclusion is reached on the requirement.

January 1953
Another draft of the Air Staff Requirement for a supersonic interceptor is drawn up.

February 1953
Draft requirement is circulated to operational requirements staff for comment.

April 1953
It is decided that a working party should be established to study the future air defence requirements of the UK.

July 1953
The terms of reference for the proposed working party are still being discussed.

October 1953
The interceptor requirement is re-drafted and re-circulated.

December 1953
The Air Ministry publishes a new paper: 'Future Air Defence of the UK'.

December 18, 1953
Another paper, 'The Future Requirement for Manned Supersonic Interceptors', is published by the Ministry of Supply.

January 1954
The composition and terms of reference of the Air Defence Committee Working Party are finally approved by the Chiefs of Staff – nine months after the initial decision to set it up. The working party is to be led by Sir Arnold Hall. The third draft of the requirement is produced.

February 1954
The fourth draft of the interceptor requirement is produced.

March 1954
A fifth draft is produced, finally with a number – OR.329 – and this time circulated to the Ministry of Supply, Scientific Advisor to the Air Ministry and Fighter Command for comments. Eleven firms are also sent copies of the fifth draft so they can prepare design studies.

April 1954
The working party under Hall publishes its first report – 'Defence Against High Altitude Bombers by Mach 2 Fighters'.

May-June 1954
Comments on OR.329 fifth draft are received and compiled.

July 1954
The sixth draft of OR.329 is produced.

August 1954
The sixth draft is finally issued, officially, as OR.329.

October 1954
OR.329 is sent to 11 aircraft firms for advance information. The Ministry of Supply publishes its first draft of Specification F.155T.

November 1954
Specification F.155T is redrafted and amended.

February 1955
F.155T is issued to eight firms complete with operational requirements for associated equipment. The firms, Armstrong Whitworth, de Havilland, English Electric, Fairey, Hawker, Saunders-Roe, Short and Harland, and Vickers Supermarine, are given six months to tender.

March 1955
Short and Harland withdraws from the tendering process.

April 1955
Conference held between the Ministry of Supply, the Air Staff and the seven remaining firms' chief designers. The tender date is pushed back to October 5, 1955.

July 1955
The revised second issue of Specification F.155T is sent to firms.

October 1955
Firms' tender brochures are received by the Ministry of Supply. Fairey offers two brochures, making a total of eight submissions.

November 1955
Tenders are discussed and three are earmarked for elimination: English Electric's P.8, Saunders-Roe's P.187 and Fairey's single seat project.

January 1956
English Electric submits a two-seater version of its P.8, which allows the company to continue in the competition.

March 1956
Tender design conference. It is recommended that only Fairey's two-seater project should be ordered and the remaining projects rejected.

April 1956
It is agreed that Fairey's two-seater and Armstrong Whitworth's AW.169 should continue in development for a year before a final decision is made. The English Electric, de Havilland, Hawker and Vickers Supermarine designs are finally rejected.

May 1956
The Thin Wing Javelin is cancelled and the decision is made to cease consideration of the Avro CF.105.

June 1956
At an Air Council meeting on June 7, the Secretary of State for Air, Nigel Birch, announces that the Chancellor of the Exchequer Harold Macmillan has not approved progress on the OR.329 fighter but that "it should be considered further when a complete review of fighter requirements is prepared". Macmillan sends Birch and others a confidential 'note' outlining his view that RAF Fighter Command should be dissolved, and work on all fighters but one stopped.

November 1956
Armstrong Whitworth is informed that its AW.169 is to be cancelled and that OR.329 now applies solely to the Fairey two-seater.

February 1957
At a special Air Council meeting on February 21 it is agreed that OR.329 should be cancelled "in view of the decisions arising from the Defence Review".

DRAMATIS PERSONAE

Ministry of Supply
Baker, Sir John (CA) – Controller of Aircraft (1953-1956)
Curtis, W H (AD/TD Plans) – Assistant Director of Technical Development, Plans
Gardner, George (DGTD) – Director General of Technical Development (Air) (1953-1955)
Hockmeyer, Ian Otto – RAF/F.1(f) and F.155T project development officer
Jones, Aubrey – Minister of Supply (January 16, 1957-October 22, 1959)
Lloyd, Selwyn – Minister of Supply (October 18, 1954-April 7, 1955)
Maudling, Reginald – Minister of Supply (April 7, 1955-January 16, 1957)
Pelly, Sir Claude (CAS) – Controller of Aircraft (1956-1959)
Roberts, Glynn Silyn (DMARD) – Director of Military Aircraft Research & Development (RAF) (-1956)
Sandys, Duncan – Minister of Supply (October 31, 1951-October 18, 1954)
Serby, John Edward (DGGW) – Director General of Guided Weapons
Shaw, Ronald Andrew (AD/ARD) – Assistant Director of the Aircraft Research Department
Woodward-Nutt, Arthur Edgar (PDRD [A]) – Principal Director of Research and Development (Aircraft)

Air Ministry
Balmforth, Thomas – Operational Requirements officer
Bennell, Anthony – Private Secretary to the Deputy Chief of Air Staff
Birch, Nigel – Secretary of State for Air (December 20, 1955-January 16, 1957)
Bower, Leslie William Clement (SASO) – Senior Air Staff Officer of Fighter Command (1954-1957)
Boyle, Sir Dermot (AOCC/CAS) – Air Officer Commanding-in-Chief of Fighter Command (1953-1956), Chief of the Air Staff (1956-1959)
Broad, Harold Peter – Deputy Director of Operational Requirements 1
Broadbent, Ewen – Private Secretary to the Secretary of State for Air
Clifton, L (DoC (A)) – Director of Contracts (Air)
Davies, Handel (SAAM) – Science Advisor Air Ministry
Isherwood, A W (Doc (A)) – Director of Contracts (Air)
Kirkpatrick, Herbert James 'Jimmy' (DOR [A]) – Director of Operational Requirements Air (1954-1957), Assistant Chief of the Air Staff (Operational Requirements) (February 1, 1957-July 24, 1957)
Kyle, Wallace Hart (DOR [A]) – Director of Operational Requirements (Air) (1952-1954)
Melville, Ronald Henry (AUS [A]) – Assistant Under-Secretary of State (Air)
Pike, Sir Thomas (DCAS) – Deputy Chief of the Air Staff (1953-1956)
Roulston, Jack Fendick (DOR (A)) – Director of Operational Requirements Air (1957-1958)
Satterly, Harold Vivian 'Harry' (ACAS [OR]) – Assistant Chief of the Air Staff (Operational Requirements) (1954-1957)
Sidney, William Philip – Secretary of State for Air (October 31, 1951-December 20, 1955)
Soames, Christopher (US [A]) – Under-Secretary of State (Air) (1955-1957)
Tuttle, Sir Geoffrey (ACAS [OR]/DCAS) – Assistant Chief of the Air Staff (Operational Requirements) (1951-1954), Deputy Chief of the Air Staff (1956-1959)
Ward, George (US [A]) – Under-Secretary of State (Air) (1952-1955), Secretary of State for Air (January 16, 1957-October 28, 1960)
Wheeler, Neil 'Nobby' (DDOR 1) – Deputy Director of Operational Requirements 1 (1953-1957)

Ministry of Defence
Alexander, Harold Rupert Leofric George – Minister of Defence (March 1, 1952-October 18, 1954)
Brundrett, Sir Frederick – Chief Scientific Advisor
Head, Antony – Minister of Defence (October 18, 1956-January 9, 1957)
Macmillan, Harold – Minister of Defence (October 18, 1954-April 7, 1955)
Monckton, Sir Walter – Minister of Defence (December 20, 1955-October 18, 1956)
Lloyd, Selwyn – Minister of Defence (April 7, 1955-December 20,1955)
Sandys, Duncan – Minister of Defence (January 13, 1957-October 14, 1959)

Royal Aircraft Establishment
Hall, Arnold Alexander – director (1951-1955)
Jones, Dr Francis Edgar 'Frankie' – deputy director (1953-1956)
Morgan, Morien Bedford – deputy director (1956-1959)
Nicholson, Lewis F 'Nick' – head of aerodynamics
Stephens, William – head of guided weapons

The companies
Bishop, Ronald Eric – de Havilland chief designer
Brennan, Maurice – Saunders-Roe chief designer
Butler, H F – Armstrong Whitworth project designer
Camm, Sir Sydney – Hawker chief designer
Creasey, Raymond 'Ray' – English Electric chief engineer
Davies, Stuart Duncan 'Dave' – A V Roe chief designer (to 1955)
Elliott, Albert G – Rolls-Royce chief designer
Ewans, Roy – A V Roe chief designer (from 1955)
Hall, Geoffrey – Fairey Aviation director
Henson, George – Vickers-Armstrongs designer
Keen, E D 'Dixie' – Armstrong Whitworth assistant chief designer
Keith-Lucas, David – Shorts and Harland chief designer
Lickley, Robert – Fairey Aviation technical director and chief engineer
Lindsey, William Henry 'Pat' – Armstrong Siddeley Motors chief designer
Page, Frederick William 'Freddie' – English Electric chief designer
Roberts, H – Fairey Aviation chief aerodynamicist
Russell, Archibald E – Bristol Aeroplane chief designer
Smith, J P 'Phil' – de Havilland designer
Smith, Joe – Vickers-Armstrong's chief designer
Stanbury, Vivian – Hawker designer
Stanton-Jones, Richard – Saunders-Roe designer
Trevelyan, Geoffrey – de Havilland designer
Twiss, Peter – Fairey Aviation test pilot
Walker, Richard W – Gloster Aircraft chief designer
Watson, Henry Romaine – Armstrong Whitworth chief designer

ROYAL AIRCRAFT ESTABLISHMENT

Two-seat fighter with guided weapon armament

❖

April 1954

Artwork by Luca Landino

— *Specification* —

Crew: Two   **Length:** 71.4ft   **Wingspan:** 34ft   **Height:** 13ft
Wing area: 386sq ft   **Empty weight:** N/A   **Loaded weight:** 31,000lb
Powerplant: 2 x unspecified turbojet   **Maximum speed:** Mach 2
Service ceiling: 65,000ft   **Armament:** 2 x Infra-red homing missile with 50lb warhead

4

THE THREAT

British intelligence on Soviet bombers 1955

The RAF needed an interceptor capable of destroying
next-generation Soviet bombers but a lack of intelligence
made it hard to say for certain what those bombers might
be capable of. So the British designed some themselves
to find out.

Producing a specification for an aircraft intended to guard against an aerial threat on uncertain capability proved to be rather difficult. The fierce debate over what requirements to set before Britain's aircraft manufacturers was founded on shifting sands – none of those arguing for a faster climb, a higher ceiling or a collision course attack really knew what the Soviets were working on.

A variety of scenarios were postulated, ranging from the mildly gloomy to the apocalyptically pessimistic. If enemy bombers appeared doing Mach 1.3 at 60,000ft or below there was a real chance of tackling them; if they showed up doing Mach 2 or above, or flying at 75,000ft, the chances of Britain's interceptors stopping them fell away rapidly.

It might be imagined that British intelligence had at least some idea of the sorts of large military aircraft being designed and developed by firms such as Tupolev, Myasishchev and Ilyushin – but unfortunately they had very little to go on. The result was a sort of semi-scientific best-guess.

In September 1955, a month before the firms' tenders for F.155T were due to be handed over, the Air Ministry's scientific advisors produced a paper, Science 2 Memo. No. 249, entitled 'An Estimate of the Likely Performance of the Next Generation of Russian Manned Bombers'.

This began: "The fighter being designed to OR.329 is required to defend the UK against the type of manned bomber which the Russians are expected to have in 1962 as a successor to the present Type 39 (Badger). The performance of the new bomber is at present a matter of conjecture although it has been necessary to make certain assumptions to enable planning to proceed. For example, a speed of Mach 1.3 and a height of 60,000ft have been used."

Under 'possible types of threat', it stated: "The successor to the present bomber might be any one of several broad categories of vehicle: a subsonic bomber carrying a long range guided bomb; an unmanned supersonic bomber; a bomber capable of supersonic flight while within our defences; a bomber capable of supersonic flight throughout its sortie; a ballistic rocket.

"The guided bomb and the unmanned supersonic bomber would be of relatively small size and capable of very high performance both in speed and height. We cannot expect a fighter to be of much use against them. Moreover, the electronic development effort associated with these projects is such that it is most unlikely that the Russians would be able to mount these types of attack by 1962. The ballistic rocket is even later in time, and even further outside the field of fighter defence.

"An aircraft with a supersonic burst would not involve any major difficulty of design: it would use turbojet engines and have a conventional wing loading which would present no operational problems. On the other hand, the bomber capable of supersonic flight

Tupolev Tu-16R – the reconnaissance version of the Soviet jet bomber in flight. The British OR.329 interceptor was intended to defeat its successor. *via author*

The Myasishchev M-4 was another Soviet strategic bomber. It might not have lasted long in the teeth of UK air defences even circa 1955 but had the Soviets fielded it in large numbers, some may well have got through. *via author*

throughout its sortie would be much more difficult to design.

"The adoption of thin, low aspect ratio, highly loaded wings would require assisted take-off and possibly arrested landing. If very high performance were required, ramjet engines could be used but auxiliary turbojet engines would still be required for landing.

"The speed would have to be at least Mach 2 to achieve a practicable size of aircraft. Consequently,

the supersonic-all-the-way bomber appears to be much more difficult to design and operate than a bomber capable of high performance flight only when within our defences. For the attack of the UK, such an aircraft is in any case superfluous. It is therefore submitted that the most likely successor to the Type 39 will be a bomber capable of a supersonic burst."

Next the report tried to imagine how such an aircraft might perform

and even what it might look like. It was assumed that the next generation Soviet bomber would carry "the same military load as the V bombers, viz. a 10,000lb bomb and 10,000lb of equipment, but the effect of halving the bomb size is considered. It has a still air range of 3000 miles (which is equivalent to an operational radius of action of 1200 miles, sufficient to permit the enemy to operate from airfields within the USSR).

"The bomber flies at maximum speed only during the 500 miles when it is within our defences, the remainder of the sortie being flown at economical speed and height. The basic engine performance data as regards specific thrust, weight and fuel consumption are assumed similar to those of the RB.106. During the high performance part of the sortie, reheat to 2000°K has been assumed.

"In accordance with current views on optimum configuration for this type of aircraft, it is assumed that the body has a diameter of 7½ft, the wings are swept at 45° and the tail is geometrically similar to the wings."

Exactly what the British feared – a supersonic Soviet bomber. The Tu-22 was a failure, however. Its top speed was Mach 1.4 and its ceiling was only 43,600ft. *via author*

An extensive study had been carried out based on a huge range of different potential bomber designs, each with a different aspect ratio and wing thickness to chord ratio. Each set of wings was then tried with three different potential take-off weights – 150,000lb, 200,000lb and 300,000lb – and three different runway lengths – 6000ft, 8000ft and infinite. With these parameters to play with, the scientists had tried to work out what maximum speeds and altitudes were possible.

They eventually deduced "that the enemy attack may be at speeds up to about Mach 2 and at heights between 60,000ft and 70,000ft. It seems unlikely that with the early warning, AI range and weapons likely to be available, the OR.329 fighter could hope to deal with a Mach 2 bomber.

"All that we can do is to make the fighter as flexible as is economically possible, so that it can deal with rather higher speeds than the Mach 1.3 originally specified. Whether the enemy can achieve a speed of Mach 2 depends of course primarily upon his state of engine design, but it is suggested that he might achieve a speed of Mach 1.7 at a height of 65,000ft."

According to the final conclusion: "There are good grounds for believing that the next generation of Russian bombers will be essentially subsonic but capable of a supersonic burst while within our defences. Their precise height and speed will depend upon the state of engine development, but it is likely that speeds up to Mach 1.7 or even Mach 2 will be achieved and that the height will be about 65,000ft.

"The OR.329 fighter should not therefore be designed only against a Mach 1.3 threat but should have the maximum flexibility which is economically attainable to allow it to have some measure of effectiveness against attacks at higher speeds. So far as height is concerned, it is probably adequate especially in view of the fact that the associated missile can take up some of the height deficiency."

The reality

Despite their admitted lack of evidence, the Air Ministry's scientific advisors painted a worrying picture of potentially unstoppable Soviet bombers capable of penetrating Britain's defences with ease – whether the RAF was operating the OR.329 interceptor or not. But what were the Soviets actually doing?

During the early years of the Cold War, the Russians concentrated on trying to develop their Tupolev Tu-4 – a clone of the Boeing B-29 Superfortress, reverse-engineered from USAAF aircraft impounded after they were forced to land on Soviet soil during the closing stages of the Second World War.

First came the Tu-80, which first flew in December 1949, then the scaled-up Tu-85 – nearly 40m long, compared to the 30m B-29 original and a 56m wingspan compared to 43m – which was first flown in January 1951 but then cancelled.

The Soviets' next bombers were the turbojet Tu-16 Badger, the turboprop Tu-95 Bear and the Myasishchev M-4 Bison, also turbojet powered. These subsonic swept-wing aircraft were developed side-by-side, the first Tu-16 flight being on April 27, 1952, the first Tu-95 flight on November 12, 1952, and the first M-4 flight in 1953.

What worried the British was what might replace these three during the early 1960s. The answer was the Tupolev Tu-22 Blinder – development of which only began in 1954 while the British, having anticipated it, were already trying to decide what sort of aircraft to build to defeat it.

First flying in 1959, the supersonic Tu-22 could manage Mach 1.4 but with a ceiling of only 43,600ft. And even with this barely adequate performance, the bomber was plagued with technical and maintenance problems. Another design to make its first flight in 1959 was the Mach 1.6 Myasishchev M-50 Bounder, with a reported ceiling of 54,000ft. This might have proven more of a challenge for the OR.329 interceptor but it still fell some way short of the British 'worst case scenario'. In fact, only two prototype M-50s were built before the programme was cancelled.

The Myasishchev M-50 would have challenged British defences but it never entered service, arriving only when ballistic missiles were already beginning to take over from bombers. *via author*

5

A FEW SHORT STEPS

English Electric P.8

With development work on the P.1 research aircraft well
advanced and the F.155T in-service date looming, English
Electric designed an interceptor which was, effectively, a
heavily modified Lightning.

As the enfant terrible of the British aviation industry, English Electric had seemingly come out of nowhere at the end of the Second World War to produce a string of highly advanced aircraft designs – the radical supersonic P.1 being the main focus of its efforts during the early 1950s.

The P.1 was designed as a supersonic fighter and the company had great faith in the fundamental soundness of its design. Therefore, when the ER.134T requirement was issued for a Mach 2 research aircraft, it put forward a proposal largely based on the P.1 – the P.6.

Four different versions of the P.6 were initially proposed in a brochure dated May 11, 1953: the P.6/1 with notched delta wing and a single Rolls-Royce RB.106R engine, the P.6/2 with notched delta wing and two Armstrong Siddeley Sapphire Sa.7 engines, a straight wing design which completely departed from the P.1, and had its two Sa.7 engines in wing nacelles, and an otherwise unnumbered delta wing P.6.

The P.6/1 had been worked on in more detail than the others. It shared the P.1's wing form and tail shape, but having just one powerful engine meant its fuselage was more slender. With this configuration it was expected to top Mach 2 in nine minutes and thirty seconds at 45,000ft. However, despite tendering it for a research aircraft contract, the EECo team nevertheless depicted the P.6/1 with a quartet of Aden cannon in one of the brochure drawings – leaving little room for doubt about the company's expectations for the design.

The twin-engine P.6/2, presented in an appendix, was expected to hit Mach 2 in just nine minutes at 50,000ft. The unnamed straight-winged design, shown in drawing number EAG 2333, was naturally also intended for Mach 2, but other details were lacking. The fourth design, the delta, was similarly undetailed.

As the date for a decision on the seven ER.134T contenders drew closer, in September 1953, a fifth and final P.6 design was drafted which differed completely from what had gone before – although it was originally intended to be a development of the earlier unnamed straight wing design. This featured a revised wing form and canards rather than the sharply swept tail surfaces envisaged in the original.

Once again, armament was shown, but this time it took the form of four Aden cannon fitted into the centre of the fuselage and pointed slightly upwards – pre-dating the slanted cannon weaponry

Concept painting produced for the English Electric P.8 brochure. *BAE Systems*

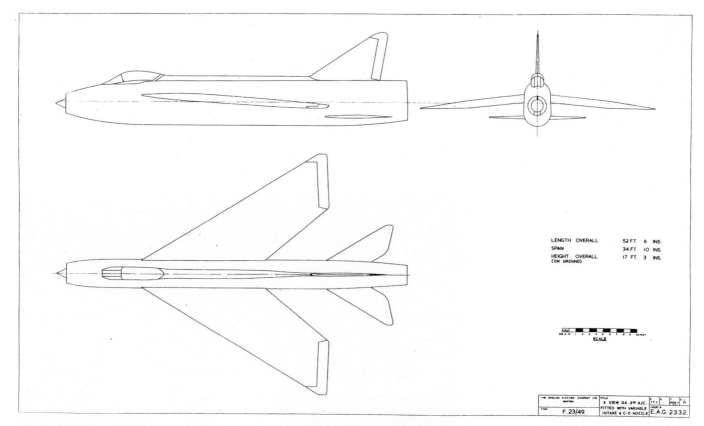

LENGTH OVERALL   52 FT   6 INS.
SPAN   34 FT   10 INS.
HEIGHT OVERALL   17 FT   3 INS.
(ON GROUND)

SCALE

THE ENGLISH ELECTRIC COMPANY LTD. TITLE 3 VIEW GA. 3RD A/C.
PRESTON
TYPE F.23/49 FITTED WITH VARIABLE E.A.G. 2332
INTAKE & C-D NOZZLE

The English Electric F.23/49 (P.1) as it stood in May 1953, at the point when the P.6 brochure was being drafted. *BAE Systems*

suggestion of the Hall interceptor report by seven months. However, as previously mentioned, despite English Electric's argument that the P.6 could be built cheaply because most of the research and development had already been carried out for the P.1, it was decided in December 1953 that the Bristol Type 188 should be built instead. But English Electric did not give up on the idea of an advanced P.1 for Mach 2+.

The company was among those given an advance preview of OR.329 on March 17, 1954, and when its brochure for an aircraft to meet the F.155T specification was handed over 18 months later it must have come as no surprise to the Ministry of Supply and Air Staff that yet another design based on P.1 technology was offered – the P.8 – Fighter Weapon System to Specification F.155T (OR.329).

At the beginning, the brochure offers a summary: "It is concluded

that the only certainty of a successful aircraft being in service in the required time scale will result from Short Step developments of the existing F.23/49 – AI.23 – IR weapon combination. The developments outlined are the results of a considerable study of the operating conditions against Mach 1.3 and other probable targets, resulting in a closer integration into a Weapon System."

This set out the company's stall immediately: the lack of time meant the best way of defeating the Soviet threat was by bundling three existing pieces of kit together to form the weapon system – the P.1, the AI.23 radar and a passive infra-red homing (heat seeking) missile.

Next a series of "considerations leading up to the present design" were offered. Firstly, "it was emphasised to the designers' conference that the preliminary requirement is stated on Page 1 of the F.155T and of OR.329 i.e.

to develop a day/night fighter into a weapon system capable of intercepting Mach 1.3 targets at 60,000ft. In order to do this, it is necessary to examine such targets more closely.

"…Mach 1.3 targets would probably cruise at high subsonic speeds with elaborate radar countermeasures and a supersonic burst near the target, giving considerable infrared radiation from its jets. The prospect of much faster supersonic targets after 1962 is also discussed.

"It is noted from Page 1 of F.155T that the remainder of the requirements 'present the current official views on the best way of achieving the operational aim and any proposal which can be shown to be superior in any important respects should be presented'. It is also noted that the aircraft is required in service by January 1962. This implies that the flight development of the aircraft and all its equipment must be completed in 1961."

Guns as an insurance policy

English Electric "agreed" with the specification that guided weapons would be the best and only form of armament for the P.8 "since this will considerably improve the efficiency of the system. We share the hope, with Air Staff and MoS, that the simpler forms of these weapons will have been developed to a sufficient state of reliability in the time scale. As an insurance policy in this respect it is assumed that sufficient numbers of F.23/49 aircraft will be in service, with Aden guns and rocket batteries to fall back on.

"Attempt has been made to reconcile the carriage of both IR and radar weapons, but this has been found impossible. We agree with RAE that it is impossible to obtain the specified pursuit performance, whilst carrying a radar weapon system, in any practical size of aircraft.

This analysis is based on first-hand knowledge of the design of a practical supersonic fighter system, for which even 10% optimism on engine and structure weights or drags can show a completely unrealistic picture."

The sheer size of radar-guided weapons, particularly Vickers' Red Dean/Red Hebe, made them unattractive for a fast interceptor and a system based on much smaller infrared homing missiles

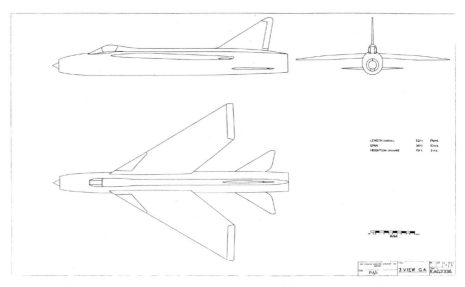

The P.6/1 featured a single powerful engine in place of the F.23/49's two less powerful units and therefore had a slimmer fuselage. The drawing is from the May 1953 brochure. *BAE Systems*

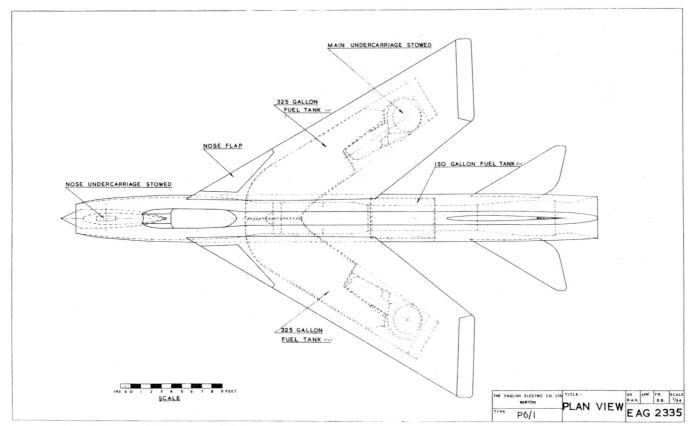

Plan view of the P.6/1 showing its fuel tanks and undercarriage positions. *BAE Systems*

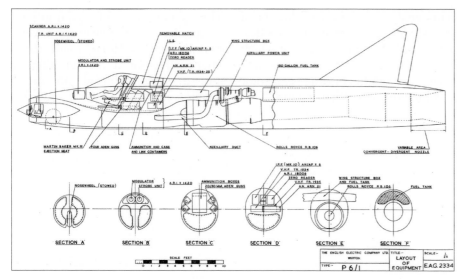

Although it was tendered for an experimental requirement, the P.6/1 was designed with development as a fighter in mind. Four Aden cannon are shown in the side view. *BAE Systems*

"must therefore be much quicker, less costly, more reliable and more certain of success than the larger and more complex radar collision system, all of which is completely new".

This appeared to be English Electric committing itself to a pursuit-course attack when the F.155T Issue 2 specification called for the use of "all-round collision-course tactics" but this was not necessarily the case.

The brochure went on: "Design is therefore based on the use of the IR weapon, but this is not restricted to that at present represented by Blue Jay. In this form, the weapon may be regarded as the first logical step in the development from the gun, in that it may be fired at rather greater ranges and closing speeds with improved accuracy.

"This greatly improves the fighter's chances of success, particularly in the face of tail armament, but does not otherwise help the fighter system. Since the present Blue Jay must be fired from short range within a narrow cone dictated by the target, the fighter must still follow out a complete pursuit interception, usually involving sharp turns in a high drag condition, followed by a chase back from behind the target."

Evidently when it was fitted to the P.1 for testing, the Blue Jay Mk.I had created such a degree of extra drag that the aircraft burned 100 gallons more fuel when climbing to 50,000ft than it did without it. The use of rocket motors to intercept targets above 55,000ft would require the aircraft to carry 2700lb of rocket fuel in place of kerosene – making the situation even worse.

However, English Electric had the solution: make the missile do the work. It was stated that "the

next logical step in the development of the IR weapon is therefore to convert this performance penalty on the aircraft into a performance gain. This may be done by giving the weapon greater firing range from all round the target".

Guidance range could be improved through the use of a system which locked-on to the CO_2 emissions produced by the jet engines of the target – something that could not be masked and would be visible to the missile from a wide range of angles, even the front, as long as the fighter attack from below.

English Electric had worked with the Radar Research Establishment and the Blue Jay's manufacturer, de Havilland Propellers, to determine that this would actually allow the missile to be released from much further away without reducing its chance of a kill. Releasing it from further away would still mean more fuel had to be carried – but it would be a small additional amount inside the missile itself rather than a much larger amount in the aircraft's own tanks.

"It is therefore possible to investigate the proper division of interception performance between the fighter and weapon in order to give a better two-stage weapon," the

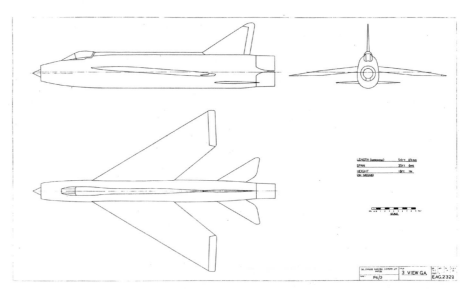

A three-view drawing of the English Electric P.6/2. At first glance it was very similar to the F.23/49 but a closer look reveals a broader fuselage, greater wingspan and longer fuselage. *BAE Systems*

brochure argued. "In the case at present envisaged, the addition of rocket fuel to the weapon will save about 100 times as much rocket fuel in the fighter to complete a given interception, so that a relatively small penalty on the weapon can eliminate the need for rocket boost in the fighter.

"Similarly, if the interception is limited by manoeuvrability then it is a much smaller overall penalty to increase the wing area of the weapon, rather than that of the fighter. Any improvement in weapon performance should not however cause appreciable deterioration in performance of the fighter, or its flexibility will suffer."

With all this in mind, English Electric went on to boldly state: "It is not generally realised that the present AI.23-Blue Jay system is already a weapon collision system, although it is at present being used in a manner approximating to

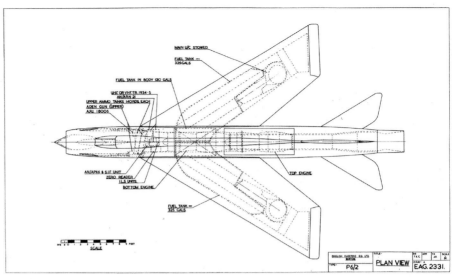

Plan view of the twin-engine P.6/2. *BAE Systems*

simple pursuit, due to the narrow angle and range limitations of guns and of the sulphide cells in Blue Jay Mk.I."

Whether pursuit or collision course was necessary would depend on the target, but English Electric was confident that Blue Jay could handle either. Slow targets would require pursuit from behind, where all the heat and CO_2 was coming from, but "higher performance targets, such as those specified, should give

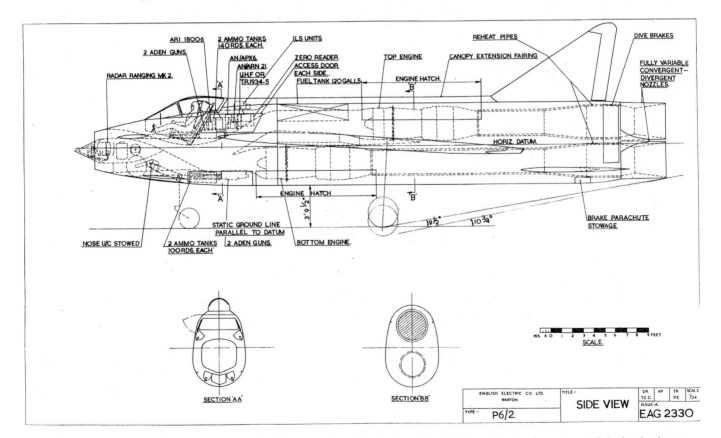

The side view of the P.6/2 shows more marked differences from the single engine P.6/1. Again, the 'experimental' design is shown fully armed with cannon. *BAE Systems*

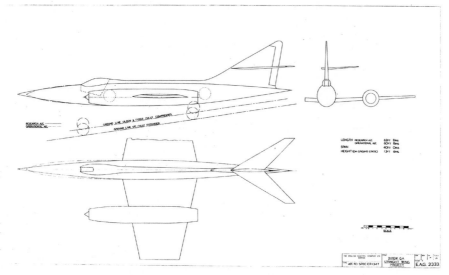

A complete departure from the other F.23/49ish or P.1ish versions of the P.6 was this straight-wing version. The engines in wing nacelles are more Canberra-like and the fuselage is extremely slender. Two versions are depicted overlaid on top of one another – the research aircraft and the 'operational' aircraft. *BAE Systems*

sufficient radiation from below for a lead pursuit attack from the side".

In other words, the interceptor would approach the bomber at right angles from the side but ahead. Anticipating the target's speed, it would then fire its missiles at the place where the bomber was about to be.

At the uppermost end of the spectrum however: "The high supersonic speed bomber may be attacked from any direction, but it will be very desirable to try and attack from in front before it reaches the target. Interception is very difficult even with more complicated systems and precise radar control, but it may be necessary to try and develop the present system if other systems do not materialise, or are unserviceable.

"It may be possible to do this, since a high-speed bomber will give a much larger amount of IR radiation to the front, and the lead pursuit system can follow a fighter collision course initially, turning automatically towards a weapon collision course as the target comes within firing range. This prospect of development will be examined in more detail at a later stage."

It should be pointed out that English Electric wanted to develop Blue Jay based on the Mk.2, rather than the Mk.4 (Blue Vesta), commonly specified by other F.155T

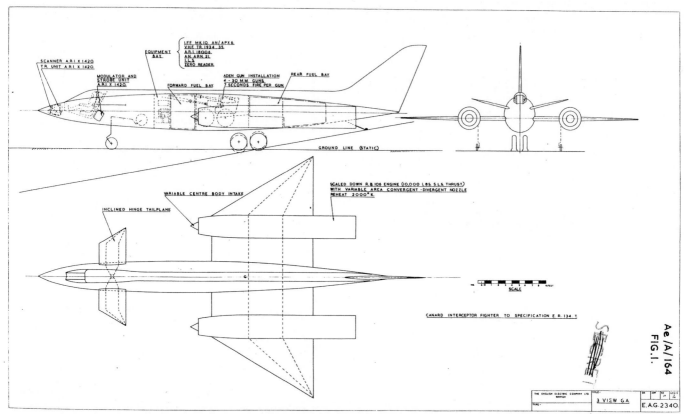

This development of the straight-wing P.6 appears to have been the last of the series – produced months after the other versions. The upwards-angled Aden cannon show its intended development as an interceptor. *BAE Systems*

competitors – even though the brochure drawings clearly depicted the P.8 with Blue Jay Mk.4s rather than Mk.2s.

According to the brochure: "The IR weapon developments already described are different from those proposed for Blue Vesta, but are less extensive, particularly in relation to the insulation requirements. It is possible that if this weapon were developed only to our own requirements, it would be no larger than Blue Jay and differ only in detail.

"It seems certain that airborne guided weapons can be designed successfully only with the emphasis on one supersonic fighter system, so that this problem must be solved by the tender competition."

This approach to Blue Jay/Blue Vesta would later lead to conflict between English Electric and de Havilland Propellers.

The 'short steps'

Throughout the English Electric brochure it is evident that the design team's eye was firmly on the clock. It had already taken years to get the P.1 to the point of being ready for supersonic flight and it was evident that time was already beginning to run short for developing the F.155T aircraft.

Time and again, the company stresses the need to build on existing technology before trying to jump ahead with new systems and materials. It says: "Our studies have shown that the above system can best be based on logical developments of all the components in the present F.23/49 – AI.23 – Blue Jay – auto-control system. This is fortunate, since this is the only method of ensuring success in the required time scale.

"Each development must be integrated properly into the complete weapon system but the existing components act as some insurance against the failure of any development."

The P.8's airframe was to be a direct development of that used by the P.1: "The design emphasis on the present airframe is for steady flight and manoeuvres at transonic, as well as supersonic speeds. This

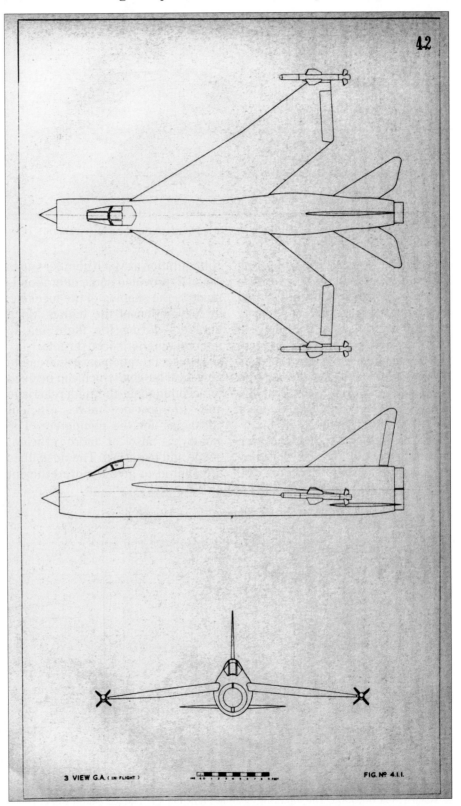

Basic three-view drawing of the English Electric P.8 as its configuration would appear while in flight and armed with a pair of developed Blue Jay missiles. *BAE Systems*

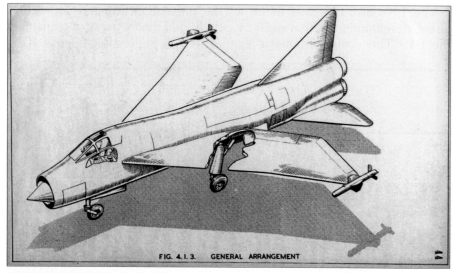

FIG. 4. I. 3.   GENERAL ARRANGEMENT

The gently curving fuselage of the Mach 2+ P.8 is shown in this brochure general arrangement drawing. *BAE Systems*

is still the critical period during the supersonic climb, the critical part of the turn and the aiming of the weapon. The superiority of the F.23/49 configuration in handling and performance at such speeds has already been proven by flight test, and has revealed no problems in any way resembling those encountered by less swept or tailless configurations.

"Extensive analysis by the area rule shows no reason for any performance inferiority of the configuration at Mach numbers up to Mach 2, provided some alteration is made to the shaping of the fuselage, in recognition of the higher Mach numbers during the flight out to intercept higher speed targets.

"These alterations are such as to give local bulges, which can be used to accommodate the undercarriage and to provide more efficient packaging for the equipment. The canopy is also of more efficient shape and materials. The nose lines are altered to give a more efficient

intake for the higher Mach numbers and to allow a larger AI scanner.

"The removal of the undercarriage from the wing gives ample internal fuel capacity without need of external tanks. In view of the proven handling characteristics, the wing, tail and control shapes will be changed as little as possible, and only in ways that can be checked on F.23/49 prototypes. For example, the wing leading edge and tip will be altered to accommodate the guided weapons at the wing tip, and our wind tunnel tests have already confirmed that this will reduce the drag.

"Wherever possible, the structure will be redesigned so as to effect the maximum weight saving. It is considered that the extensive strength and stiffness testing, resonance and flight testing and the experience obtained by detail analysis and manufacture will result in a structure that is much lighter than that which could be designed without such experience."

So it would be a Lightning but with a re-profiled 'Coke bottle' fuselage housing the undercarriage, rather than it retracting into the wings, and with different leading edges on its wings too.

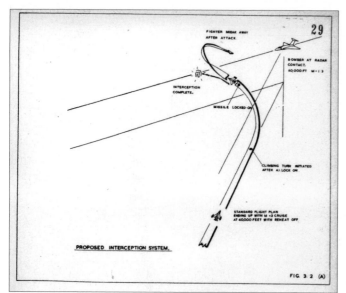

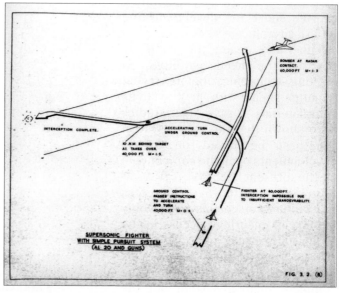

These two brochure drawings map out English Electric's approach to the problem of intercepting incoming Soviet bombers travelling at Mach 1.3 at 60,000ft. The top drawing shows how the P.8's attack would work. The bottom drawing is intended to show how a pursuit-course interception from 40,000ft could actually be more successful than one where the fighter matched the target's altitude in a collision-course attack. *BAE Systems*

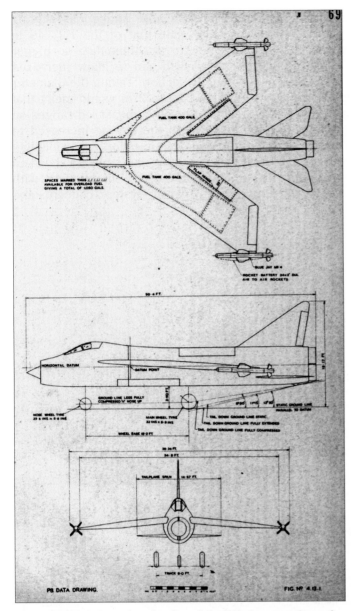

This annotated three-view drawing of the P.8 shows sections of the wings where overload fuel could be stored. *BAE Systems*

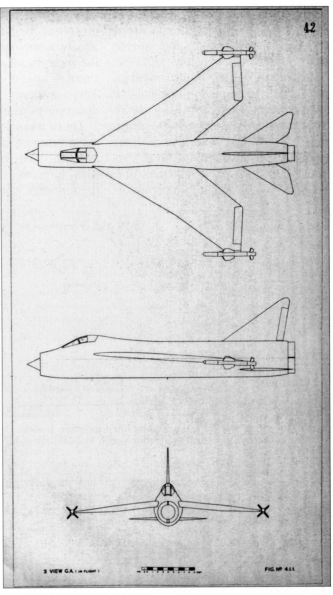

The P.8 on the ground. The most striking difference between the P.8 and the F.23/49 was its undercarriage – which retracted into the fuselage rather than the wings. *BAE Systems*

Even the engines were to go largely unaltered: "No basic change is proposed in the propulsive system, after consideration of the alternatives. Our detailed study of a single-engine arrangement [the P.6/1] showed that this still has the disadvantage in (thrust-drag) compared with our staggered twin-engine system. This can only be recovered by a greater degree of reheat and hence more weight of fuel, jet pipe and nozzle. The greater specific weight of a single large turbojet, compared with two turbojets designed for identical conditions, more than offsets any reduction in installation weight.

"The overwhelming argument comes from the pilots that have flown the present arrangement. Their confidence in duplicated power plants on the centre-line of a supersonic fighter with high landing drag and power operated controls is such that it must be assumed that the service would also dislike a reversion to any other arrangement. The nose intake is also essential to guarantee peak performance over the full range of Mach number without an extensive high-speed tunnel programme that would jeopardise time scale."

There would be some tweaks, however: "Detail changes in the matching of the intake-turbojet-nozzle system can give considerable improvements in performance and fuel consumption at the higher Mach numbers that are now of interest. The Rolls-Royce RB.126 is a straightforward development of the RA.24 and relies for its improved performance on increased mass flow and turbine temperature. The possible improvements from the associated intake and nozzle systems are even greater.

"These detail improvements in the complete propulsive system, combined with the detail improvements in supersonic drag, make it possible to cruise without reheat at Mach numbers up to two above 40,000ft. This improves the economy of a supersonic interception

very considerably. A certain amount of reheat is however desirable to allow a supersonic climb and improve the acceleration, so as to increase the average speed of the interception. This system must not cause disproportionate weight or drag."

There would then be no need for rocket motors on the P.8, since the aircraft's own turbojets, combined with improved performance from the missiles, would get the job done.

The P.8's nose intake was slightly wider than that of the F.23/49 in order to accommodate a bigger radar dish and to allow increased engine airflow. Taking the diameter from 24in to 27in would mean that "the presently measured ranges on AI.23 will thereby be increased to 20 nautical miles for 75% probability of detecting a Canberra head-on (20sqm target)". In keeping with the Weapon System concept, and

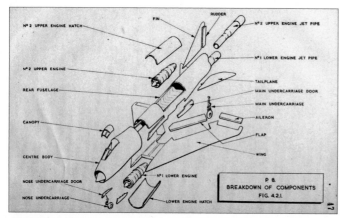

Drawing showing how the P.8 would be fitted together. It was nothing if not a practical and straightforwardly buildable design. *BAE Systems*

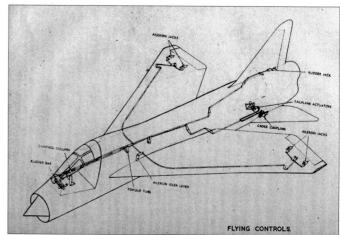

The P.8's flying controls. *BAE Systems*

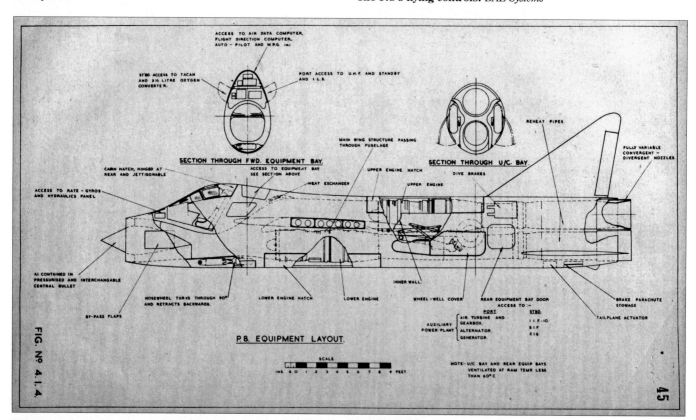

Side-view of the single-seater P.8. Its origins as a developed F.23/49 are clear. *BAE Systems*

once again with an eye on the clock, English Electric was keen to ensure that the P.8's radar would be ready in time: "…it is considered that Ferranti should be encouraged to start immediately on their J-band variant of AI.23, so that a prototype can be ready in 1959. This will not only increase the range to 25 nautical miles but, even more important, will make jamming much less likely.

"Detail changes will be required in the associated instrument systems to accommodate the revised fighter-weapon kinematics. No great change in principle is involved, since a lead-pursuit system is essentially weapon-collision course, and the net increase in weight will be less than 5lb. If, after further reflection, it is decided to replace the gunsight by an alternative presentation, there will in fact be a considerable saving in weight and cockpit space."

A system which provided automatic lock-on to the target would be helpful to the pilot, if Ferranti could manage it, "but it will be regarded only as an adjunct to the pilot's facility since this is one job that a human being will always do better than a guided weapon, particularly in a complex situation. A more important task is therefore to relieve the pilot of his flying duties, so that he can get greater value from the displays".

One man or two?

The F.155T specification was very definite about the number of crew that the Air Ministry expected to have aboard their new interceptor: two. English Electric had not been privy to the months, years even, of heated debate which had resulted in this particular aspect of the spec. If it had, it might not have so easily dismissed the two-crew option, presenting instead a single-seater.

From a technological standpoint, English Electric struggled to understand why the 'back seater'

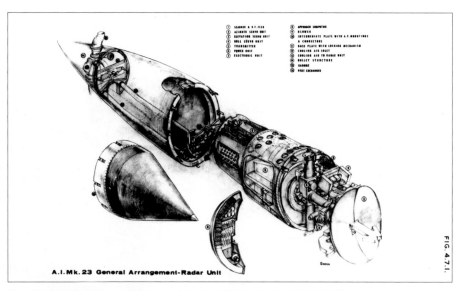

A.I.Mk.23 General Arrangement-Radar Unit

The AI Mk.23 radar unit intended for installation in the P.8. *BAE Systems*

was necessary since automated electronic and hydraulic actuation systems were available which could ease the pilot's workload: "The performance and handling problems resulting from trying to add a second crew member are being investigated in the present airframe, since there appears to be no advantage in increasing the size of the fighter for this purpose. Our wind tunnel tests suggest that these problems will delay the development of the 'short step' system and that the penalties may not be justified in a simple pursuit supersonic fighter, particularly if the pilot is aided by auto-control.

"But the auto-control system becomes an important component in a single-seater system. There is little need or intent to further revise the present Hobson hydraulic jacks, which are already being integrated with the Elliott autopilot system and with the Newmark system as an insurance policy.

"The hydraulic motor-screw jack system on the tailplane is not very suited to the further autopilot developments envisaged and may be exchanged for simple jacks, with the autopilot earthed through a simple clutch so that it will fail safe."

The goal was to provide the pilot with a system which let him choose the aircraft's speed, direction and altitude and then let the autopilot get on with the business of accelerating, climbing and turning. The autopilot, it was hoped, could also follow a course set by controllers on the ground.

And the "ultimate aim is therefore to convert the fighter towards a guided weapon with a man in it, so that his greater reliability and flexibility, provided he is not overworked, can always be relied upon. This would seem a fair compromise between the alternative extremes of completely automatic ground-launched weapons and large complicated multi-seaters."

The threat

English Electric was a large and well-connected company even before it became involved in aircraft manufacturing, and it continued to have its own intelligence sources, particularly through a strong relationship with American firms.

Rather than rely on the worst-case scenario Air Ministry assessment of the threat posed by Soviet bombers, the company put forward its own view on 'the threat' in the P.8 brochure, based on Ministry of Supply data, which with hindsight was just as inaccurate – but more optimistically so.

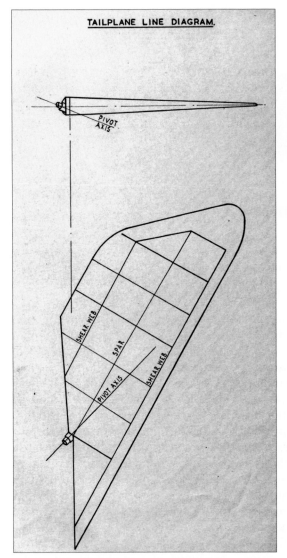

TAILPLANE LINE DIAGRAM.

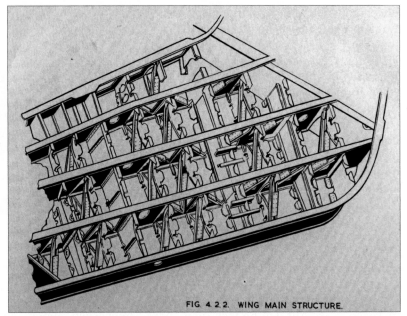

FIG. 4.2.2. WING MAIN STRUCTURE.

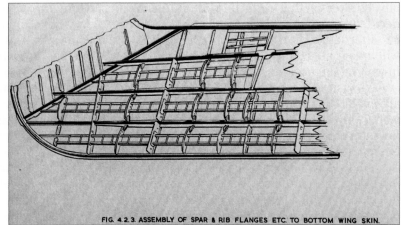

FIG. 4.2.3. ASSEMBLY OF SPAR & RIB FLANGES ETC. TO BOTTOM WING SKIN.

English Electric already had a good idea of how the P.8 would be constructed in detail before it submitted the brochure in October 1955. *BAE Systems*

There was a large increase in bomber capabilities when the first turbojet types entered service after 1950 but "since then, there has been slow improvement towards the limits imposed by high subsonic design. The Russians and Americans appear particularly laggard in respect of this improvement but it should be remembered that, in addition to the universal problems of large highly swept aircraft, the primary concentration of these countries is now on long range bombers.

"Thus, whereas most British requirements range up to 4000 miles still air, the American and Russian types are all designed from 4000 miles up to 8000 miles. This imposes severe additional problems on their designers, which must react back on their altitude and speed performance.

"Discounting any fundamental new discovery unknown to ourselves, this would suggest that enemy bombers should not have a performance in excess of our own developments.

"As knowledge and experience improve, it seems certain that all countries will develop their bombers up to the economical limits set by high subsonic design. This would appear to be about 50,000ft at Mach 0.9, although the probability of lightly loaded aircraft up to 60,000ft should not be discounted in a few years' time.

"The Canberra PR.9 is the first example of such developments, but the cruising Mach number is unlikely to exceed Mach 0.75 and its normal manoeuvrability will be lost, making it a possible target for the rocket-boosted version of the F.23/49.

"The problems of large long-range supersonic aircraft are such as to delay their introduction into service for many years and then only in small numbers. The enemy can therefore be certain of a strong bomber force, only if he continues to concentrate within the Mach 0.9 and 60,000ft bracket.

"An enemy must eventually realise that this performance is inadequate against fighters of the F.23/49 type. It therefore seems certain that he will turn to extensive radar countermeasures as a major offensive aid. This would be consistent with a 'saturation' philosophy and should be quite practical in large, moderate performance aircraft which need only be partly filled with fuel when attacking this country."

Under a heading of 'possible supersonic developments after 1962', the brochure outlines the problems associated with cruising just above Mach 1 and concludes that "in consequence, design for low supersonic Mach numbers is limited at present to short range aircraft with a small payload, such as fighters".

But "as design Mach number increases towards 2 and beyond there is a progressive restoration in range and/or payload towards values already possible at subsonic speeds. This is due to the removal of the need for structural sweepback and the progressive improvement in propulsive efficiency, first with the turbojet and then with the ramjet".

This suggested that the Soviets might work on a supersonic bomber for the long term, aiming for a top speed of Mach 3 with the aid of ramjets – but this was unlikely to be ready before 1965.

Finally, the brochure comes to what it describes as the 'interim Mach 1.3 aircraft in 1962', the year that the non-rocket boosted Mach 1.4 cruise-capable Tu-22 entered service with the Soviet air force: "The above argument suggests that, having faced up to the problems of a supersonic aircraft, there is no merit whatsoever in designing for steady cruising Mach number as low as 1.3. It would be no more difficult to design for a Mach number nearer 2,

and rather easier for a large range or payload. An enemy with long-range aspirations might go straight for Mach numbers in excess of 2.

"It is therefore necessary to envisage the Mach 1.3 target, specified for 1962, as being basically a high subsonic design with thin enough surfaces to allow a supersonic burst near the target. To illustrate this possibility, we imagine a scaled-up version of the Thin-Wing Javelin, rather nearer to the size of a thin-wing version of the Vulcan. Even with six turbojet engines it is necessary to keep the aircraft weight down to about 120,000lb in order to allow the aircraft to cruise in at 60,000ft. This allows only limited manoeuvrability.

"The use of reheat is insufficient for a supersonic burst at this altitude and it is necessary to boost the thrust still further by rockets. Allowing for the heaviness of the large thin wing and primary propulsive system, it is difficult to spare even 15,000lb of weight for this purpose and the weight control problem is one of the primary reasons for not expecting such an aircraft in service before 1962."

Having imagined a completely different sort of aircraft to what the Soviets were actually beginning

to develop at this time, English Electric offered a conclusion that was closer to the fate that befell the Tu-22: "The problems associated with these interim types are such that they may well be abandoned in favour of the ultimate supersonic type and eventually ballistic missiles. The interim phase may therefore continue with the subsonic type carrying extensive countermeasures and possibly powered bombs to allow stand-off from the target."

A modest development

The P.8 was designed as a thoroughly practical, buildable solution to Britain's interceptor problem. It relied on relatively modest developments of existing technology and might well have been ready to enter service exactly when the company said it would. However, it failed to meet the specification in terms of both the guided weapons it could carry – no radar guided missiles – and the number of crew it was designed to carry. And the Air Staff were very particular about both.

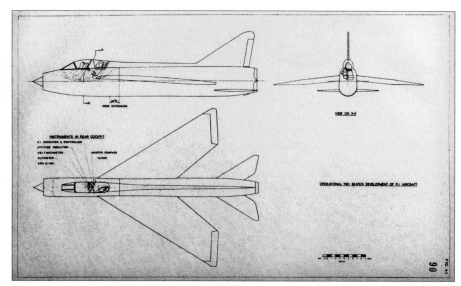

A drawing of the P.1 adapted as a tandem two-seater was included in the P.8 brochure to show how the adaptation might be carried out. *BAE Systems*

ENGLISH ELECTRIC
P.8

October 1955

Artwork by Luca Landino

— *Specification* —

Crew: Two **Length:** 50.4ft
Wingspan: 38.36ft **Height:** 18.17ft
Wing area: 471sq ft **Empty weight:** 24,616lb
Loaded weight: 31,768lb
Powerplant: 2 x Rolls-Royce RB.126
development of 13,400lb static thrust each,
with reheat
Maximum speed: Mach 2
Service ceiling: 65,000ft
Armament: 2 x Infrared homing
missile with 50lb warhead

6

CHASING SUPERSONIC

Hawker up to the P.1103

The Hunter was Britain's most advanced fighter when it entered service in 1954 but its top speed in level flight was only Mach 0.9. Regarding itself as Britain's pre-eminent fighter firm, Hawker really wanted to produce something supersonic.

While designing the Hunter, Hawker experimented with different jet intake, fuselage, tail and wing arrangements – attempting to find the ideal combination for the best possible performance.

One of the earliest drawings to show what would later become the Hunter, dated December 13, 1948, shows a thick forward fuselage to house four cannon, tapering very gently towards the tail. It features a nose intake and swept wings, with a pronounced spine stretching from the rear of the cockpit to the T-tail. The undercarriage and internal layout are basic and unrefined.

Then a drawing dated January 2, 1949, shows a much more detailed design – the fuselage has lost its bulge and the internal arrangement is fleshed out with a practical looking inward-retracting undercarriage, mapped out intake ducts and cannon arrangement. The T-tail now has a swept leading edge too.

While these nose intake designs would ultimately be rejected in favour of the more familiar wing-root intakes of the Hunter, this layout reappeared in Hawker's trio of scaled transonic experimental designs – the P.1069, P.1070 and P.1071. Whether any of these, designed in late 1948, would have been capable of reaching Mach 1 is debatable – although the latter two each featured a rocket engine for an extra boost of speed.

Hawker's aim was made plain by the inclusion of two cannon in the potentially supersonic P.1071.

A more concerted effort to produce a Mach 1+ fighter began in May 1950, shortly before the outbreak of the Korean War, with the P.1082 then P.1083 – a development of the P.1067 with 50° swept-back wings instead of the standard version's 35° sweep. The P.1083 was the subject of an official brochure in May 1951, by which time the thickness of the strongly swept wings had gone from 8.5% down to 7.5%.

The reduction in drag this was expected to produce, combined with the more powerful Armstrong Siddeley Sapphire turbojet in place of the Rolls-Royce Avon RA.7, would result in speeds of up to Mach 1 albeit only on reheat. The P.1083 was ordered in December 1951 – but not before Hawker had produced a larger, more radical

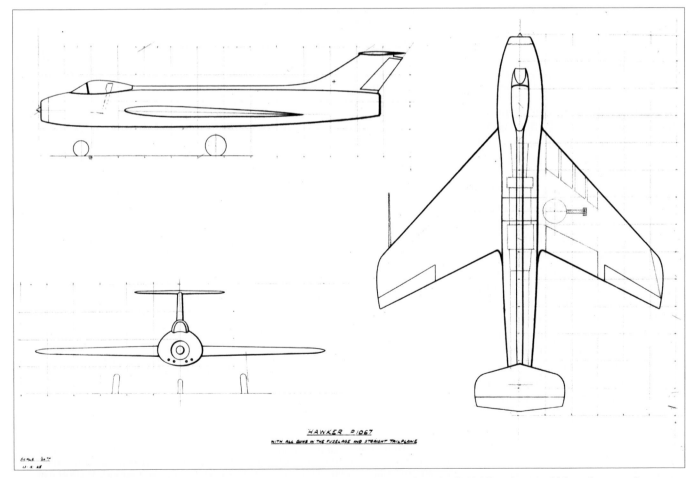

HAWKER P1067
WITH ALL GUNS IN THE FUSELAGE AND STRAIGHT TAILPLANE

This controversial design, dated December 13, 1948, is one of the earliest to show the P.1067 – what would later become the Hawker Hunter. *BAE Systems*

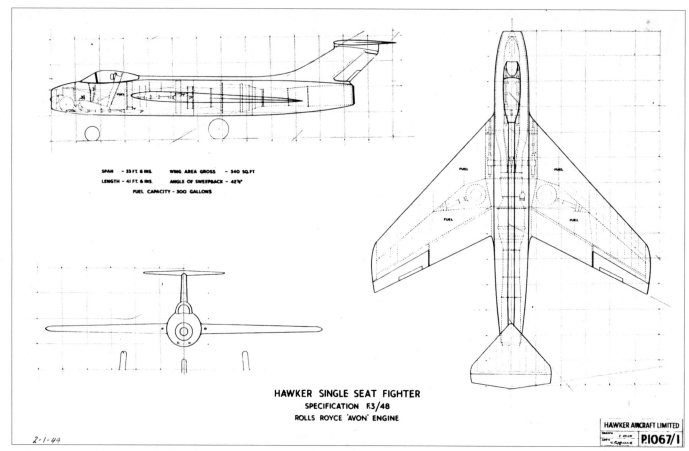

SPAN   - 33 FT. 6 INS.   WING AREA GROSS - 340 SQ.FT

LENGTH - 41 FT. 6 INS.   ANGLE OF SWEEPBACK - 42½°

FUEL CAPACITY - 300 GALLONS

HAWKER SINGLE SEAT FIGHTER

SPECIFICATION F.3/48

ROLLS ROYCE 'AVON' ENGINE

HAWKER AIRCRAFT LIMITED

P.1067/1

2-1-49

A drawing of the P.1067 with circular transonic fuselage as it apparently appeared in a full design proposal during August 1948. However, the drawing is dated January 2, 1949, making it later than the bulbous fuselage layout. *BAE Systems*

development of the Hunter into a Mach 1 aircraft, the P.1090, and a design which envisioned a much more streamlined all-weather supersonic fighter, the P.1092.

The latter boasted a 65° swept delta wing which, it was thought, would allow it to reach speeds up to Mach 1.5. Drawings of the P.1092 produced in early November 1951 showed a futuristic looking interceptor complete with AI radar and a back-seater to operate it. Its armament was four Aden cannon, rather than guided weapons, and it also featured a huge bulbous drop tank shaped around its belly for carrying an additional 550 gallons of fuel on top of its internal capacity of 650 gallons.

This was followed up with another supersonic delta design in February 1952, the P.1093. Then in August 1952, Specification F.119D was issued for a prototype of the P.1083

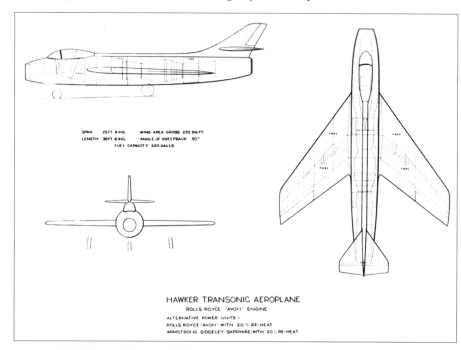

SPAN   25 FT. 9 INS.   WING AREA GROSS 235 SQ.FT.

LENGTH 36 FT. 6 INS.   ANGLE OF SWEEPBACK 50°

FUEL CAPACITY 320 GALLS.

HAWKER TRANSONIC AEROPLANE

ROLLS ROYCE 'AVON' ENGINE

ALTERNATIVE POWER UNITS :-

ROLLS ROYCE 'AVON' WITH 20% RE-HEAT

ARMSTRONG SIDDELEY 'SAPPHIRE' WITH 20% RE-HEAT

While the Hunter went on to assume its familiar form with wing root intakes, the nose intake form was recycled as a three-stand 50° wing-sweep experimental transonic aircraft proposal from late 1948 or early 1949. This is the first strand, P.1069 with a span of 25ft 9in and a length of 36ft 6in. This drawing shows fuel capacity as 320 gallons but another, which otherwise appears to be identical, shows 300. *BAE Systems*

50° swept-wing Hunter. Work on a mock-up commenced towards the end of the year and continued into 1953. In April however, with the Air Staff now increasingly involved in preparing a requirement for Britain's bomber interceptor, it was decided that if the P.1083 was to be built at all it would need to be able to carry guided weapons – specifically the Blue Jay.

However, the P.1083 had been conceived as a Mach 1 research aircraft with potential for development into a cannon-armed fighter. Guided weapons had never been part of the programme up to this point and Hawker decided that if they were required, rather than attempt to tweak the existing P.1083, a new blank-sheet design would be necessary.

Hawker carried out some preliminary work to see just how much effort was required to bring the P.1083 up to the required standard – a great deal as it transpired. A drawing from spring 1953 shows the original P.1083 with all the upgrades added to it; including a Rolls-Royce RA.19 engine with reheat, a modified Hunter Mk.6 centre fuselage, new rear fuselage, new low tailplane, lengthened nose, fuel-carrying under-fairing and modified windscreen.

In parallel to this, Hawker now worked on a host of other advanced supersonic designs. The company had been invited to tender for the ER.134T research aircraft requirement, drafting the closely related P.1096 and P.1097 for it in April 1953. Rather than struggling to hit Mach 1, as Hawker's earlier efforts had done, these two were intended to hit Mach 2 and Mach 1.9 respectively.

A third project, also of April 1953, involved creating a practical single-seat Mach 1.5 interceptor with fully integrated guided weapons systems. Labelled 'Supersonic Hunter', the P.1100 was an almost entirely new aircraft only loosely

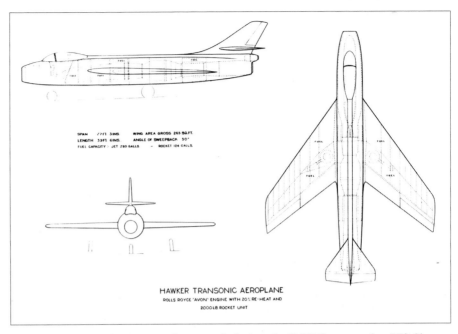

Hawker's medium sized transonic research design, the P.1070, measuring 27ft 3in span by 39ft 6in long. Fuel capacity for the turbojet was reduced to 280 gallons so that 124 gallons could be carried for a rocket motor positioned just below the tail fin. *BAE Systems*

based on the Hunter's form. It was intended to carry a pair of Blue Jays plus a pair of Aden cannon. An AI.20 radar was to be fitted and buried in the wing roots were a pair of auxiliary rocket motors.

Unfortunately for Hawker, none of these three strands went any further than the drawing board. The two ER.134T designs were defeated by Bristol's 188, the P.1100 was a design study only – however much, with hindsight, it appears

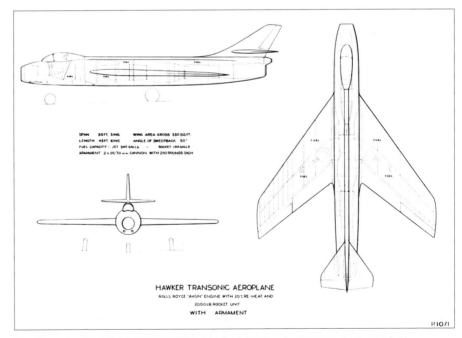

The largest of Hawker's 1948/49 transonic designs, the P.1071, had a 30ft 3in span and was 43ft 6in long. Now the jet got 340 gallons of fuel and the rocket motor 190 gallons. A pair of cannon were also pictured. *BAE Systems*

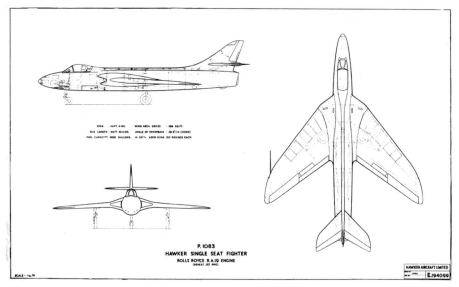

The most concerted attempt to create a supersonic Hunter was the P.1083 – a prototype was ordered but then cancelled in 1953. *BAE Systems*

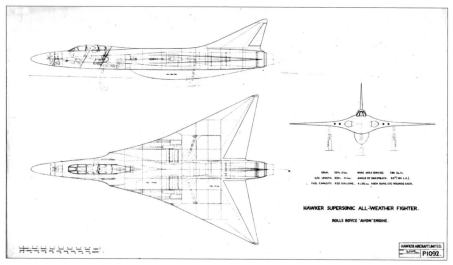

The Hawker P.1092 all-weather supersonic fighter was a remarkable design. Drafted on November 5, 1951, it embodied numerous advanced features – particularly its wing and cockpit design. *BAE Systems*

to predict what would come later – and rather than suffer all the delays that an extensive redesign would entail, the P.1083 was cancelled in July 1953.

The first P.1103s
During November 1953, Hawker designer Ralph Hooper drafted a 'Hawker Mach 2 Fighter' which, according to aviation historian Paul Martell-Mead, was probably the first iteration of the P.1103. It was equipped with Blue Jays and a long, sharply pointed fuselage housing its single

turbojet with relatively small swept wings.

At this point Hawker, with its many contacts at the Air Ministry, had undoubtedly heard about the latest discussions surrounding what would become OR.329 but exactly how much of the then-current version of the requirement it knew about is uncertain. Nevertheless, even without formal notification the company now began to focus its efforts on designing Mach 2-capable interceptors equipped with guided weapons, particularly Blue Jay.

In December 1953, designer John Fozard drafted a speculative approach to ER.151 – an experimental requirement which in the end was never issued – showing an elegant slender dart-like supersonic research aircraft powered by a single engine. The most notable aspect of the design was the positioning of the wide split intake, centrally and directly underneath the fuselage.

At the same time, P.1104 was now progressing in parallel to P.1103. Where the latter encompassed relatively lightweight Mach 2 designs using only a single fuselage-mounted turbojet, the former aimed to reach Mach 2 with a pair of turbojets positioned in nacelles beneath its wings. As a result, the numerous designs produced for P.1104 between November and December 1953 – at least four are known – tended to resemble the RAE's 'basic design' and indeed the sample fighters that Hall and his team would suggest four months later in their Mach 2 interceptors report.

Work on the 'engine in fuselage' P.1103 continued, however, and by February 1954 it appears to have been chosen over P.1104 as the most promising layout for a Mach 2 fighter. Another Ralph Hooper drawing from this time shows the P.1103 as a two-seater but now armed with a pair of Aden cannon rather than guided weapons. Two relatively narrow D-shaped intakes protruded from the sides of the fuselage.

The company finally received the fifth draft of what was now numbered OR.329 on March 17, 1954, from Kyle. Hawker chief designer Sydney Camm wrote back two days later saying: "Thank you very much indeed for your letter of the 17th March, and for the OR for the new fighter. This will give us plenty to think about for some time. As soon as I have prepared a statement of military load etc. I should like to come and discuss our conclusions with you. I confirm that I shall hold myself personally responsible for the safe custody of the document."

During April 1954, Hooper drew up another P.1103 that was superficially similar to the February design but which now featured Hunter-ish wing root intakes and a pair of Blue Jays. Further P.1103 designs continued to emerge from the Hawker project office throughout 1954.

By January 1955, the project solidified into two choices – a lightweight single-seater with wing root intakes or a much large two-seater with a split under-fuselage intake similar to that seen over a year earlier on Fozard's ER.151 design. When the official specification, F.155T, finally arrived shortly after February 17, 1955, the choice was clear: the Air Staff wanted a two-seater with exceptional climbing capabilities. The single-seater was abandoned and Hawker

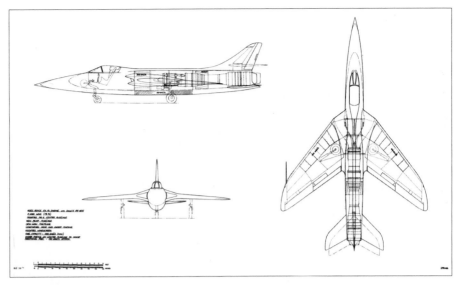

When the Air Staff decided that the P.1083 needed to carry guided weapons, Hawker decided it would need a total redesign. This spring 1953 drawing shows the outline of the original P.1083 with the point-nose, deep fuselage additions deemed necessary to bring it up to modern standards added over the top. *BAE Systems*

focused its energies instead on the two-seater.

On May 20, 1955, Hawker sent its then-current brochure for the two-seat P.1103 through to Gardner at the Ministry of Supply. An accompanying letter from Camm said: "We are submitting herewith our proposals for a supersonic all-weather fighter, based on a military load which is lower than that recently discussed in connection with the requirements of OR.329. Nevertheless, with the military load

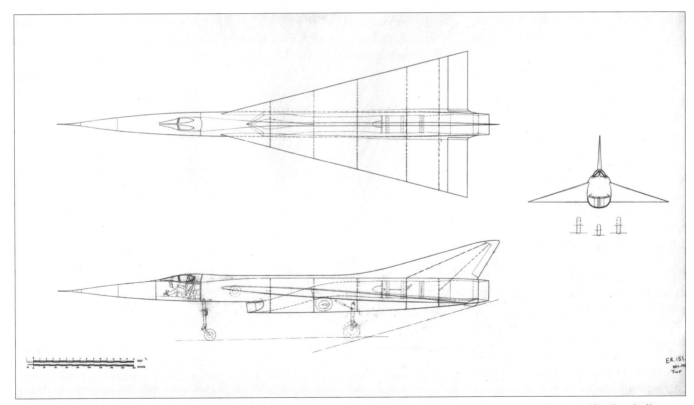

This dart-like design for an experimental requirement which never materialised – ER.151 – featured a split ventral intake similar to the one that would later be used on the P.1103 design submitted for F.155T. *BAE Systems*

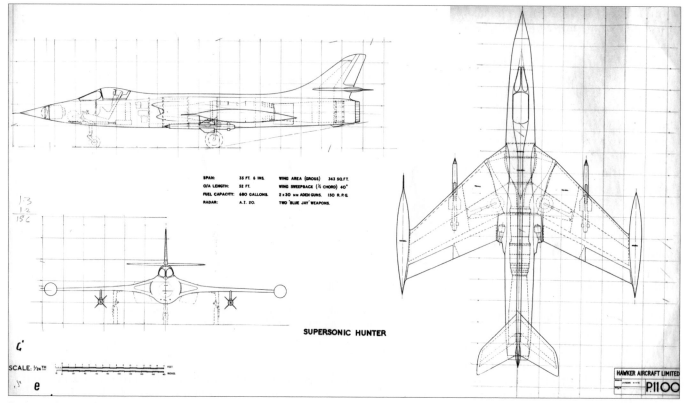

SPAN: 35 FT. 6 INS. WING AREA (GROSS) 343 SQ.FT.
O/A LENGTH: 52 FT. WING SWEEPBACK (¼ CHORD) 40°
FUEL CAPACITY: 680 GALLONS. 2 x 30 mm ADEN GUNS. 150 R.P.G.
RADAR: A.I. 20. TWO 'BLUE JAY' WEAPONS.

SUPERSONIC HUNTER

SCALE: 1/24TH

HAWKER AIRCRAFT LIMITED
P1100

Even as the P.1083 was heading towards cancellation, Hawker produced this attractive design for a radar-equipped, Blue Jay-carrying, rocket motor-boosted supersonic Hunter – P.1100. The drawing is dated April 4, 1953, in the bottom right hand corner. *BAE Systems*

we are suggesting the AUW of this aircraft is approximately 35,000lb, which is just over double the weight of the Hunter.

"As you will readily appreciate, the problems of strength and structure weight increase rapidly with size, and we are strongly of the opinion, therefore, that our design does represent an advance which is the maximum which could be obtained in a reasonable time."

The brochure was handed on to Hockmeyer who then wrote a note saying that the Ministry of Supply was being "pestered" by Camm for its views on his concept but the ministry could not "spare the necessary effort to study the proposals in detail until the R.156 assessment is disposed of" – R.156 being the concurrent RB.156T requirement for a Mach 3 reconnaissance aircraft/bomber which was ultimately won by the Avro 730.

In October, after months of exhaustive work, Hawker submitted its final brochure for F.155T. This is discussed more fully in the next chapter but it is interesting to note that just a month later, in November 1955, Hawker designed the P.1115, a two-seater all-weather fighter

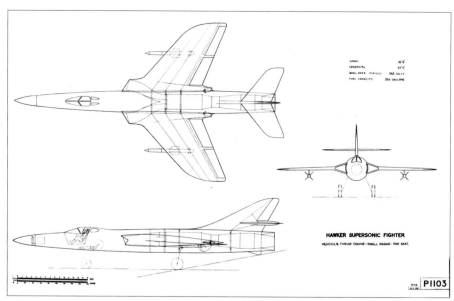

SPAN: 30'6"
LENGTH: 55'0"
WING AREA (GROSS) 565 SQ.FT.
FUEL CAPACITY: 720 GALLONS

HAWKER SUPERSONIC FIGHTER
14,000LB. THRUST ENGINE - SMALL RADAR - ONE SEAT.

P1103

During January 1955, a month before the F.155T specification was issued (the F.155T document has the date '15th January, 1955' printed in it – but this was only the date the spec was finalised; it was not sent out to the firms until February 17) Hawker was pursuing two lines of development for the P.1103. This was the lightweight single-seater version, dated January 10, 1955. *BAE Systems*

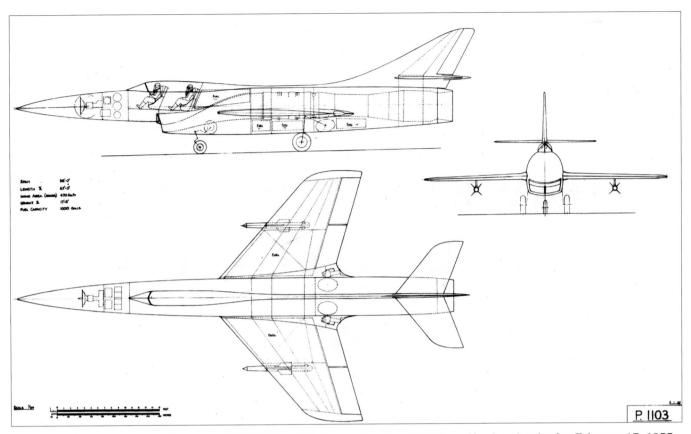

SPAN   36'-0"
LENGTH X   61'-0"
WING AREA (GROSS) 470 Sq.Ft
WEIGHT X   171-6"
FUEL CAPACITY   1000 Galls

P. 1103

The heavyweight two-seater version of the P.1103. When Hawker received the F.155T specification shortly after February 17, 1955, this design was clearly in a better position to meet it and the lightweight version was dropped. *BAE Systems*

obviously based on the two-seat trainer version of the Hunter. It is shown with a pair of Aden cannon but had it been able to carry guided weapons it might have made for a useful interim fighter ahead of the introduction of the F.155T design.

HAWKER AIRCRAFT
SINGLE-SEAT P.1103

January 1955

Artwork by Luca Landino

— *Specification* —

Crew: One **Length:** 57ft **Wingspan:** 32.5ft Height: 18.17ft
Wing area: 365sq ft **Empty weight:** N/A **Loaded weight:** N/A
Powerplant: 1 x unspecified turbojet with 14,000lb static thrust
Maximum speed: N/A **Service ceiling:** N/A **Armament:** 2 x de Havilland Blue Jay

7

THE SMALLEST POSSIBLE AIRCRAFT

Hawker P.1103

Performance was everything for Hawker's P.1103.
The design brochure gave little consideration to tactics,
strategy or even the weapons system concept and related
everything to increasing power and reducing weight. The
result was undoubtedly a fearsome combat machine.

Hawker made no bones about it – the P.1103 was going to be relatively small, relatively light and packing the largest, most powerful single engine that could possibly be squeezed into it.

Rather than attempting to discuss the problem of tackling Soviet bombers via a pursuit course or head-on attack, the brochure begins instead with a straightforward description of the aircraft itself: "An attempt to meet the requirements of Specification F.155T with the smallest possible aircraft is the design philosophy behind the weapon system described in this brochure. A single engine design has been chosen, since it is the cleanest aerodynamically and has the highest thrust/weight ratio."

The powerplant was to be "the most powerful engine available,

namely the de Havilland Gyron". Other engines were being kept under consideration however: the Armstrong Siddeley P.173, the Rolls-Royce RB.122, and the Orenda Engines PS.13.

Rather than fit rocket motors internally, where they and their fuel would add weight and take up valuable space, Hawker intended the P.1103 to have aerodynamic rocket fuel tank/motor units which could be easily put on or taken off the aircraft as required: "The detachable rocket booster units are … carried on the wings. These units are completely self-contained and hold sufficient oxidant and fuel for 3.7 minutes rocket firing time."

They were also, evidently, the result of some confusion about the specification. Hawker's engineers had read between the lines and

thought they could discern what the Air Staff really wanted out of the F.155T aircraft – range and loiter time. It was therefore a good job that the mounting points for the rocket motors could also be used for drop tanks: "Although the Specification places particular importance on rate of climb and acceleration, it is understood that emphasis has recently swung towards increased endurance. Since there is this conflict in requirements and, indeed, the strong possibility that both characteristics will be required at different times, the rocket booster has been designed as a detachable self-contained unit, so that the aircraft is equally efficient in either role.

"An advantage of this arrangement is that rocket motors of greater thrust can be substituted and it is

This dramatic piece of concept art, showing the Hawker P.1103 literally rocketing skywards, was used to open the October 1955 brochure on the design. *BAE Systems*

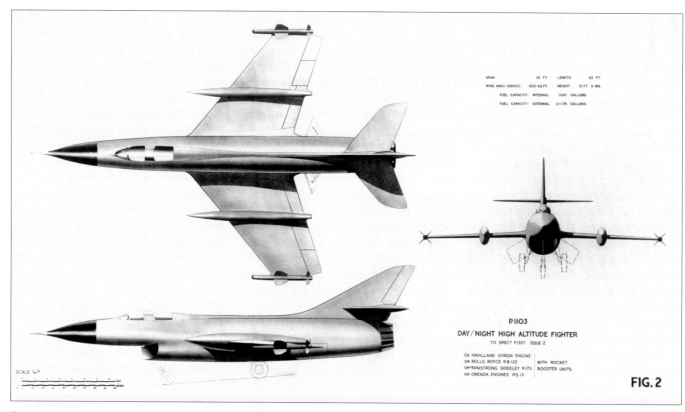

Toned three-view drawing of the high-tail P.1103 from the brochure. The high tail was preferred over a low-tail layout, presented as an alternative, as it was thought to prevent the problem of pitch-up. *BAE Systems*

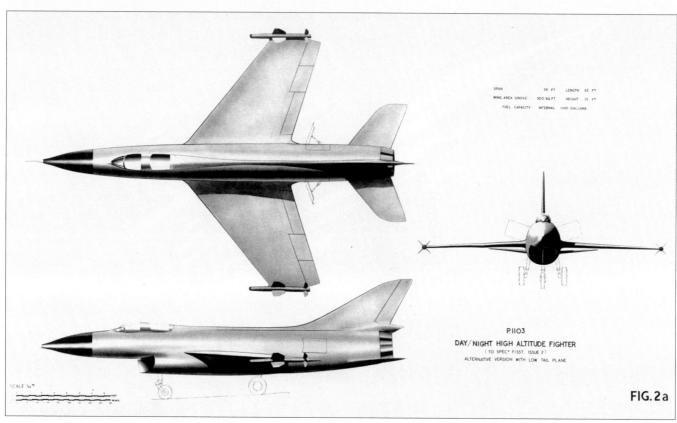

A low-tail version of the P.1103 was also presented in the brochure as an alternative. On paper, the only real difference in spec was a reduction in overall height by 6in, despite a taller undercarriage. *BAE Systems*

further suggested that the present 1100 gallons internal fuel capacity could be augmented by carrying additional fuel in containers similar to, but in lieu of, the rocket booster units. This configuration would provide some 1500 gallons total fuel capacity."

The actual motor used for the rockets would be an Armstrong Siddeley RB.6/1, rated at 2000lb – the same as the late-1940s Armstrong Siddeley Snarler. The rockets would be controlled using "a single on-off switch mounted on the throttle handle" and the pilot would get a 'firing time left' indicator along with a warning light operated by a pressure switch connected to the combustion chamber to show when each motor was in operation.

Weaponry would consist of either two Blue Jay Mk.4 infrared homing missiles, or a pair of Vickers "small radar missiles". Hawker accepted that the spec called for the ability to mount either infrared or radar

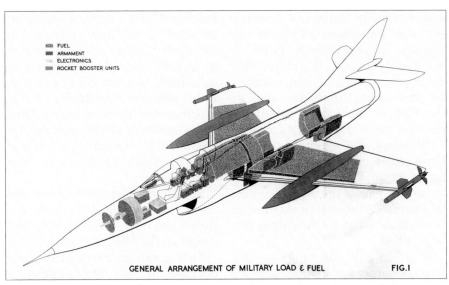

GENERAL ARRANGEMENT OF MILITARY LOAD & FUEL   FIG.1

The P.1103's clean but conventional layout belies the huge number of configurations that led up to it. The fact that it resembles the hugely successful General Dynamics F-16 – designed some 20 years later – gives an indication of just how 'right' the Hawker team got it. *BAE Systems*

homers, but intensely disliked the enormous radar weapons Vickers was developing at that time, stating: "The Red Dean replacement type of weapon, as at present designed, is so large and aerodynamically

dirty as to be completely out of harmony with this aircraft or any other aircraft on which it is mounted externally.

"The alternative of mounting a pair of these weapons internally or

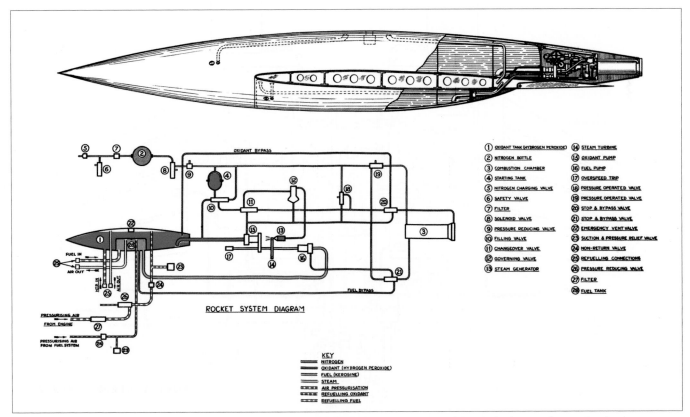

Providing the P.1103 with detachable boosters that housed all their own fuel was one of the design's more innovative features. *BAE Systems*

semi-internally implies a fuselage (or other container) which, in our opinion, is prohibitively large. It is strongly urged, therefore, that all efforts should be concentrated on developing Blue Jay and/or the Vickers small radar missile to perform the Red Dean mission.

"However, the weight of the Red Dean replacement missile is not excessive and it may be possible to carry a pair of these weapons on this aircraft if the severe sacrifice in performance due to their drag can be justified."

Every single drawing in the Hawker brochure which showed the P.1103 fitted with missiles depicted Blue Jays. The company had drawings prepared which showed it armed with Red Hebes, Raytheon AIM-7 Sparrows and

Hughes AIM-4 Falcon missiles, but declined to put any of them into its tender submission. However, it appears that the brochure, as submitted, actually came complete with a little model of the P.1103. The brochure introduction noted: "Blue Jay is shown in all the pictures, but the model kit contains a set of both types of missile which can be fitted as alternatives."

So anyone interested to see how the aircraft might look with Red Deans had only to tinker with their model a little. The brochure went on: "The weapons are carried externally because of the impossibility of stowing such irregularly shaped articles within this small compact aircraft. Moreover, the carriage of the weapons externally has the advantages of simplicity, light

weight, and flexibility of operation. Further, it affords the best possible field of view for the weapon sensing-heads."

The P.1103's all-up weight was given as 35,000lb or 40,000lb if the rocket booster packs were installed. The brochure goes on to comment on the P.1103's handsome shape, being evidently rather proud of it: "It is apparent from the Frontispiece and Fig. 2 (three-view G.A.) that the aerodynamic layout is conventional. A swept wing has been chosen because of its favourable transonic characteristics, load relieving ability and structural suitability for the single engine arrangement.

"The thickness/chord ratio is 5% at the root and 3½% at the tip."

Two tail arrangements, high and low, were offered but, "in our opinion

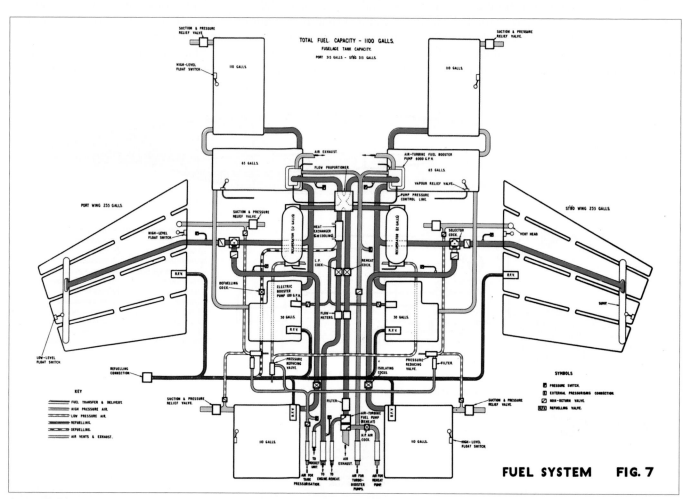

A straightforward kerosene fuel system was all the P.1103 needed – because the aircraft itself was not required to house the fuel for its rocket boosters. *BAE Systems*

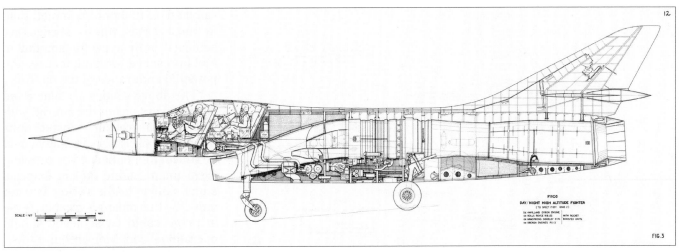

Although the P.1103 was not a particularly small aircraft, its interior layout was impeccable as this brochure drawing makes plain. *BAE Systems*

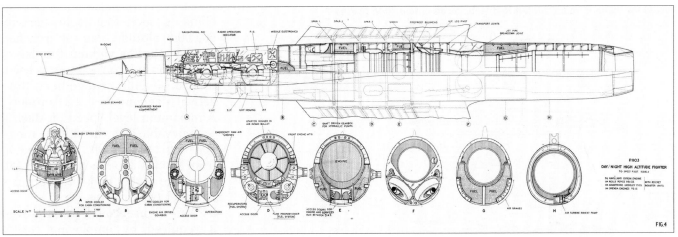

Barely an inch is wasted in the P.1103's slender fuselage. *BAE Systems*

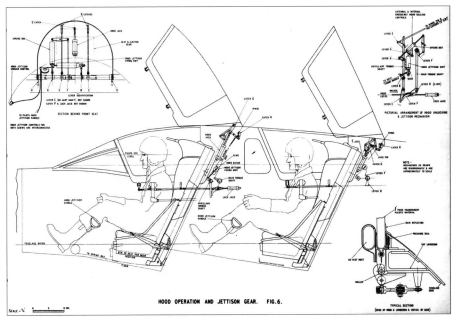

The P.1103's crew were provided with simple ejection seats – there wasn't room for anything more elaborate. *BAE Systems*

an aircraft layout incorporating a high tail position can, with the aid of wind-tunnel experimentation, be developed satisfactorily against pitch-up, and this position is strongly preferred from all other aspects.

"An alternative low position has, however, been investigated in detail."

The pitot-static head was mounted in front of the radome, a familiar position today. The engine's air intake featured a retractable debris-guard, and a fairing at the rear of the tailplane/fin junction housed braking parachutes, which would be essential during landing:

"Take-off presents no problem on account of the extremely high power to weight ratio. The landing requirement, on the other hand, is severe for this type of aircraft and in

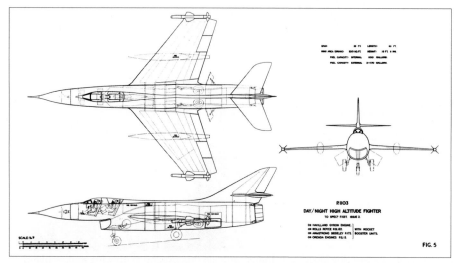

Every image of the P.1103 included with the F.155T tender brochure deliberately showed the aircraft armed with Blue Jay Mk.4 missiles – even though the specification asked for Vickers' radar-guided Red Hebe as an option. *BAE Systems*

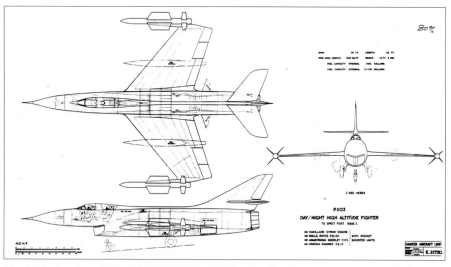

Hawker's drawing of the P.1103 with Red Hebe missiles bears out a point made in the brochure – that they would cause a huge amount of drag and badly affect the performance of the aircraft. *BAE Systems*

order to meet it, a braking parachute installation has been provided. Wheel brake developments are in hand with a view to shortening the ground run as much as possible. The nose wheel is steerable and it should be noted that the tyre pressures are 170psi."

The P.1103 would carry three 7ft diameter parachutes stowed in the fin/tailplane trailing edge bullet, assuming the high tailplane version was adopted. If the low tailplane option was chosen, a "special fairing above the reheat nozzle" would be used. Only two of the parachutes would be deployed during a normal

landing, the third being reserved for emergencies, and it was possible for all three of them to be jettisoned.

Outright performance

Having designed what they regarded as an aircraft with a winning combination of flexibility and outright performance, the Hawker team were supremely confident that it could not just meet but significantly exceed the F.155T performance requirements.

The brochure stated: "Both the Normal Warning Time and the Extended Warning Time sorties outlined in the Specification are

satisfied … it should be noted that, in most cases, these sorties are achieved with a useful amount of fuel in reserve, which increases the potential endurance of the aircraft.

"The above sorties are illustrated for both versions of the aircraft with and without rocket booster units fitted. The aircraft's versatility could be still further enhanced by carrying extra main engine fuel in external tanks similar to the rocket booster units. By this means a great increase in range could be achieved should operational conditions require this.

"A 1½g ceiling of 65,000ft is achievable with the aid of the rocket boosters. The maximum rate of climb is such that from start-up, 60,000ft altitude can be reached in four minutes without the use of rocket boost. If rocket boost is used, this can be achieved together with an arrival Mach number of 2.0 or more. A maximum level speed of Mach 2 is achievable over the altitude range 30,000ft to 65,000ft. Acceleration from Mach 1.3 to Mach 2 at 60,000ft, using the rocket boosters, occupies just over two minutes.

"This figure could be improved if required by employing rocket motors of greater thrust (approximately 2½ times i.e. 10,000lb rocket thrust would give one minute acceleration time from Mach 1.3 to Mach 2) but something approximating to a pro-rata reduction in rocket endurance would have to be borne.

"This is because the characteristically high fuel consumption of the rocket motor would increase the aircraft weight disproportionately such that the law of diminishing returns would predominate. However, it is possible that a compromise could be reached if the issue is vital."

In other words, bigger rocket motors would cut the time to go from Mach 1.3 to Mach 2 in half. However, the cost in extra weight would be substantial, ultimately defeating the whole point of making the P.1103 such a lightweight machine in the first place.

In spite of its general flexibility, the performance demands likely to be placed on the P.1103 meant some of its stats were severely curtailed.

Under a heading of 'combat radius on supersonic cruise sortie (reheat only)' the brochure noted: "The effective combat radius of the aircraft, without rocket boosters, is shown to be in excess of 200 nautical miles when the speed used for pursuit and combat is restricted to Mach 1.5. This type of sortie

is likely to be used only against subsonic raiders." Two hundred miles was not much of a combat radius and it would only really be acceptable for a pure interceptor.

Furthermore, under 'combat performance above 60,000ft (reheat plus booster)' it was stated: "By carrying rocket boosters the aircraft is shown to be capable of reaching 80,000ft in a steady climb at a speed of Mach 2.

"Unfortunately the combat time remaining at this altitude is very short (one minute) and only very

gentle manoeuvres are possible if speed and altitude are to be retained. However, the height advantage over a target at, say, 60,000ft will enable a very rapid overtaking pass to be made by diving. The height limit to this steady climb is incurred by the exhaustion of the rocket fuel and not by lack of thrust."

Limited freedom

When it came to the weapon system concept, Hawker struggled. Rather than even feigning an acknowledgment that a combined

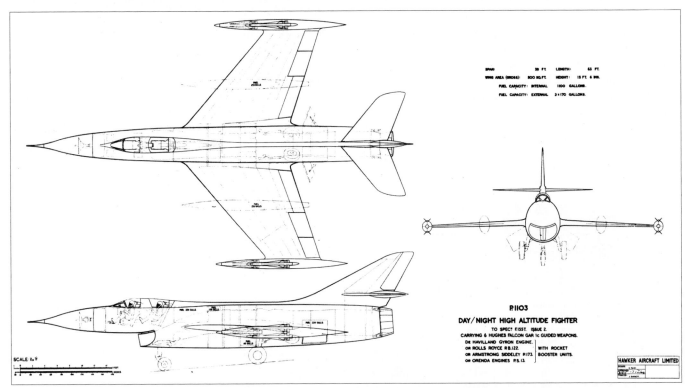

It was possible to fit the aircraft with no fewer than six Hughes AIM-4 Falcon missiles, carried in aerodynamic wing-tip fairings. *BAE Systems*

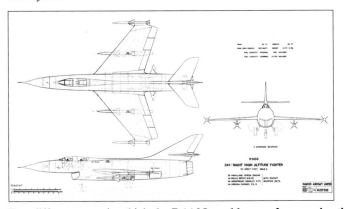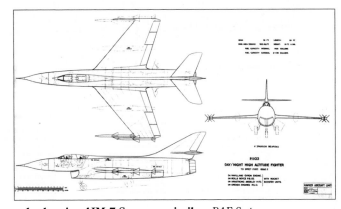

Two different ways in which the P.1103 could carry four semi-active radar homing AIM-7 Sparrow missiles. *BAE Systems*

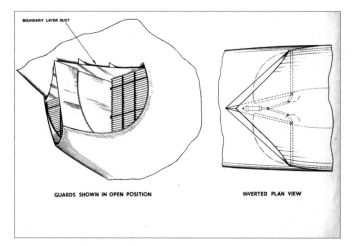

Intake debris guards designed to fit over the P.1103's low-down intakes. *BAE Systems*

The P.1103's generator and hydraulic pump arrangement was compact and well-positioned. *BAE Systems*

and integrated approach to radar, missile and aircraft could make the united trio greater than the sum of their parts, Hawker's attitude was that this simply wouldn't work in practice.

It stopped short of calling the idea nonsense, but only just. Under the heading 'weapon system' the brochure said: "The components of the Weapon System which can be under the control of the aircraft designer, in addition to the aircraft automatic control system, are the weapons, the AI radar, the navigation and the radio communication equipment.

"It is agreed that ideally they should come under one authority but, in this country, technical ability is too thinly spread to afford the duplication of effort which will occur if the aircraft firm is to be able to influence the design of, say, the guided weapons or AI equipment to more than a superficial extent.

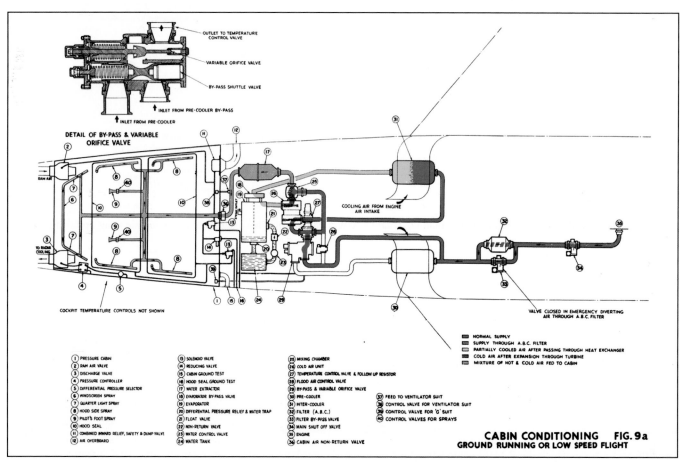

CABIN CONDITIONING FIG. 9a
GROUND RUNNING OR LOW SPEED FLIGHT

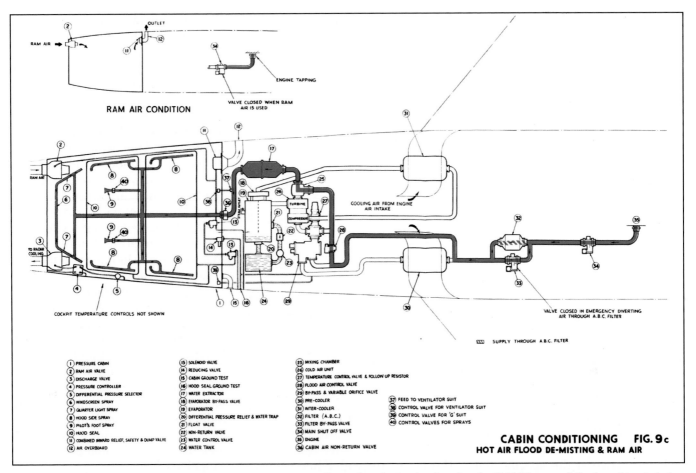

CABIN CONDITIONING FIG. 9c
HOT AIR FLOOD DE-MISTING & RAM AIR

ABOVE, BELOW and BELOW LEFT: Hawker went to extraordinary lengths in showing that the P.1103 was a fully thought-out design rather than a mere concept, as demonstrated by these brochure diagrams showing how the air conditioning system would work in different situations. *BAE Systems*

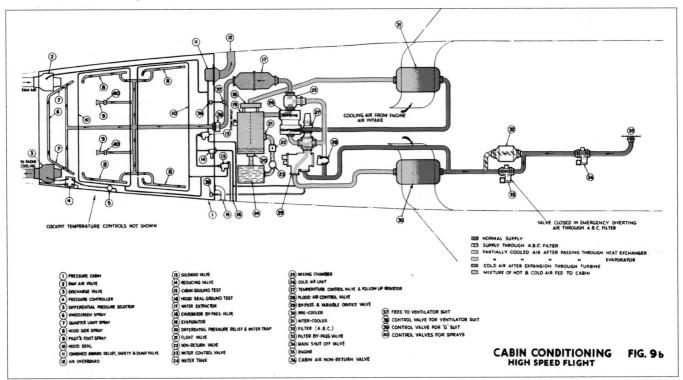

CABIN CONDITIONING FIG. 9b
HIGH SPEED FLIGHT

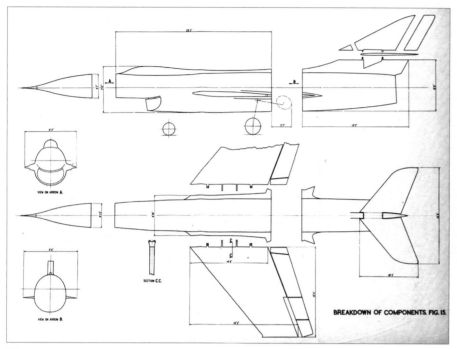

There was nothing particularly unusual about the way the P.1103 was intended to be put together – but this deceptive simplicity was the point. *BAE Systems*

"Also, by the time the aircraft designer is called in, preliminary studies of the overall system must have been carried out in order to arrive at the specification requirements. Hence the aircraft designer is presented with a partially determined solution. We are of the opinion therefore that the aircraft designer's contribution, during this next era, is limited to close collaboration with the designers of the various items of military load.

"Whilst the overall requirements determine the approximate characteristics of each component, these components are still being developed by different organisations in various forms, and for that reason a certain amount of latitude is available to the designer of the aircraft and its equipment. Within this limited freedom the smallest possible aircraft is presented in this brochure and, where alternatives exist, the smallest or lightest equipment is specified."

With Red Hebe

Following the submission of the Hawker brochure, at an unspecified later date, a new appendix was produced and circulated so that it could be attached to the back of existing copies. This was entitled 'Hawker P.1103 with 2 Red Hebes – descriptive notes' and came complete with its own mini table of contents. This was, belatedly, Hawker's note on tactics and strategy – the use of its aircraft in combat rather than a simple description of the aircraft itself.

The introduction started: "The performance penalty, in terms of the specification (F.155T) requirements, when two Red Hebe weapons are carried on the Hawker P.1103, is stated overleaf and on the attached tables and graphs.

"In spite of this rather severe penalty, however, it is still possible by using the frontal attack technique for which Red Hebe is specifically designed, to intercept enemy bombers flying at Mach numbers up to 2.0 at 60,000ft over a wide front with the accepted Normal Warning Time."

The Vickers missile would be mounted "at the wing tips in a manner similar to the Vickers Small

Weapons in our F.155T brochure, but considerably farther forward. This forward position has been chosen for the following reasons: to minimise aerodynamic interference, to ease the stability problem with and without the weapon, to provide adequate ground clearance in the tail down and one wing low attitude.

"Special attention will be paid to the rigidity characteristics of the mounting arrangements and suitable production to that part of the wing affected by the rocket blast will be provided. It is not expected that the blast will have a detectable effect on the aileron control."

The grisly details of Red Hebe's impact on the P.1103's performance were then listed: maximum speed at 60,000ft cut by Mach 0.25, ceiling lowered by 4000ft, time to climb to 60,000ft and Mach 2 increased by 1.87 minutes, fuel use in doing so increased by 152 gallons. Turning radius at height and Mach 2 was increased by 1.9 miles and extra fuel used in this manoeuvre was 44 gallons.

Hawker argued that the much smaller and more aerodynamic infrared homing Blue Vesta – the Blue Jay Mk.4 renamed – was suitable for tackling both Mach 1.3 and Mach 2 targets, offering belated descriptions of how an interception with this missile would be effected. First, against Mach 1.3 targets: "The fighter performs an energy climb reaching Mach 2.3 at 40,000ft. The remainder of the climb and the flight out to the target is continued at this Mach number (Mach 2.3 is chosen as the maximum sustained Mach number to which the light alloy structure may be subjected). The missile is limited in direction of attack, by consideration of minimum time of flight, to within 114° of astern target. A minimum radius turn is therefore commenced at the last moment to bring the fighter into a line of sight at the assumed missile lock-on range of three nautical miles and at the limiting angle of 114°

(the kinematics of the final stage of attack are thus in error since a missile collision course should be the aim. However, the effect on the kill line will be very small indeed).

"A front of 284 nautical miles is thus defended (limited by fuel exhaustion if the fighter is to return to its home base). Over the whole of this front the missile is operating at its minimum time of flight."

The Blue Vesta interception got a little trickier where Mach 2 targets were concerned however: "Here at small angles from ahead of base the fighter climb terminal Mach number must be reduced or the bomber will pass above the fighter before its climb is completed. Hence the fighter Mach number is held at 2.3 when the bomber approaches at more than 70 nautical miles to either side of base, but is progressively reduced to give Mach 1.5 in the case of attack directly in line with base.

"The higher bomber speed further restricts the direction of attack to the rear hemisphere and a minimum radius turn is performed as previously described to bring the fighter in at 90° (in all cases where the bomber is reached ahead of base). A front of 315 nautical miles can be defended (limited by fuel exhaustion) but within 138 nautical miles of base the missile operates at its minimum time of flight; and within 70 nautical miles to either side of base, the turn is commenced immediately as the top of the climb is reached."

The add-on appendix concluded that Red Hebe was "slightly superior" when it came to dealing with enemies when they were almost on top of the interceptor's base – within 180 nautical miles – but "high speed (Mach 2) targets attacking outside this lateral range and all subsonic and transonic targets are better countered with smaller and lighter weapons".

Looking at Hawker's brochure today, it is difficult to escape the conclusion that simple poor presentation almost doomed the P.1103 from the outset. The aircraft itself was highly advanced and embodied some great ideas – such as the detachable boosters – not to mention outstanding performance, but the brochure failed to address any of the key issues that both the Air Staff and Ministry of Supply had agonised over. If Hawker had at least paid lip service to the weapons system concept, offered persuasive arguments in favour of pursuit-course attack with Blue Jays and given a full (or indeed any) explanation of how automation and ground-control guidance would be utilised, the firm's chances of success might have been dramatically improved.

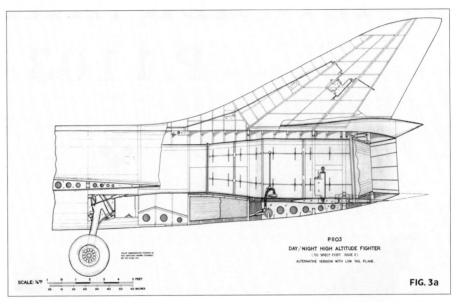

A more detailed view of the alternative low tail version of the P.1103. As the drawing notes in tiny writing, a slightly taller undercarriage would be required to give the tail plane tips sufficient ground clearance. *BAE Systems*

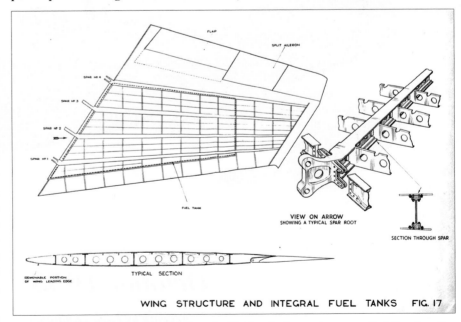

Another detailed drawing showing how far Hawker had gone to ensure that the aircraft would be buildable within the given timescale, if it was chosen for further development. *BAE Systems*

12

HAWKER AIRCRAFT P.1103

❖

October 1955

Artwork by Luca Landino

— *Specification* —

Crew: Two **Length:** 63ft
Wingspan: 39ft **Height:** 15.5ft
Wing area: 500sq ft
Empty weight: 20,760lb
Loaded weight: 35,000lb
Powerplant: 1 x de Havilland Gyron
or Rolls-Royce R.B.122 or
Armstrong Siddeley P.173 or Orenda
Engines P.S.13 with rocket booster units
Maximum speed: Mach 2.9 with rockets and
reheat (structural limit Mach 2.3)
Service ceiling: 70,200ft
Armament: 2 x Vickers Red Hebe

8

MARGINAL PERFORMANCE

Fairey ER.103 Development

The slender experimental Fairey Delta 2 had made its
first flight a full year before the tender submission date for
F.155T and the company naturally offered a straightforward
development of this promising design for the competition –
but it also harboured ambitions to go a step further.

Fairey designed what would later be known as the Delta 2 during 1949, following on from studies carried out during 1948. The delta-wing project, intended to reach speeds up to Mach 1.5, had experimental requirement ER.103, issued on September 26, 1950, written around it.

ER.103 stated: "This specification is issued to cover the design and construction of a 60 degree delta-wing research aircraft which is required to enable problems associated with flight at transonic and supersonic speeds up to a Mach number of 1.5 and up to altitudes of at least 45,000ft to be investigated."

The engine was to be a modified Rolls-Royce Avon RA.3 with 8300lb thrust with provision for reheat to $1500^{\circ}K$ and a variable nozzle. The fuel system was to be "suitable for aerobatics including inverted flying for a period of 15 seconds whether the reheat system is on or off" and a pressure cabin was to be fitted.

It was to have enough fuel for a mission sequence involving engine start and take-off without reheat, climb to 45,000ft without reheat, 15 minutes cruising at 45,000ft without reheat, eight minutes on full power with reheat, powered descent and return to base. Take-off distance was to be not more than 1500 yards and landing no more than 1550 yards at maximum design weight.

Company documents show that during the first four years of its development the aircraft was known to Fairey and the Ministry of Supply as the Type 'V', often referred to as 'the 'V' aircraft', 'the 'V' Type' or simply as the ER.103. Its unveiling as the Fairey Delta 2 or F.D.2 seems to have taken place in October 1954, but even then reports continued to refer to it by its earlier name.

A mock-up was made during the first half of 1951 and, following delays caused by Fairey's heavy workload, construction of the first of two prototypes ordered began

The first Fairey Delta 2 – WG774 – in flight, from the cover of a 1956 publicity brochure. *via author*

When sitting on the ground in readiness for take-off, the Delta 2 had a pronounced nose-up attitude. *via author*

during the summer of 1952. The aircraft, serial WG774, was meant to make its first flight in March 1954 but this was delayed due to a range of difficulties.

At a progress meeting at Fairey's offices in Hayes, Middlesex, on March 1, company chief engineer Robert Lickley "said that the cockpit canopy had not been received, but the most serious hold-up arose from non-delivery of the engine. Rolls-Royce development of the reheat system was seriously behind schedule and the delay was the more serious because the mock-up engine was not fully representative". He further "reported that, apart from these component parts remaining to be delivered, the outstanding difficulties were fuel tank sealing and obtaining agreement on satisfactory engine operating conditions".

Sealing the tanks apparently proved to be a near-insurmountable obstacle because "all British sealants had failed to prevent leaks from the integral fuel tanks" so a product supplied by the Minnesota

Mining & Manufacturing Co was being tried. But the tanks still weren't sealed by April 9.

The fifth draft of OR.329 was sent out to 11 firms on March 17, 1954, but Fairey never received a copy and presumably remained ignorant of its existence.

A Ministry of Supply Aircraft Research Department memo from early 1954, giving consideration to what the press might and might not be told about the ER.103, gave an outline of its design and function at that point: "It is a single seat, tailless delta aircraft intended for research at transonic and supersonic speeds. With the present RA.14 engine, with reheat, it should be capable of Mach 1.3 in level flight and of operating at heights up to 55,000ft.

"The wing has 60° leading edge sweepback and the thickness/chord ratio is only 4%. The trailing edge wing controls provide separate longitudinal and lateral control, the inboard control acting as an elevator and the outboard control as aileron. Directional control is a conventional rudder. All flying

controls are completely power operated by a system of duplicated tandem hydraulic jacks. There is no feedback to the pilot's control of aerodynamic loads, as all stick forces are purely artificial, derived from springs.

"Air brakes are provided in the form of four 'petal' brakes mounted circumferentially on the rear fuselage. These air brakes are intended for flight deceleration only and are not expected to be used for landing run retardation. A 10ft diameter parachute is designed primarily as a landing parachute, but may also be used for anti-spin precautions. To provide extra downward vision dead ahead for landing and take-off, the whole fuselage nose to just aft of the cockpit can be drooped to an angle of 10° nose down, relative to the fuselage datum line.

"This aircraft is complementary to the F.23/49 although it has no immediate military application. Its configuration is promising for a very wide range of operating speeds including Mach numbers in excess of 2. Hence there is considerable interest in the research to be done with the aircraft, two of which are being built."

There were further delays when Rolls-Royce revealed they were, according to a June 4, 1954, Ministry of Supply letter, "not happy with the intake design". The firm had held talks with Fairey, at which it was agreed that several modifications were needed: "These comprise the extension forward of the air intake, the fitting of vanes in the air intake and certain modifications to the engine including the incorporation of steel blades in the early stages of the compressor". This resulted in another four months of delay. Rolls-Royce had apparently pointed out these problems two years ago but did not blame Fairey for failing to act because the matter had not been properly communicated.

Another progress report was held at Hayes on June 23, 1954, at which Lickley "reported that the aircraft is now fully assembled and receiving its final tests". The Minnesota Mining & Manufacturing Co sealant had proven effective in the wing tanks and an interim engine supplied by Rolls-Royce was allowing taxi tests. According to the minutes of the meeting, "the intake position was rather confused and discussions with Rolls-Royce were still open". The flight engine had been promised by the end of September but would be 500lb less in thrust than it was officially rated. While the company was waiting, a rigorous programme of wind tunnel testing was carried out with a particular focus on the engine intakes.

When the earliest list of potential participants for the OR.329 competition was drawn up on July 21, 1954, Fairey was not included. Finally, the missing engine was delivered on September 4 and its installation, commencing after taxi tests on September 11, took another month.

WG774 made its first flight from 4.57pm to 5.23pm on October 6, 1954. At Boscombe Down on November 17, during the 14th flight of its test programme and having yet to go supersonic, the aircraft suffered engine failure at 30,000ft at 1.06pm and was brought in for a forced landing at 1.12pm. According to the crash report, issued on November 22, pilot Peter Twiss "succeeded in landing the aircraft on the runway on the nose wheel and tail skid only. He ran along level for about 1000ft and only then slewed off the runway. The aircraft is now on its main undercarriage and will be brought back to Fairey's works by road on Monday.

"There is some damage to the nose wheel, the underside of the rear fuselage and to the wing tips and ailerons. It is intended to remove the wing and check for

A selection of four photos from the Delta 2 publicity brochure – two show the aircraft's 'droop nose', designed to give the pilot good visibility on landing despite the rest of the aircraft being tilted up for increased lift. *via author*

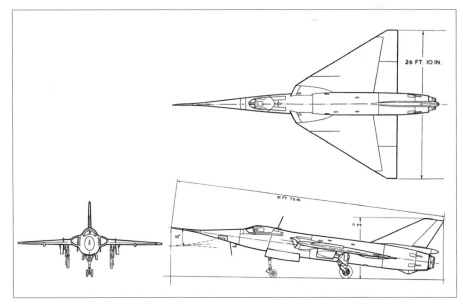

A three-view drawing of the single-seat experimental Delta 2 from Fairey's brochure. The aircraft was 51ft 7½in long and 11ft tall, with a span of 26ft 10in. *via author*

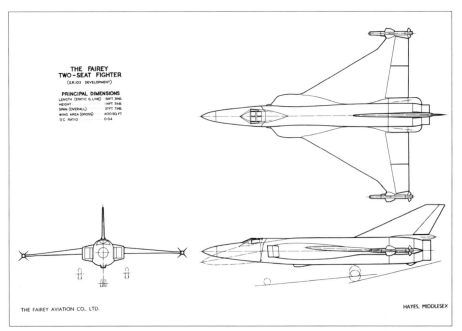

Brochure drawing of the Fairey ER.103 development fighter, one of the company's two proposals to meet F.155T. Its origin as a scaled-up Delta 2 is clear, complete with 'droop nose', but it is substantially bigger at 56ft 3in long and 14ft 3in tall, with an overall span of 37ft 7in. *Leonardo Helicopters*

distortion in the jigs. Until this is done it will be uncertain how much damage has been sustained."

On November 24, 1954, Fairey's chief aerodynamicist H Roberts wrote to the Ministry of Supply to return details he had been borrowing on the Convair YF-102, noting "these have given me more or less what I wanted and I am very grateful for their loan". The YF-102, at this time entering the closing stages of a major redesign to incorporate area rule into its fuselage shape for reduced transonic drag, had a similar single engine delta-wing layout to the Delta 2.

Fairey wrote to the Ministry of Supply on December 16 asking for permission to dispose of the ER.103 wooden mock-up: "Will you please confirm that this is no longer required, and may be disposed of as scrap, as the mock-up at present occupies valuable floor space required for other work."

Even by January 5, 1955 – just over a month before the first issue of F.155T – Fairey was still not on the list to tender for it, only being added on January 6 because Westland was being relegated to the B-list and a replacement was required. At this stage, if Fairey had any thoughts on turning the Delta 2 into a fighter, it kept them to itself.

In February 1955, M Booth, of the Ministry of Supply, wrote to the ministry's liaison at the British Joint Services Mission in Washington, DC, W Stewart, asking for data from the YF-102 test programme. The letter was headed 'Convair F-102': "As you know, the above aircraft is very similar in general configuration to our ER.103, having a wing of similar sweep and t/c ratio. When the ER.103 resumes its flight programme, the next stage to be explored will be the transonic region, and in view of the lack of knowledge on control surface flutter, we are endeavouring to draw on experience on other aircraft, and by comparison of the configuration, to form some idea of whether the ER.103 will be better or worse than these in this respect.

"We understand that the F-102 has flown transonically and should be grateful if you could find out if any control surface flutter experience has been encountered, together with any details which may be available, so that we can relate this experience to the ER.103."

Stewart wrote back on February 7 to thank him for his letter asking for information on the F-102: "This aircraft has flown supersonic, the latest version achieving supersonic speeds in level flight. As far as we know there has been no difficulty associated with flutter. The aircraft

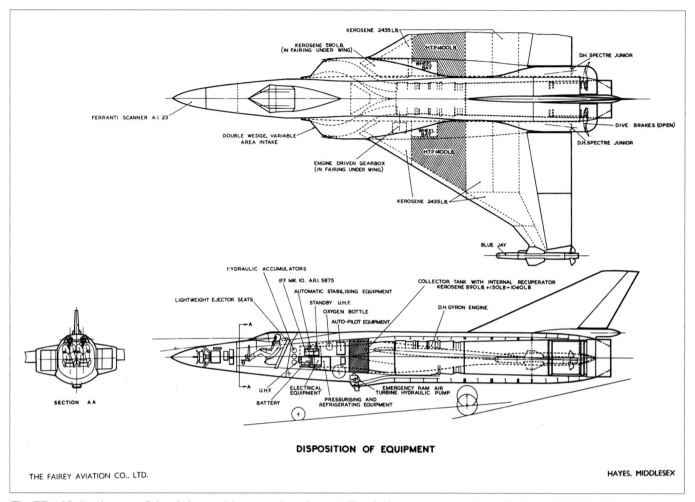

The ER.103 development fighter's internal layout and equipment. The design was comparable to Hawker's P.1103, with a centrally positioned de Havilland Gyron engine – but featured side-by-side seating and built-in rocket engines. *Leonardo Helicopters*

details you asked for are already available in our previous reports."

As investigations into the cause of WG774's engine failure, focusing on fuel starvation, continued on March 18, 1955, Lickley sent Ronald Andrew Shaw, Assistant Director of the Ministry of Supply's Aircraft Research Department, a letter headed 'ER.103 Development'. He wrote: "As you know, we have been looking into developments of the ER.103, and the enclosed brochure is an attempt to summarise our thoughts and ideas.

"We have based it mainly on the fact that by making use of the lead-in time already available in the ER.103 prototype, a very high performance fighter can be available in squadron service, well in advance of any new type. The interim version would

give much useful data, and would represent a research type of considerable value.

"The whole project would seem to fall into the shorter development stages now envisaged, but gains greatly by making use of aircraft research programmes already under way. Should you wish to discuss further any aspect of this, I would be very pleased to do so with you." Scribbled at the bottom of Lickley's original letter is a note from Shaw: 'Spoke on telephone 22.3.55'.

The brochure itself set out a two-step programme. The Delta 2 was regarded as ER.103A and the next step was ER.103B, the interim experimental version mentioned in Lickley's letter. This was to be slightly enlarged from the base model with a wingspan increase

from 26ft 10in to 28ft, length increase from 52ft 3in to 54ft 4in and height from 10ft 2in to 12ft 4in. The engine would be replaced with either a de Havilland Gyron or Rolls-Royce RB.122, taking top speed at 45,000ft from Mach 1.49 to Mach 2.72.

If this proved to be successful, the final development would be a fighter powered by a Gyron and two de Havilland Spectre rocket engines. Its size would be significantly increased, with a wingspan of 37ft 7in, length of 58ft 4in and height of 14ft 2in. The 'A' weighed 13,600lb and the 'B' 20,650lb, but the 'C' would tip the scales at 27,000lb. Speed at 45,000ft would drop slightly to Mach 2.54 and armament would be two Blue Jay missiles. It is evident that Lickley's thoughts were now firmly fixed on F.155T.

The Delta 2 mock-up was still taking up valuable space at Fairey by June 8, 1955, when the Ministry of Supply, whose position had previously been that it should be scrapped, wrote to the company to say: "Arrangements have been made for the Air Ministry to take over the mock-up of the above aircraft … the mock-up will be collected by Service transport from RAF Station Henlow on the 9th or 10th June. This letter authorises you to hand over the aircraft and engine mock-ups to the officer in charge of transport."

The fact that the Air Ministry had taken over the Delta 2 mock-up, rather than see it scrapped, would seem to suggest a strong interest from the Air Staff in the aircraft as a potential basis for future fighters, even at this early stage.

Flight testing of WG774 had resumed on June 26 but fuel system problems were experienced almost immediately and on July 13 the aircraft suffered an engine failure during the early part of its take-off run. The engine was removed from the aircraft and sent back to Rolls-Royce for detailed examination. A de-rated engine was fitted in the meantime and subsonic flights resumed – 26 being carried out between August 23 and September 26. The Delta 2 had not yet broken the sound barrier.

When the October 6 deadline for submission of the F.155T tenders came, uniquely among the competitors, Fairey offered two designs. The first was a direct development of the Delta 2 and amounted to a two-seater version of the 'ER.103C' outlined in Lickley's brochure of seven months earlier. The second, outlined in the next chapter of this publication, was something new which – though still based on Delta 2 technology – represented a bigger and riskier step forward.

During adjudication, the ER.103 development tended to be referred to as either the 'Fairey Small' or 'Fairey Little'. The title on the brochure was simply 'The Fairey Fighter Aircraft (ER.103 Development)' and the three-view drawing was titled 'The Fairey Two-Seat Fighter (ER.103 Development)'. The second proposal, much larger and more powerful, was referred to as 'Fairey Large' or 'Fairey Big'.

The ER.103 development had its own brochure but there was no accompanying text – just drawings and technical statistics. This 'Fairey Small' had the ER.103C's single Gyron engine with two Spectre rocket motors but slightly different dimensions, being 56ft 3in long

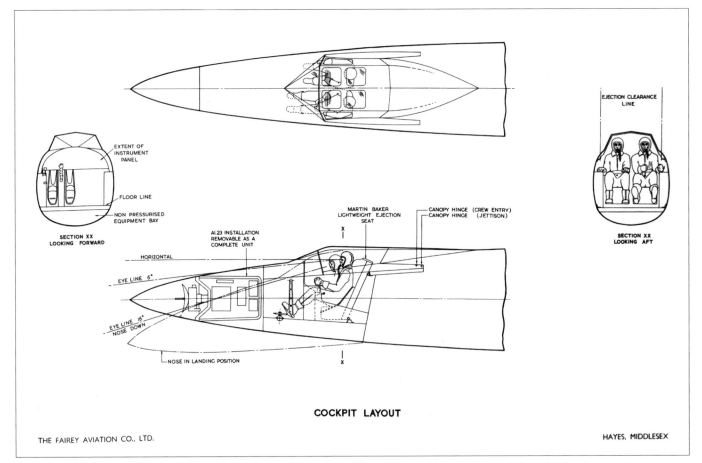

The crew of the ER.103 development 'Fairey Small' design had ejection seats – whereas the 'Fairey Large' offered a complete escape capsule. *Leonardo Helicopters*

and 14ft 3in tall though the overall wingspan was identical at 37ft 7in.

However, as the 'Fairey Large' brochure explained: "A single engine type was just possible (see our alternative submission); designed round the de Havilland weapon only, but both altitude performance and range would be marginal."

The Delta 2 would surprise everyone – including Fairey itself – by breaking the absolute World Speed Record by a huge margin in March 1956 but in October 1955 its potential was viewed in a much more pessimistic light.

The company's hopes were pinned on something much less substantial.

FAIREY AVIATION TWO-SEAT FIGHTER (ER.103 DEVELOPMENT)

❖

October 1955

Artwork by Luca Landino

— *Specification* —

Crew: Two   **Length:** 56ft 3in
Wingspan: 37ft 7in   **Height:** 14ft 3in
Wing area: 600sq ft
Empty weight: 18,950lb
Loaded weight: 30,100lb
Powerplant: 1 x de Havilland Gyron
with reheat plus 2 x de Havilland Spectre
Junior rocket engines
Maximum speed: Mach 2
Service ceiling: 67,000ft
Armament: 2 x de Havilland Blue Jay Mk.4

9

MAXIMUM PERFORMANCE

Fairey Large

The second of Fairey's two submissions for F.155T was
a gigantic two-jet rocket-boosted monster of an aircraft –
underpinned by technology developed for the ER.103/
Delta 2. This was the one Fairey really wanted to build and
it shows in the well thought-through brochure tendered in
support of it.

ad it not been for the existence of the flying Delta 2 prototype, Fairey's Two-Seat Fighter Aircraft (Day/Night High Altitude) might have seemed a little too good to be true.

In straightforward dimensions alone it was enormous: 74ft 4in long compared to the ER.103 Development's 56ft 3in, 17ft 3in tall compared to 14ft 3in and with a span of 46ft 10in compared to 37ft 7in. All-up weight was 48,000lb.

But the introduction to the brochure made it plain that Fairey wasn't about to play games or ignore the specification given – and it wouldn't shrink from making hard decisions about the aircraft's size: "This specification calls for an aircraft of extremely high performance, capable of considerable development as a 'weapon system', and able to meet any likely enemy threat.

"As a fighter, it is also essential that it should be as small as possible,

but this highly desirable object should not be allowed to prejudice the primary function, namely to destroy the enemy bomber at a safe distance from the coast line. In making our preliminary studies for this design, we considered single and twin engine layouts of various sizes, and of various plan forms, and reached the conclusion that the specification was best met by a twin-engined type, with rocket assistance, using a delta planform.

"The choice of two engines stemmed from the need to have development potential in the aircraft … The use of two engines also considerably increases the safety, an important point for all-weather operation."

Fairey considered that an interceptor could not fulfil its primary function effectively without the combined use of jets and rockets – the engines chosen being a pair of Rolls-Royce's RB.122 jets and a pair of de Havilland's

Spectre Junior rockets. Using smaller jets but bigger rockets had been considered and dismissed because this would limit the type's operational flexibility. "In fact, on many missions with RB.122 engines, particularly with collision-course weapons, it will be possible to carry out the mission without using rockets, thus simplifying refuelling, etc. and alternately, permitting longer range by replacing HTP with kerosene."

A pair of Gyrons could be fitted as an alternative if the RB.122 took too long to develop, but this would have a detrimental effect on range. In either case, the engines would be mounted side-by-side with fully variable reheat units. The Spectre Juniors were to be installed on the centre line of the aircraft at the aft end of the rear fuselage, in the wells formed between the jet engine re-heat units, "their outer fairings forming only a small excrescence outside the main fuselage contour".

The concept artwork frontispiece of the Fairey 'Large' brochure, sporting a fictitious serial – ZA436. This remains unallocated but now falls within a block of Tornado serials. *Leonardo Helicopters*

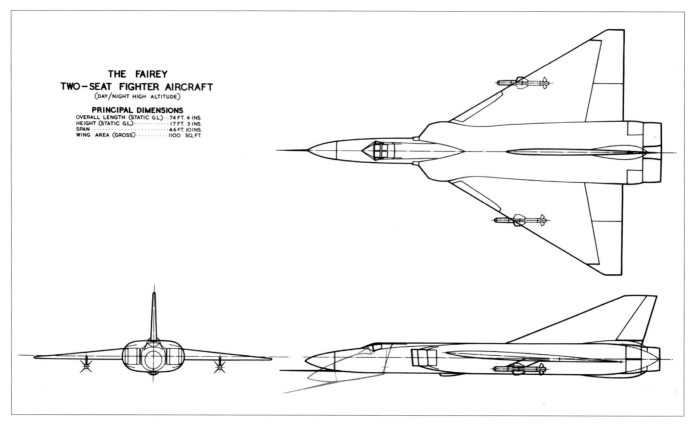

Three-view drawing of the Fairey Two-Seat Fighter Aircraft (Day/Night High Altitude). It was never referred to as the Delta 3 but had it made the transition from drawing board to physical aircraft, as with the Type 'V'/Delta 2, the company might well have given it that name. *Leonardo Helicopters*

Their nozzles would be covered with small expendable fairings until they were fired, when these would be automatically ejected.

This positioning meant that the jets and rockets were conveniently separated from one another and it would be relatively easy to reach the rocket motors for maintenance

by removing the outer fairings. If the motors needed to be removed completely, they would come out as a 'complete package', as Fairey put it.

Unlike, for example, the Hawker rocket boosters which were either on or off, the Spectre Juniors could be powered up or down: "As these motors are of the variable thrust

type, twin throttle controls similar to standard engine throttles are installed in the cabin immediately aft of the main jet engine controls in the port console. They are conveniently positioned so that they can be manipulated by the pilot whilst still operating the jet engine controls".

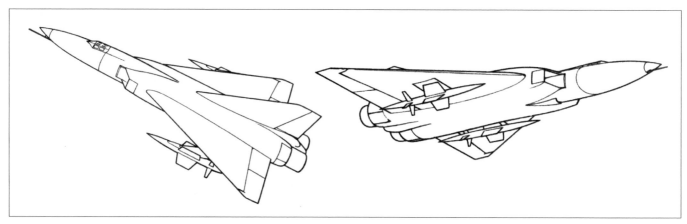

Whatever else the adjudicators might have thought about Fairey's design, the brochure certainly succeeded in portraying it in the most favourable possible light. As these two drawings show, the aircraft was one of the few designs tendered upon which the Red Hebe missile did not look outsize. *Leonardo Helicopters*

The steel delta

The aircraft's delta-wing planform was chosen because "in brief, we consider that it gives excellent manoeuvrability at high altitude, the best landing and take-off characteristics, and the lightest structure weight. The choice was also dictated in considerable measure by our decision to house the engines in the fuselage, the position which we feel gives the simplest and lightest installation, and which leaves the wings clear for the carriage of weapons, drop tanks, etc. and it gives a low moment of inertia in roll.

"In addition, our experience on the E.10 and ER.103 delta wing aircraft will enable us to save many months in the design and development of this new aircraft. While a light alloy structure would be capable of successful operation up to the minimum performance required by the specification, the aerodynamic and power plant parameters we have chosen give an actual performance far greater than this, and still have room for development; and in consequence, we have chosen structural materials which will enable full use to be made of the considerable potential of this aircraft.

"For the wing, centre fuselage, and fin, our investigations have shown that steel is the most efficient material, and we intend to use high tensile stainless steel similar to the American 17.7 P.H. We are already engaged on a programme of development of this material in connection with our large helicopter blades and consider it to be a most effective material. Other parts of the aircraft where heat resistance is of greater importance than strength and stiffness will be fabricated in titanium alloy.

"The structure layout chosen is based on that developed for the ER.103, which has given a low structure weight, and our experience with this type of layout

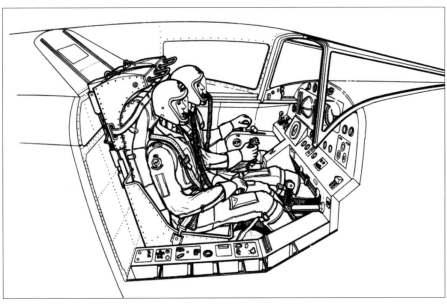

A side view of the cockpit, showing the crew wearing full pressure suits and strapped into their ejection seats. The amount of headroom available is surprising. *Leonardo Helicopters*

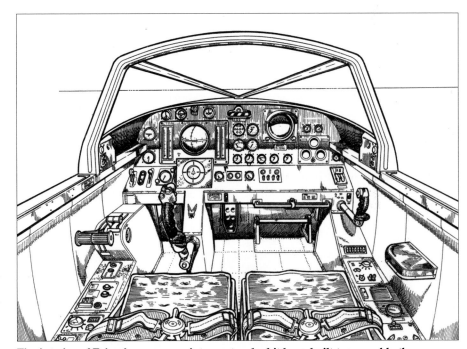

The interior of Fairey's enormous interceptor, had it been built to resemble the scene portrayed in this drawing, would have been a remarkably spacious place to sit. *Leonardo Helicopters*

will again save time in the design of this larger aircraft. The main fuel system is also based on our experience with the ER.103, and we are confident that our system of integral tank construction and sealing gives a leakproof system under operational conditions. The use of the delta wing enables the large volume of fuel required to be carried in a wing of low (4%) t/c ratio."

Fairey's interceptor was to benefit from a modular construction technique that the firm had developed during the course of its work on other types. If something needed maintenance, it could simply be entirely removed and swapped with a pre-prepared unit:

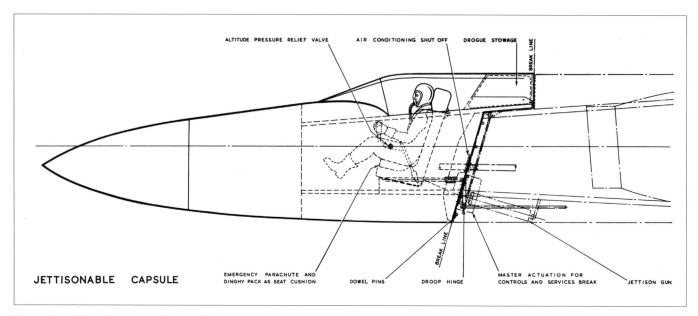

ALTITUDE PRESSURE RELIEF VALVE   AIR CONDITIONING SHUT OFF   DROGUE STOWAGE   BREAK LINE

JETTISONABLE   CAPSULE

EMERGENCY PARACHUTE AND
DINGHY PACK AS SEAT CUSHION   DOWEL PINS   DROOP HINGE   BREAK LINE   MASTER ACTUATION FOR
CONTROLS AND SERVICES BREAK   JETTISON GUN

The entire tilting 'droop snoot' nose of the Fairey large interceptor was designed with conversion to a self-contained escape capsule in mind. *Leonardo Helicopters*

"The layout of the equipment and the design of the structure ensures easy maintenance and access to main items of equipment. The equipment is further 'packaged' to a high degree to maintain speedy servicing by replacement."

Structurally, the design utilised semi-monocoque stressed skin construction throughout and was to be "mainly of Firth Vickers 'Stayblade' steel or titanium alloy. Modern techniques of welding,

machining and precision casting are used wherever practicable thus contributing to the overall stiffness of the structure. The wing structure in particular has been influenced by the experience gained in the design and construction of the Fairey ER.103 aircraft".

The fuselage was to be made in three main parts comprising the section forwards of the leading edge spar, which would be made of titanium alloy, a centre section

of steel housing the engines and providing the main spar attachment points for the wings and fin, and a rear fuselage of titanium alloy containing the engine reheat, rocket motors and dive brakes.

The forward section itself was subdivided into two bits – the pressure cabin and radar-housing nose, and the bit aft of that, housing the nosewheel gear, equipment and fuel collector tank.

Escape pod cabin

The aircraft's pressure cabin offered side-by-side seating for the crew, both facing forward, because "this arrangement permits the maximum view for pilot and observer and allows for full co-operation between the crew. Every effort in the design has been to provide adequate clearance with good visibility above, forward and to port and starboard with an excellent instrument layout and accessible controls, while setting up minimum drag."

Putting the crew next to one another meant that the observer could see all the essential instruments on the pilot's panel and the pilot could, if necessary, see what was happening on the observer's radar display. The brochure noted:

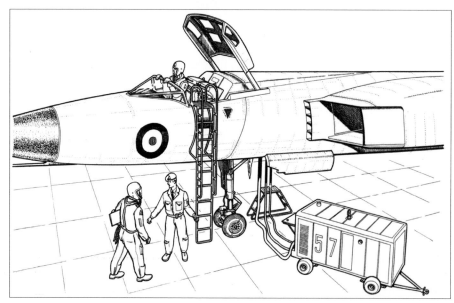

Brochure drawing showing the ease with which the crew could climb up to take their stations aboard the Fairey interceptor. *Leonardo Helicopters*

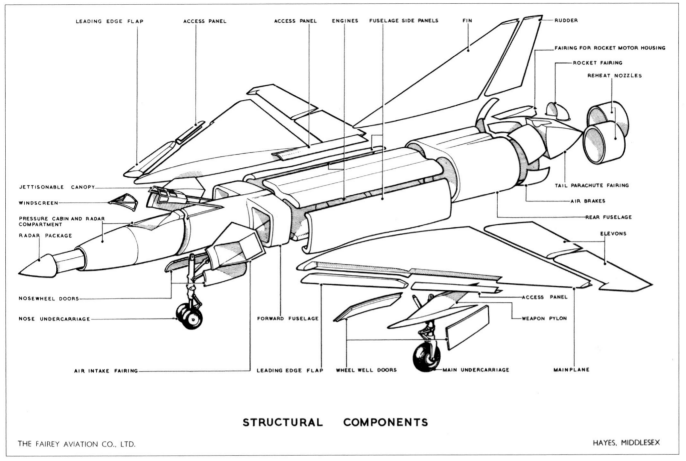

LEADING EDGE FLAP · ACCESS PANEL · ACCESS PANEL · ENGINES · FUSELAGE SIDE PANELS · FIN · RUDDER
FAIRING FOR ROCKET MOTOR HOUSING · ROCKET FAIRING · REHEAT NOZZLES
JETTISONABLE CANOPY · WINDSCREEN · PRESSURE CABIN AND RADAR COMPARTMENT · RADAR PACKAGE · TAIL PARACHUTE FAIRING · AIR BRAKES · REAR FUSELAGE · ELEVONS
NOSEWHEEL DOORS · NOSE UNDERCARRIAGE · FORWARD FUSELAGE · ACCESS PANEL · WEAPON PYLON
AIR INTAKE FAIRING · LEADING EDGE FLAP · WHEEL WELL DOORS · MAIN UNDERCARRIAGE · MAINPLANE

STRUCTURAL COMPONENTS

THE FAIREY AVIATION CO., LTD. · HAYES, MIDDLESEX

Part of Fairey's sales pitch for its large interceptor was the relative ease with which it could be constructed, based on experience with the ER.103. *Leonardo Helicopters*

"The latest ideas in display are incorporated and combine to give a compact layout with the attitude display facing the pilot and the plan display tilted upwards to his view. Entry to the cabin is by hinging the hooding on the jettison rails." Not only that, if the drawings provided with the brochure were strictly accurate, the cockpit would also offer a near-ridiculous amount of headroom.

A key feature, carried over from the Delta 2, was the downwards-tilting cabin: "To ensure adequate forward view for landing and taxying, we have used the 'droop snoot' principle, which has proved so successful on the ER.103". Initially, lightweight ejection seats were to be provided with the actuator being "centrally placed for either crew member" but the eventual goal was to develop the movable cabin

into a self-contained jettisonable escape pod.

This would be water and airtight, and once jettisoned from the presumably crippled aircraft would float down to earth on a cluster of drogue chutes housed in the front fuselage just aft of the capsule itself. All control and service connections would be broken by automatic mechanical means on firing the jettison gun.

Even then, the crew would still each get a personal parachute and survival pack, and the cabin was to be fitted with emergency lighting and power for signalling equipment. According to Fairey: "The overall weight of this system will not be appreciably less than the conventional ejection seat installation as the lighter seats will be offset by the jettison gun and sealing, but the increase

in crew comfort and morale will be considerable."

The aircraft's radar would be housed in its nose. It would be "fully packaged and is carried by one mounting ring on to the forward end of the cabin. It is pressurised and temperature controlled and is easily removable along built-in guide rails". Evidently, "information on the radar and the transmission of data from it to the weapons has been difficult to get, and is of necessity incomplete, as no brochure is available on it, but we have, on advice, from RRE and GEC, based our installation on a developed and lightened AI.18".

Jets, wings and wheels
The centre section of the fuselage was to be a monocoque steel structure extending from the leading edge spar frame to a joint aft of the rear spar frame. Fairey decided on

steel here because it "contributes to the fire proofing of the engine installation, as this structure carries the side by side engines". Each engine was effectively housed in its own fireproof cell.

The detachable rear fuselage section was made of titanium alloy to house the engine reheat, rocket motors and retractable petal air brakes. It also had a retractable tail bumper built into the base. The whole section could be removed, when necessary, by taking out a set of bolts that were externally accessible, although "access for day to day servicing of engine accessories is provided by suitably located panels in the lower fuselage skin".

If the engines did have to come out, "guide rails are built integrally with the fuselage structure to allow the engines, after disconnection of main mountings, to be withdrawn aft. With this arrangement the engines can be changed without disturbing the reheat installation thus giving an excellent engine change time".

Once they were back in, the rear fuselage could simply be left off during ground testing, the brochure explaining that "this system is successfully used on the North American F-100". A tail parachute was fitted at the rear end of the fuselage on the aircraft centre line for deceleration during landing. Fairey had considered using thrust reversal but "the complication of this with reheat and the present lack of proposals on the subject from the engine manufacturers has caused us to omit this from our proposals".

'Stayblade' steel was also to be used for the wings, in a multi-spar stressed skin structure similar to that used on the ER.103. The justification for using steel was again "the need for minimum reduction in strength at elevated temperature". Foamed plastic was to be used for thermal insulation.

The oleo strut undercarriage main gear, which had hydraulic disc brakes fitted, retracted forward into the wing, being attached to the main spar. The retractable nosewheels would be steerable through 60° by the pilot thanks to hydraulic jacks mounted at the lower end of the main strut outer casing.

No abnormal forces

While working on the Type 'V'/ Delta 2, Fairey had been involved in discussions about the ever-advancing state of the art in autopilots and automated controls.

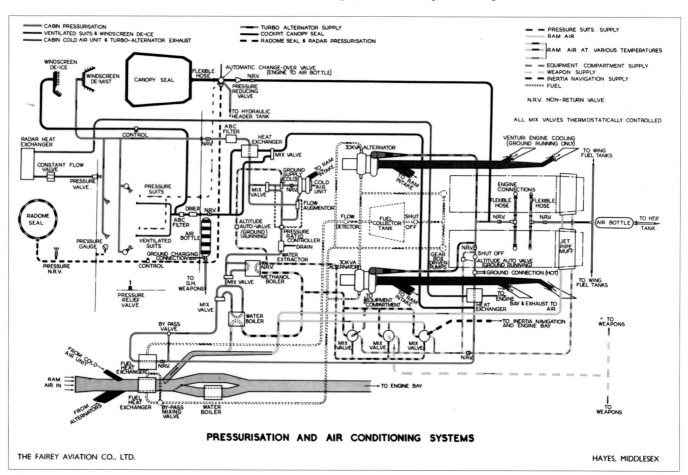

Fairey was aware that its greatest perceived weakness was its small size as a company. It therefore tried to allay fears about its ability to build Britain's next-generation interceptor by demonstrating that aspects of the design, such as the vital air conditioning systems, had been properly thought-out. *Leonardo Helicopters*

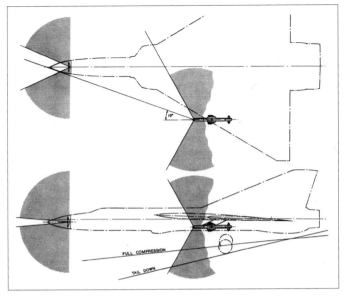

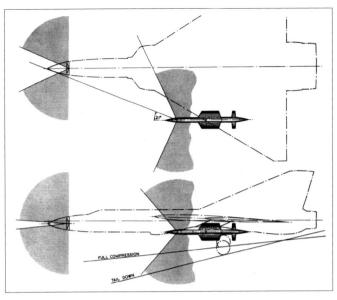

Positioning of the de Havilland Blue Jay missile on underwing pylons. *Leonardo Helicopters*

Putting the Vickers Red Hebe missile in a conventional underwing position would give its seeker head the best possible chance of finding a target, according to Fairey. *Leonardo Helicopters*

This resulted in a brochure entry on automation which allowed for measured progress and development in this area but shrewdly offered a strong safety net, should the electronic gizmos experience difficulties.

It stated: "The OR requirements for the control of this aeroplane are extremely advanced, and the final complete integration of data presentation to the pilot, autopilot control, and control links with the radar and weapon requirements, will need very considerable development, and in our opinion, not all these requirements will be met initially due to the time it will take to give this new equipment the reliability essential for use in an aeroplane.

"We have, accordingly, decided to use for the flying controls a system of duplicated hydraulic power controls with a direct mechanical link to the pilot's control column: this system uses components basically similar to those in use successfully on Hunter and CF-100 and is a logical development from that in use in the ER.103.

"Full provision is made for the control of the aircraft through autopilot and auto-stabiliser units, but should they fail or not be available in time, the system is still one such as gives the pilot full control of the aeroplane at all times, without any abnormal forces or movements. The autopilot and similar systems are so chosen that as development proceeds, the overall automatic control of the aircraft becomes more nearly complete, and when we are satisfied with the reliability of the components, all-electric operation of the controls can be made available."

Weapons platform

Part of Fairey's motivation for designing such a large aircraft was to provide sufficient room to fulfil the part of the requirement that related to the carriage of Vickers' oversize radar guided missiles. The brochure said: "The aircraft is designed as a 'weapon platform' for the two weapons put forward for OR.1131 (Blue Jay and Red Hebe). The main installations have been developed around the de Havilland weapon, as it will be ready much earlier, but the aircraft has also been laid out for the carriage of the Vickers weapon and change from one to the other is straightforward.

"The two weapons required by the OR vary greatly in overall weight and complexity, and also in the likely period of availability. It has, therefore, been difficult to decide how best to integrate the weapons with the overall design, especially as the tactical use of the aircraft may differ considerably with the differing weapons. In view of the fact that the de Havilland weapon should be available earlier, we have based our main submission on this, but have made full provision in the aircraft design for the larger Vickers weapon to be carried.

"The all-up weights of the aircraft with the different weapons should not vary greatly, as the heavier collision course weapon needs less fuel to get a 'kill' at a given distance from base. It is suggested however, that the larger weapon has tended to get too heavy and elaborate, and before it is too late, some simplification of the requirements might be considered."

Each missile was looked at separately to work out the best way of carrying it. For Blue Jay: "Consideration has been given to folding the wings of these weapons and stowing them either

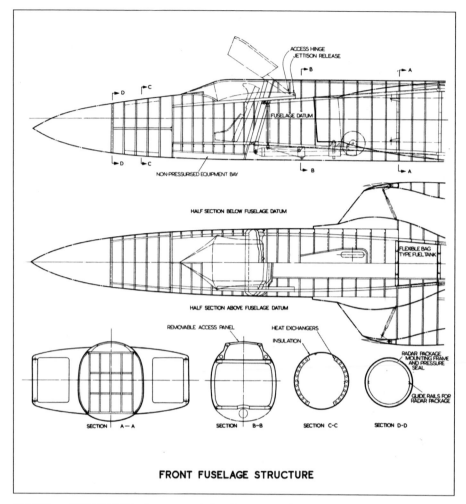

FRONT FUSELAGE STRUCTURE

ABOVE and BELOW: The interceptor's fuselage was to be built in three sections – forward, centre and rear. Each could be separated from the others for ease of maintenance or replacement if necessary. *Leonardo Helicopters*

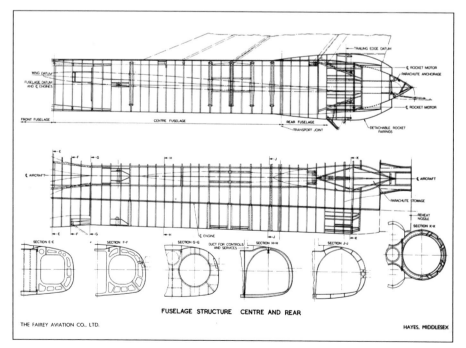

FUSELAGE STRUCTURE CENTRE AND REAR

in pods beneath the fuselage or in a weapon bay. The increased weight involved together with the complexity of the design, and the need for an external pylon carriage for the large sized alternative weapon did not outweigh the lower drag, and a common wing station is used, dictated by optimum scanning angle and ground clearance."

The Blue Jay pylon and launch rails would be quickly removable but would not be jettisonable. The pylon itself would house all the necessary weapon air conditioning, electrical and other services, with armament coolant being carried in the leading edge of the aircraft's wings.

In fact: "The pylon position is such that four de Havilland weapons could be carried as an overload if required." The Vickers Red Hebe would require its own special pylons but these would be made interchangeable with those designed for Blue Jay. It was concluded that the underwing position was also best for Red Hebe because it "gave the best compromise between drag, weight, and field of view for the weapon radar".

Nevertheless, just like the other aircraft manufacturers competing for F.155T, Fairey was concerned about the sheer bulk of Red Hebe: "It is felt that as the design goes forward every effort must be made to reduce the size and weight of this weapon and cut down its temperature control requirements in order to avoid the weight penalties compared with the small weapon."

Careful attention to design

Perhaps the most persuasive part of Fairey's presentation was the section describing the aircraft's performance and how closely this was linked to the delta-wing layout that had been chosen. Whether Fairey had really done its homework to the extent suggested is debatable but the existence of the Delta 2 and the promising nature of early test flight reports – mechanical gremlins aside – made it that much easier to believe it had. And Fairey sensibly managed to relate all this directly to the specification and example missions it outlined. The aircraft would do precisely the job that was required.

The brochure states: "In arriving at the configuration chosen for this submission, a wide range of aircraft layouts was considered. It was obvious from an early stage that concentrating on isolated performance objectives would seriously prejudice many other objectives. Hence it was decided that a particular operational mission should be chosen as a basic case with a subsequent study of other combat missions and an eventual correlation of fuel quantities to the requirements of OR.329.

"It was decided that the best case to study was the 'Normal Warning Case' as this included climb to 60,000ft 180° turn, and flight at Mach 2. The requirements of the turn at Mach 2 at 60,000ft and the overall programme time to reach the kill line in pursuit of the target make the choice of a mixed power plant (turbine-rocket) combination essential if a prohibitive weight is to be avoided.

"Of the large number of arrangements which have been considered we believe that on balance the delta-wing design submitted offers the best prospects of giving the flexible all-weather fighter called for in this specification.

"Since the operational requirements demand high manoeuvrability and good performance in high 'g' turns at Mach 2 and 60,000ft, the lift drag and trim drag in this condition are of major design importance in their effect on the fuel used in these manoeuvres. The primary variable influencing these two drag components in this flight condition is wing area, and aspect ratio is only secondary. A relatively low wing loading is

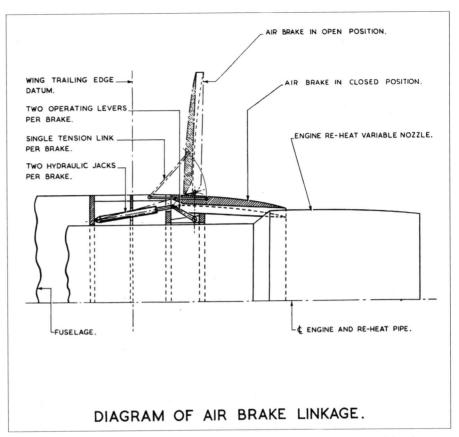

DIAGRAM OF AIR BRAKE LINKAGE.

Given the huge speeds of which the Fairey aircraft was expected to be capable, air brakes were a useful aspect of the design. *Leonardo Helicopters*

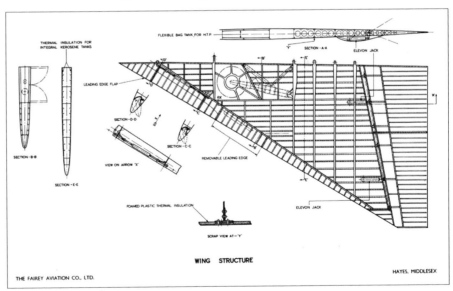

The interceptor's delta wing was to be made of steel with foamed plastic thermal insulation – use of which Fairey prided itself on having pioneered. *Leonardo Helicopters*

therefore needed on this supersonic fighter for its high-altitude manoeuvring performance at Mach 2, and the take-off and landing distances will not normally yield design limitations."

If the interceptor was to have any hope of remaining manoeuvrable at high speed and high altitude, Fairey argued, it needed to be a delta. The likelihood of severely restricted control at these extremes was

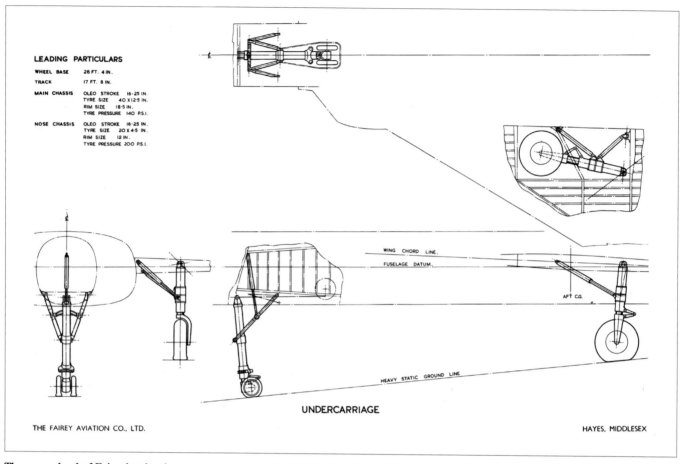

LEADING PARTICULARS

WHEEL BASE	28 FT. 4 IN.	
TRACK	17 FT. 8 IN.	
MAIN CHASSIS	OLEO STROKE	16·25 IN.
	TYRE SIZE	40 X 12·5 IN.
	RIM SIZE	18·5 IN.
	TYRE PRESSURE	140 P.S.I.
NOSE CHASSIS	OLEO STROKE	16·25 IN.
	TYRE SIZE	20 X 4·5 IN.
	RIM SIZE	12 IN.
	TYRE PRESSURE	200 P.S.I.

WING CHORD LINE.
FUSELAGE DATUM.
AFT C.G.
HEAVY STATIC GROUND LINE
UNDERCARRIAGE

THE FAIREY AVIATION CO., LTD.   HAYES, MIDDLESEX

The nosewheel of Fairey's tricycle arrangement was steerable by the pilot and the rear wheels were fitted with disc brakes.
Leonardo Helicopters

another factor which had weighed heavily on the minds of the Air Staff in considering their requirement. The fact that Fairey was proposing a delta-wing solution and just so happened to have more practical experience in this area than anybody else was convenient.

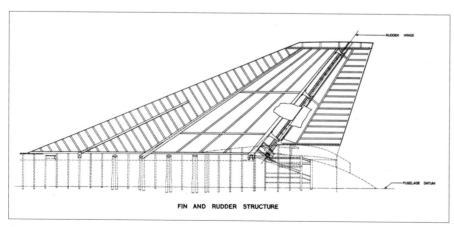

RUDDER HINGE
FUSELAGE DATUM
FIN AND RUDDER STRUCTURE

Construction of the aircraft's fin and rudder was to be relatively straightforward.
Leonardo Helicopters

The brochure went on: "The usual comparison of delta, straight and swept configurations on the basis of equal landing speeds etc. therefore breaks down and the comparison can best be made in terms of the complete interception flight, the engineering problems, and the relative state of knowledge of overall aerodynamic characteristics.

"A straight wing configuration would have very much more drag than the delta wing in the transonic and low supersonic region for the same thickness-chord ratio wings, since the wing area cannot be much smaller than the delta because of the high altitude combat manoeuvre case. In practice the thickness-chord ratio of the straight wing would normally have to be higher than the delta for strength reasons or to accommodate fuel, undercarriage, etc.

"A straight wing aircraft with the same engines would thus be heavier, use more fuel and have longer normal interception and emergency interception times for the same combat manoeuvre performance. A swept wing layout (swept trailing edge) would offer a better low supersonic performance than the delta, but the layout would demand a tailplane, and once again, unless the overall length of the aircraft were to be greatly increased, the wing area would be very close to the delta configuration.

"Structural and space problems would lead to a slightly heavier aircraft for the same engines with consequently a slightly longer overall interception time although the low supersonic performance would be improved. The final aircraft size and weight chosen takes into full account the fuel requirements of OR.329 including sufficient rocket fuel for a nearly 3 'g' turn."

Extensive model tests and flight testing with the Delta 2 would, Fairey claimed, allow it to ensure that the interceptor's controls could be designed "on an extremely realistic basis". They would "keep the overall

manoeuvring drag low and provide adequate longitudinal control power to permit development to higher speeds and altitudes".

Furthermore, it claimed, the delta layout was less susceptible to "extreme forms of instability caused by high rates of roll, or separation shock interaction 'buffet' in supersonic flight. Careful attention has been given to fin design and we have developed a very low aspect ratio moderate taper fin, which we believe, on the basis of considerable analysis and experimental results, will ensure a high level of basic directional stability at Mach numbers well above 2.0 without causing any uncomfortable characteristics for low speed flying".

Better than spec
While it was claimed that the basic fact of a delta layout would ensure

Fairey's interceptor had low drag and high manoeuvrability, the company also made strong claims for the way in which its engines would complement and improve the overall package. This really was the 'weapon system concept' as the Ministry of Supply had hoped someone would apply it.

Fairey pointed out that fitting two engines as powerful as the RB.122 was expected to be, or even two Gyrons, was actually overkill for the mission that the interceptor would be required to perform – but if smaller engines were used it would be necessary to provide the rocket motors with more fuel, which would require "either large supersonic drop-tanks containing HTP as an overload or a reduction of rocket fuel needed for the high altitude turn".

Fitting the RB.122s would result in "a much more flexible performance

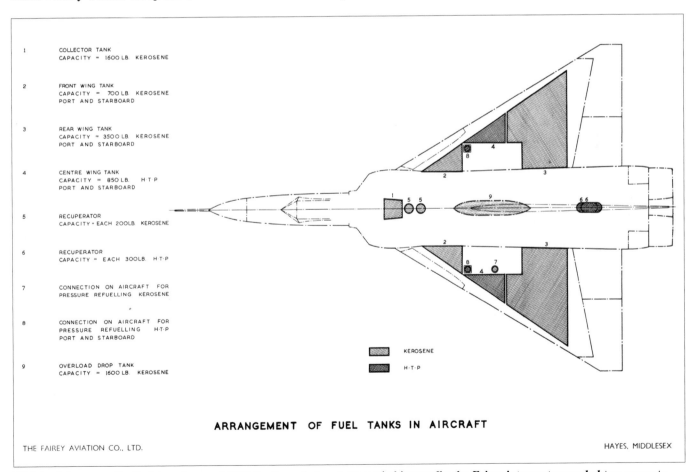

With both kerosene for its jet engines and HTP for its rocket motors carried internally, the Fairey interceptor needed two separate sets of tanks. *Leonardo Helicopters*

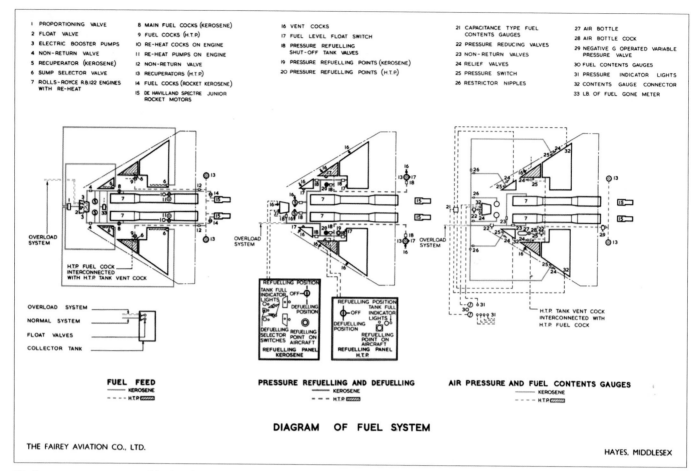

Having two separate sets of fuel tanks meant also carrying two entirely separate fuel systems – a complication which Fairey fully acknowledged in its brochure. *Leonardo Helicopters*

in which the emergency interception can be carried out on the basic aircraft still retaining the high 'g' turn for a stern attack with the de Havilland weapon. The interception times are much better than those called for in the specification.

"A further point in the twin RB.122 arrangement is that the failure of one engine would still permit the aircraft to be safely flown in the cruise condition at heights up to about 30,000ft".

The operational sorties said to be achievable with the Fairey interceptor were certainly impressive. For the 'normal warning time' mission with two Blue Jays, the aircraft wouldn't need drop tanks. From a standing start, it would take off, climb and hit 60,000ft at Mach 2, just 70 nautical miles from base in a little over five minutes and 20 seconds.

The pilot would get four minutes' level flight at Mach 2, including a 180° turn, pulling 2.9 g (only 2.15 g if fitted with Red Hebes), before firing his weapons at the target. Return to base would then take 15 minutes at 40,000ft, with sufficient fuel for an aborted landing and second approach if necessary.

For the 'extended warning time' mission, the interceptor would be kitted out with a single 200 gallon external fuel tank. From 'engines on', the aircraft would take off, climb and reach 36,000ft in just over three minutes. It would then be able to cruise for 15 minutes, covering 133 nautical miles. Then it could still accelerate to Mach 2, pulling a 5 g turn, up to 60,000ft, and fly level for two minutes and 15 seconds. Returning home, there would be enough fuel for 30

minutes at 40,000ft (28 minutes with Red Hebes) before landing with the same provision for a second approach if required.

Fairey's overall performance stats had the aircraft capable of Mach 2.28 – the engine limitation – or up to Mach 3 if more powerful engines could be fitted, this being the structural limit. Ceiling on turbojets alone on maximum reheat was 76,000ft but assisted by rockets the aircraft was expected to reach 92,000ft.

Drawing on experience

Meeting or even beating the spec was one thing, but as a relatively small company would Fairey be able to deliver the aircraft on time? It claimed that it would: "The development of this aircraft to a successful weapon system demands that the early aircraft shall be delivered quickly and we have considered, in detail, ways of doing this.

"By having more than one assembly line and by making full use of the resources of our various factories, we consider that we can have the first aircraft flying within three years from the awarding of a contract, and the next 11 can be delivered in a further two years. In view of the revolutionary methods of construction and the complexity of the installations, these dates represent, in our opinion, the best which can be achieved, and are based on our experience on the Gannet, ER.103 and Ultra Light Helicopter.

"To sum up, we consider that the design submitted meets all the requirements of F.155T and OR.329, and in many instances greatly exceeds them. By using a delta planform, we were able to draw on the experience gained in designing and flying the ER.103, and thus save considerable time on research and development relative to that needed if an entirely new concept were chosen.

"The design is such that the initial aircraft will be fully operational with the weapons available at the time, but inherent in the design is the capability of carrying other weapons and control systems as they become available. In addition, with engine development, speeds of up to Mach 3 are possible without airframe redesign."

All of this was exactly what the Air Staff and Ministry of Supply had hoped for. An advanced aircraft based, however loosely, on an existing design that could exceed what was being asked and be built within the time limit. The 'weapons system' box had been ticked and the attractive aircraft design was one that the RAF could be proud of. There remained, however, a big question mark over whether Fairey could deliver on its promises.

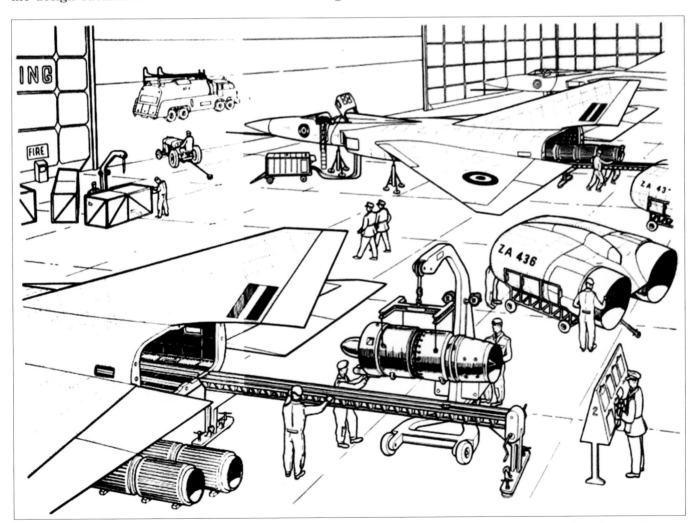

Artwork from towards the end of Fairey's brochure showing how the engines could be swapped in what, it was hoped, would be a relatively straightforward procedure. The same serial is used here as for the aircraft shown in the concept art at the beginning of the brochure – a nice touch. *Leonardo Helicopters*

FAIREY AVIATION TWO-SEAT FIGHTER (DAY/NIGHT HIGH-ALTITUDE)

❖

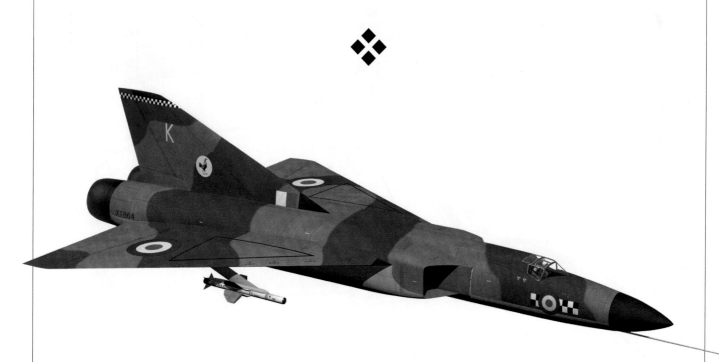

October 1955

Artwork by Luca Landino

— *Specification* —

Crew: Two   **Length:** 74ft 4in
Wingspan: 46ft 10in   **Height:** 17ft 3in
Wing area: 1100sq ft
Empty weight: 32,750lb
Loaded weight: 48,000lb
Powerplant: 2 x Rolls-Royce RB.122 plus
2 x de Havilland Spectre Junior rocket engines
Maximum speed: Mach 2.27 with reheat,
Mach 3 with reheat and both rocket engines
(structural limit)
Service ceiling: 92,000ft
Armament: 2 x de Havilland Blue Jay Mk.4

10

PRUNING THE SPEC

de Havilland DH.117

**Having just redesigned the DH.110 to become the Navy's
Sea Vixen, de Havilland's projects team should have been
ready to deliver a highly capable tender for F.155T – but
instead they offered a weary string of excuses and a
design which would work only if the specification was
'pruned' a little.**

The de Havilland team had been at the cutting edge of jet aircraft design since the 1940s, having produced the Vampire, Venom and now Sea Vixen. Not only that, the company's parent group was responsible for supplying one of the two guided weapons that were crucial to the interceptor system's success – the Blue Jay infrared homer – and one of the two engines considered most likely to power it, the Gyron.

All of this might have seemed to be a boon for the team working on the firm's F.155T submission,

the DH.117, but instead it seems to have been something of a burden. Overfamiliarity with the tendering process through long years of being put through it with one project after another and intimate knowledge of the progress being made with guidance systems, or lack of it, resulted in a deeply pessimistic brochure.

It began, not with an introduction, but with a summary and then a section headed 'prototype and production dates'. The real introduction did not start until page 19.

The summary's primary purpose seems to have been telling the reader, right from the very beginning, not to get their hopes up: "The aircraft proposed in this brochure is planned for start of service use by January, 1962, and is considered to be the most effective interceptor which can be designed and developed in the time available.

"It is not possible in the time to develop and complete service trials of an aircraft to meet in full the requirements of the Specification F.155T. In particular, the need to carry alternative weapon systems

Artwork from the start of the de Havilland DH.117 brochure. *BAE Systems*

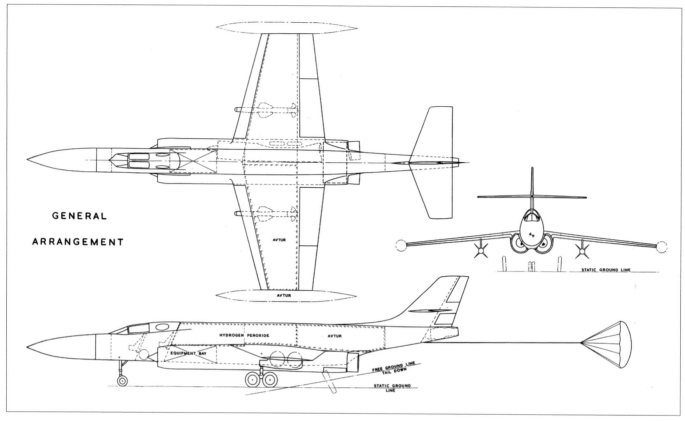

The DH.117 equipped as de Havilland intended – with a pair of Blue Jay Mk.4s. *BAE Systems*

and all the necessary equipment for a fully automatic interception would entail a very much larger and more complicated aeroplane, with consequently longer time in all aspects of the development and the co-ordination of the equipment. Therefore, Blue Jay Mk.4 has been selected for the armament, and the weapon system proposed, though not fully automatic, will enable the interception and attack to be made on a beam collision course with a high chance of success. To keep the development time to a minimum, the airframe is made of light alloy, with its fully proven methods of design and construction; this allows operation up to Mach 2.35."

The DH.117 was the very epitome of a 'safe bet'. It had thin straight wings with a conventional tail and a crew of two sitting in tandem. The powerplants were a pair of Gyron Juniors and a single Spectre rocket motor. This conservative set-up would allow the fighter to

just about meet the specification for a Normal Warning Sortie – 60,000ft and Mach 2 in six minutes. Fighter Command had lobbied for three minutes all along.

On the plus side, it could eventually hit Mach 2.35 and during the Extended Warning Sortie, with drop tanks, could manage an operational radius of 275 nautical miles with a patrol time of nearly 40 minutes, despite the spec asking for only 15. Manoeuvrability at low speed would be similar to that of "aircraft at present in service use" and landing speed would not be too high.

Ten very essential steps
By using "every possible short cut" the first hand-made prototype DH.117 could be in the air by December 1958, with the second following in June 1959. The third, the first of 12 pre-production machines, would be ready to fly in October 1959 with full production

deliveries commencing in January 1962 – bang on time. However, "it is felt that the above dates are possible to achieve, but only if certain very essential steps and decisions are taken early and adhered to.

"This aeroplane represents a large step forward in performance, and there will be a very large number of new and serious problems, so that there is not a moment to lose if the desired date of January 1962 for delivery to the RAF is to be achieved, and it is felt that it will not be possible to achieve this date unless certain changes are made in past procedure."

The brochure-proper had not yet begun and de Havilland was already setting out 10 demands: mock-ups and test pieces would have to be built while the tenders were still under consideration and "we feel strongly that a decision must be made very quickly as to which aeroplane or aeroplanes are to be ordered". Gearing up for full production would need to take place before the prototypes were finished; a production contract would be needed no later than June 1957 to allow time for jig and tool design, and it was essential that "the operational requirements for equipment should be settled at the earliest possible date, and not changed during the design of the aeroplane.

"Much delay has been caused in the past by changes in equipment being made at a late date, and it is felt that, as the equipment of this aeroplane will be closely packed, changes of equipment made at a late date may completely change the whole layout and so cause most serious delays".

And the list went on. The company wanted a senior RAF liaison officer posted to its offices "whose duties would be to keep us in touch with the latest Air Force thinking"; more specialised service test pilots would be needed at Boscombe Down;

one of the early pre-production DH.117s ought to be sent to the Central Fighter Establishment "for a preview of the operational suitability of the aeroplane"; many more wind tunnel test models would be needed – the time taken to make them was a "disturbing factor" and the need for more models "may demand some very considerable change in our present methods of manufacture".

Finally, and perhaps most tellingly of previous experience: "As much freedom of decision as possible should be given to the design team. In the past a great deal of the time of senior MoS and Air Ministry officials and senior members of the design team has been spent at meetings, and it is felt that every effort must be made to reduce the time spent in this way to a minimum, if the aeroplane is to be in service by the date stated in the Air Staff requirement."

The actual introduction itself then said: "The aircraft proposed meets the important parts of the performance requirements contained in spec F.155T. In order to meet the operational service date of January 1962, however, some pruning of equipment and weapon system requirements is thought to be necessary." Snipping bits off the specification was not a prospect likely to appeal to the competition adjudicators.

Weapons and tech

Designing the actual aircraft seems to have been of secondary importance to de Havilland, who were more concerned about providing the right 'weapon system' of missiles, automation and electronics to complete a successful interception.

When it came to the missile, Vickers' radar weapon was very comprehensively dismissed – the DH.117 would carry a pair of Blue

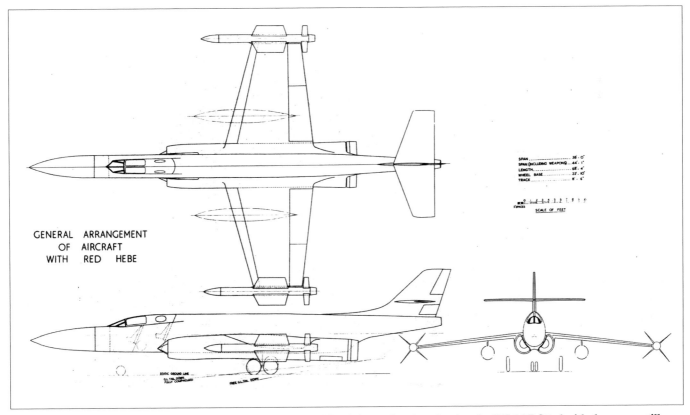

GENERAL ARRANGEMENT
OF AIRCRAFT
WITH RED HEBE

Dismissing Vickers' Red Hebe was not too difficult for de Havilland, but a drawing showing the DH.117 fitted with them was still included in the brochure. *BAE Systems*

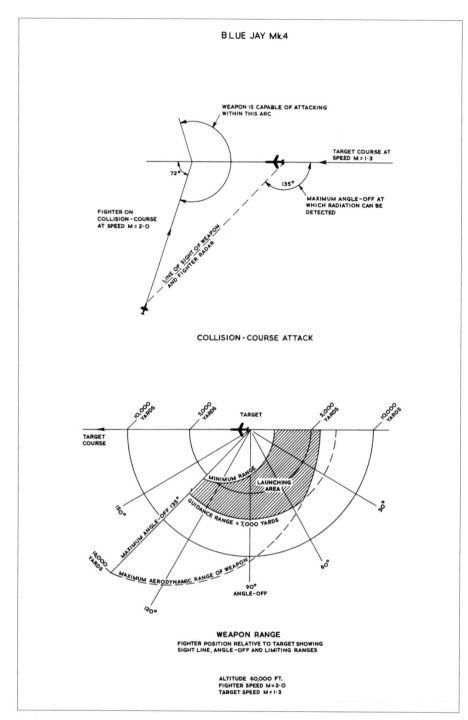

BLUE JAY Mk.4

WEAPON IS CAPABLE OF ATTACKING WITHIN THIS ARC

TARGET COURSE AT SPEED M = 1·3

72°

135°

MAXIMUM ANGLE-OFF AT WHICH RADIATION CAN BE DETECTED

FIGHTER ON COLLISION-COURSE AT SPEED M = 2·0

LINE OF SIGHT OF WEAPON AND FIGHTER RADAR

COLLISION-COURSE ATTACK

10,000 YARDS 5,000 YARDS TARGET 5,000 YARDS 10,000 YARDS

TARGET COURSE

MINIMUM RANGE

LAUNCHING AREA

GUIDANCE RANGE = 7,000 YARDS

MAXIMUM ANGLE-OFF 135°

150° 30°

14,000 YARDS

MAXIMUM AERODYNAMIC RANGE OF WEAPON

60°

90° ANGLE-OFF

120°

WEAPON RANGE
FIGHTER POSITION RELATIVE TO TARGET SHOWING SIGHT LINE, ANGLE-OFF AND LIMITING RANGES

ALTITUDE 60,000 FT.
FIGHTER SPEED M = 2·0
TARGET SPEED M = 1·3

Rather than describe in detail how the DH.117 was built, de Havilland focused more on explaining how it would be used for intercepting incoming enemy bombers with its Blue Jays. *BAE Systems*

Jay Mk.4s and only a pair of Blue Jay Mk.4s, in spite of the spec: "The new Vickers-Armstrong radar weapon is likely to take four and a half years from start of design to the first weapon firing with the complete system and, for development and proving to a satisfactory state for

service use, a further two years. It is therefore doubtful whether this weapon will be available for service use in time. The Mk.4 Blue Jay, however, will be ready for service use in the time available."

Trying to come up with a design that could carry both would simply

cause "excessive delay" and "it seems that the radar weapon has little to offer over the infrared one. Both are collision course weapons capable of attack from ahead of the beam (fighter course at right angles to bomber course). The advantages of the radar weapon over the infrared one are the ability to attack in cloud and the possibility that it may be able to attack from further ahead of the beam. Attack from the forward quarter does not provide significant benefits". And there would be no cloud above 40,000ft where the attack would take place in any case, the brochure remarks.

Then there was the size and weight of Red Hebe which would rule out "every arrangement but wingtip mounting, unless severe additional weight penalties in the undercarriage are accepted".

Next to be ruled out was the idea that a radar-autopilot system could be used for flying the aircraft remotely: "It is not considered that the design, development and flight proving of a radar-autopilot coupled attack system is achievable within the time scale. The American Hughes company allowed one year additional development time for this system over and above the time required for the radar and weapon of their MX.1179 (F-102B/F-106) system.

"Even with this extended period, they are encountering severe problems in matching the system to the airframe performance and structural limitations and expect to require an additional two years for development of the system. Bearing in mind possible radar counter-measures, this development is probably more difficult than achieving automatic blind landing.

"The need for automatic coupling is much greater on the single seater, especially if the range of radar and weapons is so short that it allows only a few seconds to carry out the attack. The two-seater has the advantage that the radar operator

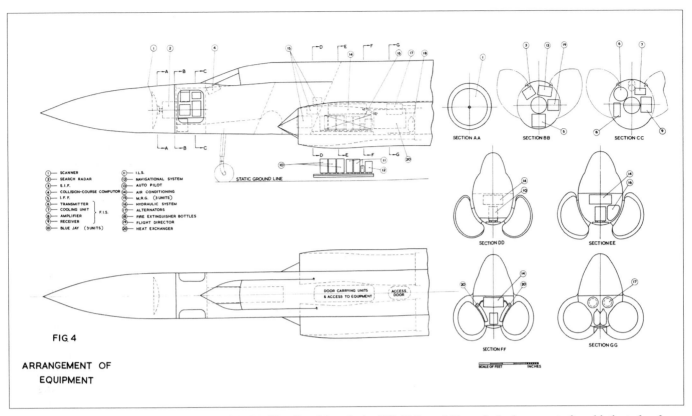

FIG 4

ARRANGEMENT OF
EQUIPMENT

①	SCANNER	⑪	I.L.S.
②	SEARCH RADAR	⑫	NAVIGATIONAL SYSTEM
③	S.I.F.	⑬	AUTO PILOT
④	COLLISION-COURSE COMPUTOR	⑭	AIR CONDITIONING
⑤	I.F.F.	⑮	M.R.G. (3 UNITS)
⑥	TRANSMITTER	⑯	HYDRAULIC SYSTEM
⑦	COOLING UNIT	⑰	ALTERNATORS
⑧	AMPLIFIER	⑱	FIRE EXTINGUISHER BOTTLES
⑨	RECEIVER	⑲	FLIGHT DIRECTOR
⑩	BLUE JAY (3 UNITS)	⑳	HEAT EXCHANGER

Packaging up electronics was a speciality of de Havilland's, although the DH.117 would have lacked any sort of sophisticated radar-linked autopilot controls due to fears of jamming. *BAE Systems*

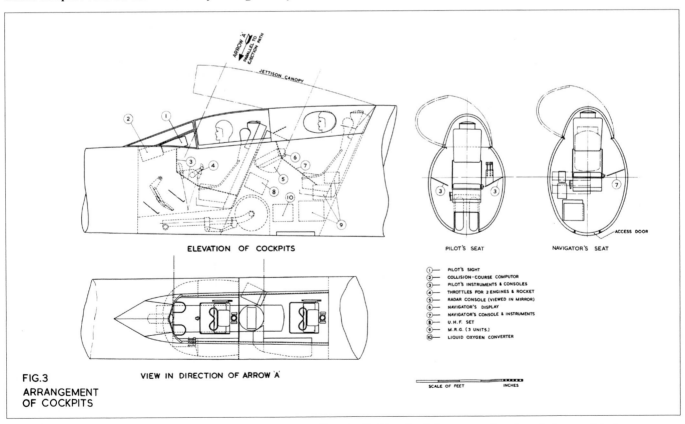

FIG.3
ARRANGEMENT
OF COCKPITS

①	PILOT'S SIGHT
②	COLLISION-COURSE COMPUTOR
③	PILOT'S INSTRUMENTS & CONSOLES
④	THROTTLES FOR 2 ENGINES & ROCKET
⑤	RADAR CONSOLE (VIEWED IN MIRROR)
⑥	NAVIGATOR'S DISPLAY
⑦	NAVIGATOR'S CONSOLE & INSTRUMENTS
⑧	U.H.F. SET
⑨	M.R.G. (3 UNITS.)
⑩	LIQUID OXYGEN CONVERTER

This rather odd view of the DH.117's cockpit shows only the disembodied heads of the crew, rather than their complete forms. *BAE Systems* can be called upon to monitor the attack, thus leaving the pilot free to fly the aircraft. It is proposed, therefore, that radar-autopilot coupling should not be provided initially for launching Blue Jay Mk.4."

The DH.117 would have AI Mk.18 for a collision course attack: "The concept of flying the fighter on an aircraft collision course, as opposed to an armament collision course, made possible by the smaller speed difference between fighter and weapon, enables a reduction in complexity to be achieved. This method of attack, which only requires bearing information, has the advantage of reducing the severity of the jamming problem by eliminating the need for range information up to the point of weapon launching."

Structure and layout

After looking into steel airframe structures, de Havilland ruled them out too, because: "There is little reliable data on steel stressed skin construction and, accordingly, much time would have to be spent in establishing the most efficient design. Additionally, it is impossible to eliminate all unessential material on castings, forgings etc. so these components always tend to be proportionately heavier than light alloy parts.

"Many new problems would arise on material supply and fabrication, and existing machine tools – which are usually designed for production runs on light alloys – would be unsuitable and inefficient. For these reasons, a light alloy structure has been chosen. A gauge indicating temperature will be provided in the cockpit to enable the pilot to operate the aircraft without exceeding the structural temperature limits."

The fuselage was to be composed mainly of conventional aluminium-copper alloys, L.65 and L.71, but "as much use as possible would be made of titanium in the pure and alloy form in regions subject to higher temperatures than are acceptable for light alloy and as a replacement for steel wherever possible. Experience is being gained of titanium sheet and forgings on the production DH.110 which will lead to their extensive use in this new aircraft". Exactly which bits of the 'mainly conventional light

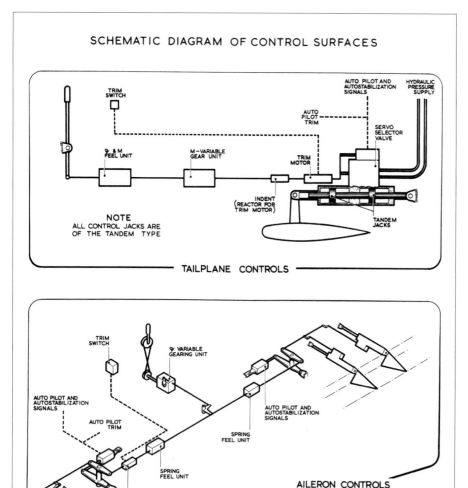

Diagram showing how the aircraft's controls would operate. *BAE Systems*

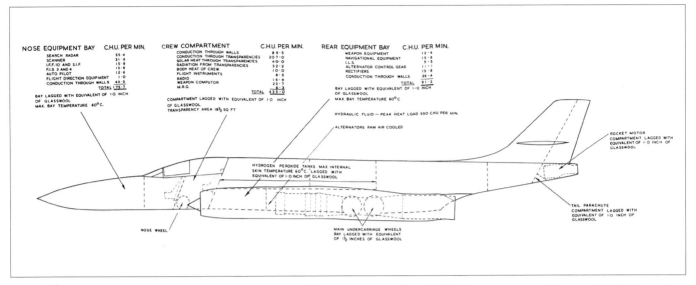

Air-conditioning, insulation and general temperature control at extreme speeds and altitudes were among the more detailed aspects of the DH.117's generally undetailed design. *BAE Systems*

alloy' DH.117 would be extensively titanium is not elaborated upon.

The fuselage was to be divided into three main subassemblies for ease of production. The forward portion, including the pressure cabin, would be split along the aircraft centre line so all the radar and associated electronic gear could be packed in. The two crew members would climb into and out of their ejector seats via a simple hinged canopy.

According to de Havilland: "The pilot's view is adequate, the wing to fuselage incidence of 3° and the lower incidences required on the straight wing assisting to provide a good view over the nose. The radar operator is seated higher in the fuselage than the pilot and thus has a good view forward through the pilot's canopy. Sideways view is provided by two large windows.

"Aft of the cockpit the lower portion of the fuselage is taken up by an air-conditioned equipment bay at the aft end of which are the engine-driven accessories. Above the equipment bay, extending from the rear cockpit bulkhead to the wing rear spar, are two hydrogen peroxide tanks of 950 gallons total capacity. Aft of the rear spar extending to the end of the reheat pipes, the fuselage houses a 500

gallon Avtur tank. The rear fuselage provides space for equipment such as Blue Jay air bottles – all moving tail accumulators etc. The tail parachute is housed in a compartment just forward of the rocket motor."

The DH.117 would have two engines "for a variety of reasons but primarily because of the importance attached to crew confidence, and for the need to ensure – as far as possible – that such an expensive aircraft (in terms of man hours expended by all those concerned to bring it and its crew to the point of service operation) should not be lost because of engine failure". Furthermore, the company could state with real conviction: "Experience with the DH.110 prototypes to date is that there would have been two possible occasions and two certain occasions on which aircraft would have been lost, owing to engine failure, if it had been of the single engine type."

And "another major point in the choice of the twin-engine layout was the wish to avoid the undesirable features of the single-engine layout, namely a fuselage almost entirely taken up with engine, jet pipes and intakes, with fuel and equipment disposed around the engine installation. This arrangement

leads to inaccessibility of engine and equipment, and difficult and complicated fuel tankage and systems, whilst increasing fire risks and the need for high operating temperature limits on equipment, more of which must be located in high temperature regions".

The firm considered that putting the two engines in the underside of the fuselage, rather than under the wings or in the rear fuselage, offered the best compromise – short intakes, good accessibility and plenty of room to fit alternative engine types without major structural revision.

The single rocket motor was housed in its own little compartment aft of the fuselage rear bulkhead and could be removed by simply opening a panel and lowering it downward. Hydraulically operated airbrakes were located in the under-surface of the engine cowling, below the reheat pipes.

Straight wings were apparently chosen only after exhaustive investigation: "From performance considerations, the straight wing is better than the swept wing; higher lift can be developed at low speed giving a smaller wing area and therefore lower weight. With the tailless delta, trim drag is a severe penalty and the tailed delta does not show any advantage over the straight wing, particularly for operation at speeds in the region of a Mach number of 2 and above.

"Flight experience to date on British and American aircraft seems to indicate that from the aircraft stability and handling point of view, the straight wing encounters fewer development difficulties."

A straight wing would have less tendency for pitch-up 'troubles' when the aircraft was close to stalling, had better directional stability at all speeds and meant the aircraft could be landed at a normal angle – avoiding the 'nose up' approach required by sharply swept deltas. It also allowed wingtip drop tanks to be carried, which could give the aircraft an impressive 'loiter' time if necessary.

Once again though, after explaining all this, that weary de Havilland voice of bitter experience re-emerges to articulate what could be seen as the real reason for preferring a nice straight set of wings: "Experience with the DH.110 has shown clearly the manufacturing difficulties arising out of the complex angles introduced by the swept and delta configurations. The straight wing and engine layout chosen gives a very straightforward structure which passes straight through the fuselage and avoids cut-outs for the undercarriage etc."

Looking to the future

While de Havilland's design was rooted in a pessimistic view of what was achievable, the firm did offer a set of plans for what might be achieved if the aircraft could be further developed while in service. The brochure said: "As discussed previously, the aircraft proposed is to a large extent dictated by the date of January 1962 for service use. This does not mean that the aircraft will be limited to this particular standard during its operational life; there are many directions in which valuable improvements can be made, and throughout the design future developments will be kept fully in view.

"The first development would be the provision of the full standard of automatic attack. When the stage has been reached when numbers of aircraft are available fully equipped with radar, autopilot and weapons, it will be possible to carry out flight tests to develop the weapon system in this way, the preliminary design and ground testing already having been completed. Automatic blind landing would also be flight tested at this stage.

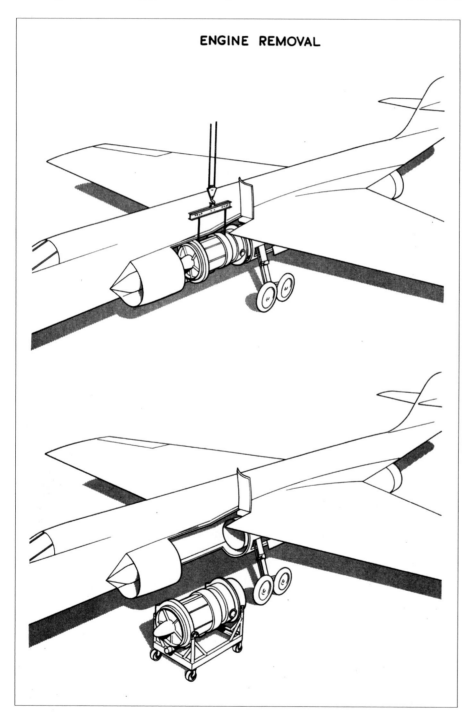

ENGINE REMOVAL

The positioning of the aircraft's engines in the centre fuselage, but mostly ahead of the wing leading edge, would have made them relatively easy to access for maintenance. *BAE Systems*

"There is potential development in the infrared weapon which will enable attacks to be made against faster targets from further ahead of the beam than is now the case with Blue Jay Mk.4. If the target speed is Mach 2 or over, homing may be possible from head on. This development will require greater range to increase the time available to complete the attack."

It was hoped that radar homing missiles might become suitable in the future if Vickers could get their size down and there was room for bigger jet engines and a larger rocket motor "if an overall operational advantage can be shown". In addition, the straight wing would allow higher Mach numbers to be reached if a steel airframe could be devised to cope with the temperature increases.

And finally, "because this is a highly specialised aeroplane requiring extensive ground facilities for its effective operation, some consideration has been given to the use of catapult take-off and arrested landing. Full examination should be made of the possibilities in this direction to determine the performance benefits which would be obtained. In this connection, the design proposed would be suitable for the use of jet deflection for lift, and skids for landing, and these will be examined".

As much as de Havilland seems to have drawn up the safest possible design that still didn't quite meet the specification, it is difficult to escape the conclusion that many of the company's complaints about the overall tendering system were entirely justified and that, had the 10 'very essential steps' actually been followed, the F.155T story might have had a somewhat different conclusion.

DE HAVILLAND AIRCRAFT DH.117

❖

October 1955

Artwork by Luca Landino

— *Specification* —

Crew: Two   **Length:** 68ft 4in
Wingspan: 44ft 1in   **Height:** 16ft
Wing area: 450sq ft
Empty weight: 28,115lb
Loaded weight: 51,175lb
Powerplant: 2 x de Havilland Gyron Junior
with reheat plus 1 x de Havilland Spectre
rocket motor
Maximum speed: Mach 2.25
Service ceiling: 70,000ft
Armament: 2 x de Havilland Blue Jay Mk.4

11

FOUR ENGINES GOOD

Armstrong Whitworth AW.169

The closest any of the F.155T competitors got to the
RAE's ideal aircraft shape was the AW.169, but the tough
requirements of the specification meant that rather than
being a small dart-like machine, the Armstrong Whitworth
design was another colossus.

Tendering for ER.134T, the same requirement that produced the Bristol Type 188, Sir W G Armstrong Whitworth Aircraft (AWA) came up with a strong contender which looked very much like the RAE 'basic design' for a Mach 2 aircraft.

The AW.166 had straight wings with mid-wing engine nacelles and a long tapering fuselage ending in a conventional tail unit. This had very nearly been enough to earn the company the contract and it only lost out because in the end it was too busy with other work to accept it.

So when it came to F.155T, it made perfect sense for AWA to utilise all the work already done on the AW.166 as the basis for its entry – the AW.169. However, whereas all the other competitors had high-performance types of entirely their own design either flying already or very close to it, the best AWA could muster by way of an example to showcase its engineering prowess was the Meteor night fighter, essentially a Gloster design, and the Gloster Javelin that it was building as a subcontractor.

Yet working on the Meteor night fighter had evidently endowed the firm with a better understanding of the weapons system concept than several of its competitors. The brochure introduction attempted to make this plain straight away: "The project has been considered under the weapon system concept and every effort has been made, by way of collaboration with the designers of specialist operational equipment, to ensure that the aircraft and its systems are co-ordinated to give the maximum assurance of enemy aircraft destruction, within the general limitations of the ground organisation likely to be available at the specified date.

"Our experience with the Meteor Night Fighter has helped considerably in our appreciation of the co-ordination problems involved in this kind of aircraft. Quite apart from the development of the basic marks with their varied AI and navigational systems, special installations for tip mounted guided weapons of the beam riding type were also provided."

It was argued that, like the Meteor Night Fighter, the best approach for getting the F.155T interceptor into the air within the time limit would be to lean on existing technology – particularly a light alloy structure. Like de Havilland with its DH.117

Striking concept art from the AW.169 brochure. *BAE Systems*

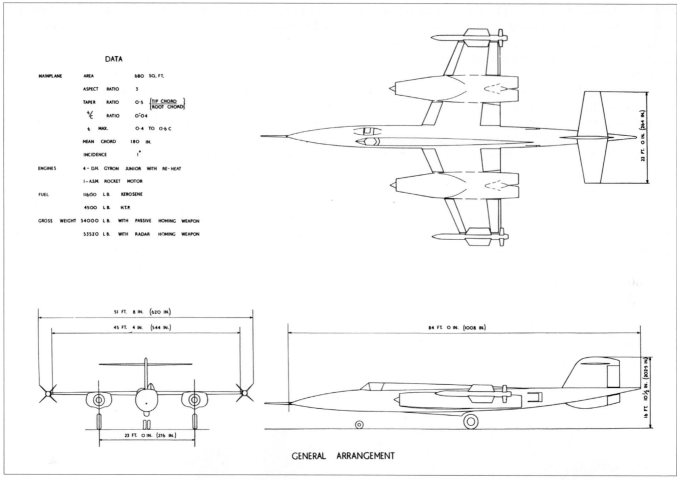

DATA

MAINPLANE	AREA	680 SQ. FT.
	ASPECT RATIO	3
	TAPER RATIO	0·5 [TIP CHORD / ROOT CHORD]
	$\frac{t}{c}$ RATIO	0·04
	t MAX.	0·4 TO 0·6 C
	MEAN CHORD	180 IN.
	INCIDENCE	1°
ENGINES	4 – D.H. GYRON JUNIOR WITH RE-HEAT	
	1 – A.S.M. ROCKET MOTOR	
FUEL	11600 LB. KEROSENE	
	4500 LB. H.T.P.	
GROSS WEIGHT	54000 LB. WITH PASSIVE HOMING WEAPON	
	53520 LB. WITH RADAR HOMING WEAPON	

GENERAL ARRANGEMENT

The AW.169's layout was the RAE's 'basic design' of three years earlier taken to the furthest extreme. *BAE Systems*

though, AWA considered that steel might eventually replace the alloys in the production of later examples of the AW.169.

Deciding on the aircraft's layout had apparently been approached by picking the wings first and AWA was entirely persuaded by the RAE's argument that thin wings were essential, meaning all the fuel had to be carried in the fuselage and the engines slung under the wings in nacelles. In fact, the brochure regurgitates all the RAE arguments for thin wings and engines in nacelles – ease of maintenance, potential to swap them for a different type later, "virtually no aerodynamic penalty", "greater safety by being separated from the main fuel system and the crew", a simpler wing structure, better landing attitude with a

better view for the pilot, and lighter undercarriage.

With the wings chosen, the design team turned to the fuselage and decided it needed side-by-side crew seats, a good view for the pilot and low drag. The rest of its size and shape was determined by what volume of fuel and equipment needed to be carried for the F.155T's specified missions.

Where the AW.169 differed significantly from the AW.166, the Bristol Type 188 and all the other thin-fuselage, thin-wing, engine-nacelles designs was in having a pair of engines in each nacelle rather than just the one. According to the brochure: "Each of our nacelles does in fact house two engines. The fundamental reason for considering the four-engine layout in preference to a twin is on the basis that, in the

size range under consideration, for a given total thrust four small engines weigh less than two large ones.

"In addition, it so happens that four Gyron Junior engines provide just the right combination for an aircraft weighing 50,000 to 55,000lb which our more general studies have shown to be about the optimum size for the specification requirements with the 7000lb military load." In addition, the space between the Gyron Juniors' intake ducts offered Armstrong Whitworth's designers a convenient location in which to position the undercarriage main wheels.

There was a performance benefit to be gained, too: "The most important advantage of all, however, turns out to be the fuel saving of about 700lb that results from being able to make the descent and landing on two engines only at a much more economical rpm. It cannot be overemphasised of course that this fuel would otherwise have to be carried throughout the entire flight to the detriment of combat performance."

The rocket motor, which would provide 15,000lb thrust at 60,000ft, was to be an unspecified "Armstrong Siddeley scheme".

It was stressed that "in all aspects of design, a striving for the greatest simplicity has been the keynote, with rapid servicing and easy maintenance the end in view". And "a great deal of work has been done to establish the current outline, far more than can ever be indicated in a brochure of this kind. Design and development is of course a continuous process and we feel that the proposals submitted are

as much as can be accomplished by 1962", although as mentioned, further developments would be possible during the service life of the aircraft.

Armstrong Whitworth had, by this point, already built a mock-up of the AW.169, mapped out an extensive wind tunnel test programme involving five separate models already under construction and planned to investigate any potential flutter or stability problems "on our new simulator".

The brochure as a whole certainly gave the impression that the AW.169 was a well-advanced design with most of the details already fleshed out.

Structure and production
The fuselage was a light alloy semi-monocoque structure of mostly

circular cross-section comprising three sections – front, centre and rear. At the front, the radome housing the scanner was a solid glass-cloth laminate of tapering thickness and between the radome and cockpit were two pressurised units, cooled with air from the cabin, containing the main AI sets.

Within the cockpit, the pilot and radar operator would sit next to one another in a pressurised air conditioned cockpit with the radar operator on a slightly lower level. Both would have lightweight ejection seats that were adjustable for height. The pilot's windscreen was fixed and is made of two pieces of conical glass joined at the centre by a structural member and supported at the rear by an arch.

Apparently, "this arrangement gives a good aerodynamic shape

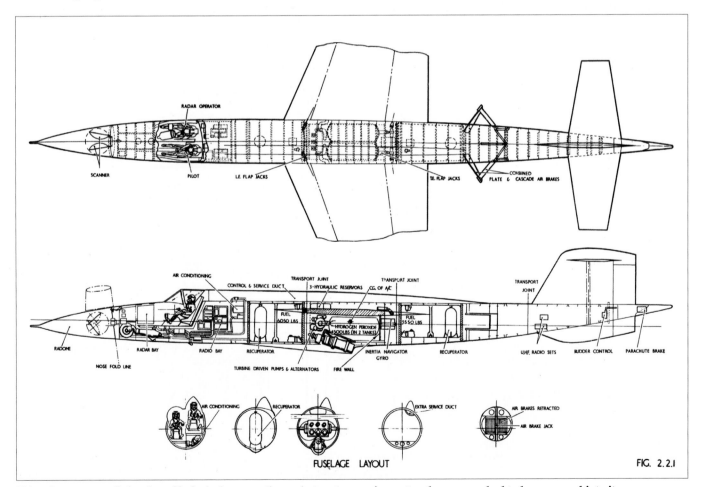

Thin wings meant all the aircraft's fuel, the crew, the rocket motor, equipment and nose gear had to be crammed into its narrow fuselage. *BAE Systems*

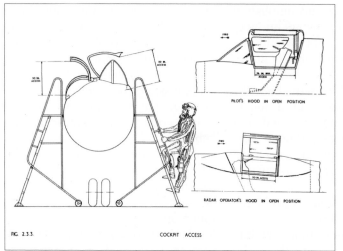

Both pilot and radar operator, wearing full pressure suits, had a 30in opening through which to enter the AW.169's cabin. *BAE Systems*

Once inside the crew compartment, the radar operator would find himself sitting low down within the fuselage, while the pilot sat high up under a conventional cockpit canopy. *BAE Systems*

and the least possible blank-off of view. A central curtain may be found necessary to prevent cockpit reflections". The hood itself would be made up of two pieces of cylindrical glass in a light alloy framework hinged at the side for access and arranged for jettisoning in an emergency. The radar operator got a hinged canopy with a cylindrical glass transparency which could also be jettisoned if necessary. Provision was made for both crewmen to wear pressure suits.

The space beneath the cockpit floor housed some of the air conditioning equipment, and between the cockpit and forward

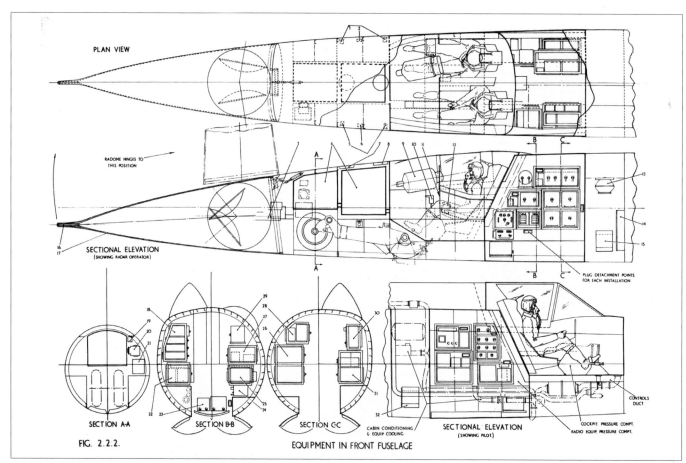

A closer look at the cramped interior of the AW.169's fuselage front section. *BAE Systems*

body fuel tank was a radio and radar bay. This was to be pressurised and air conditioned separately from the main cockpit and the various bits of equipment would be arranged in complete packages. The main flexible bag-type kerosene fuel tanks were fore and aft of the centre section and below it were the rocket fuel tanks, the air turbines, and gearbox for driving the aircraft auxiliaries, the rocket motor and the Inertia navigator gyro unit.

The rear fuselage contained the air brakes and another radar bay. The tail cone, to which the tail unit was attached, carried the braking parachute.

The wing flanges and extruded fuselage stringers were to be made from aluminium-copper alloy L.65, while the fuselage skins were made from another aluminium-copper alloy DTD.546. Titanium would be used for "secondary structure where local high temperatures warrant it e.g. jet pipe supporting structure" but more generally "in view of the unsatisfactory supply position regarding alloyed titanium and the considerable research into manufacturing techniques necessary, titanium is not felt too suitable for the primary structures of this aircraft".

Armstrong Whitworth argued that it was well equipped to take on the job of building AW.169s in quantity, primarily because of its experiences with making Gloster Javelins: "This aircraft is approximately 60% larger, on a weight basis, than the standard Javelin which is in production at AWA at the present time, but is smaller than other aircraft which have been made in this factory. Overhead runways, factory headroom, door opening, runways etc. as existing are quite satisfactory.

"For purposes of estimation the 'structure' weight to be manufactured by AWA, which includes certain equipment, has been taken as 21,000lb. The aircraft breaks down into 24 main units and

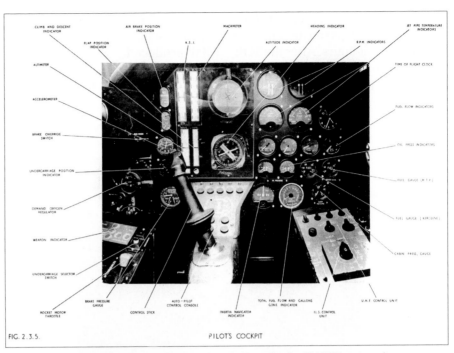

FIG. 2.3.5.   PILOTS COCKPIT

Armstrong Whitworth felt so confident that their tender for F.155T was a winner, they went to the lengths of building a full cockpit mock-up. Seen here are the pilot's controls. *BAE Systems*

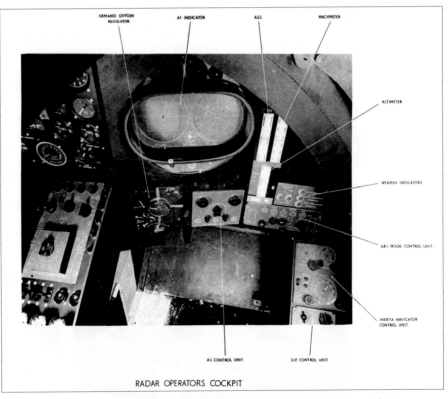

RADAR OPERATORS COCKPIT

The mocked-up radar operator's position, complete with fully analogue readouts. *BAE Systems*

can be transported by road to the final assembly factory at Bitteswell with these units fully equipped. The largest is the wing centre section, which can be transported in one piece without difficulty."

It was estimated that making the first AW.169 would require 23 man-hours per pound of weight and since the weight was 21,000lb this equated to 483,000 man-hours. After the 12th aircraft this would drop to 189,000 man-hours per aircraft, reaching a rock bottom of just 55,700 man-hours for each example by the 750th produced.

AWA was eager to stress that its factories were able to take on the work straight away, indeed, they would positively welcome it: "Firstly, a word on total factory capacity. The AWA organisation is designed to produce 40 off Hunter-type fighters per month or 16 off Javelins per month. Peak capacity for the AW.169 would therefore be about 10 aircraft per month with no other work except spares and repairs in the factory. This peak is based on the assumption that nothing would be subcontracted.

"With normal sub-contracting of 17% (this was the actual percentage of Hunter subcontracting) the peak would be raised to 12 aircraft per month. The present depleted state of our order book does, however, allow us to give an order for the AW.169 immediate attention and initial deliveries as far as production is concerned could be made with the minimum of delay."

If AWA got the go-ahead to proceed in January 1956, the first aircraft could be delivered in June 1959 with the second following in August, then another in October. By January 1962, there would already be 22 AW.169s in existence with aircraft rolling off the production line at a rate of three per month.

The first 12 would be prototypes, with Number 1 being "a more or less uninstrumented flying shell devoted to the most fundamental checks of aircraft, engine and fuel system characteristics". Numbers 2 and 3 would be fully instrumented for trials, with one going to A&AEE. Number 4 would be equipped for cabin air conditioning trials and "it might reasonably be anticipated that some time in the life of this aircraft would be devoted to trials abroad".

Number 5 would test the radio and radar, 6 the navigation and flight instruments, 7 the power control system, 8 would be a passive homing weapon test bed, 9 would test the radar homing weapon, 10 and 11 would be fully operational and 12 "might be built as a steel aircraft, with alternative power plant or with

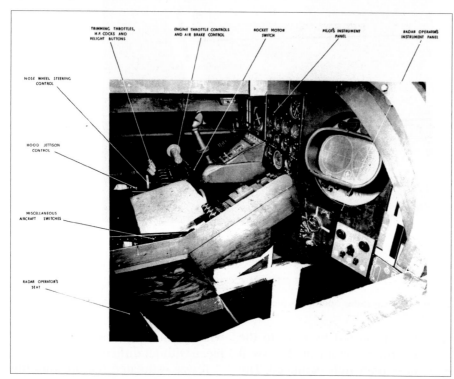

This view from the port side of the cockpit mock-up shows the difference in height between the pilot's seat in the foreground and the radar operator's position down to his right. *BAE Systems*

Looking into the radar operator's station from the starboard side. *BAE Systems* increased pressure differential, for example, as circumstances should later dictate. Otherwise it could join numbers 10 and 11 for tactical assessment".

Guided weapons

Since Armstrong Whitworth intended to accommodate loads of either Blue Jays or Red Hebes, although not both at the same time, it offered no arguments in respect of either in particular. However, it did criticise both for decidedly poor aerodynamic form: "The position regarding the drag of the weapons is somewhat unsatisfactory at present. The weapons considered as likely armament for this aircraft are the de Havilland Blue Jay Mk.4 and a radar homing weapon proposed by Vickers Armstrong to OR.1131. Both these suffer considerable drag penalties resulting from the rather blunt noses apparently necessary for efficient operation of the guidance systems.

"In addition there is a serious lack of information as to the relation between the drag of such weapons when mounted on the aircraft and when in free flight at zero lift."

Although this drag had been accounted for in the AW.169's design, Armstrong Whitworth suggested further steps could be taken to streamline the missiles: "We have accepted for our performance estimates, with consequent drag penalties, the nose shapes currently designed for the two weapons. (And we have shown) the zero lift drag of each of the weapons together with our estimates of how the drag might be improved by modest nose and tail fairings which would be jettisoned prior to combat.

"For the passive homing weapon it seems that a very reasonable nose fairing of about 2.5ft in length would restore the drag of the Mk.4 to roughly that of the Mk.1. Something along these lines may well turn out to be necessary as protection for the nose against flying through

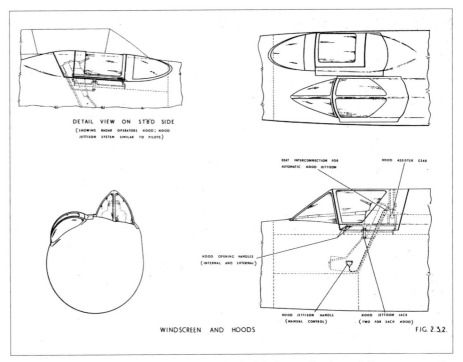

The AW.169's crew got ejection seats but AWA did plan to develop a full escape capsule at a later date. *BAE Systems*

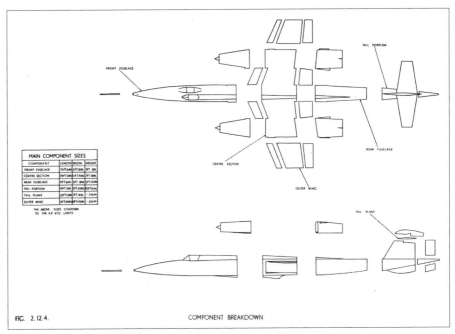

Constructional details of the aircraft were mapped out in great detail – far more than this component breakdown might suggest. *BAE Systems*

rain at low altitudes, aside from performance considerations."

Given the AW.169's high performance and the extreme speeds and altitudes it was expected to operate at, Armstrong Whitworth designed a simple weapon cooling system which consisted "of air bled from the inboard engines through a water evaporator (the storage tank for this will be well lagged) to the braked turbine. From the turbine the air is fed to the weapons or the various accessories. Some of the exhaust accessory air will be fed to the main wheel bays".

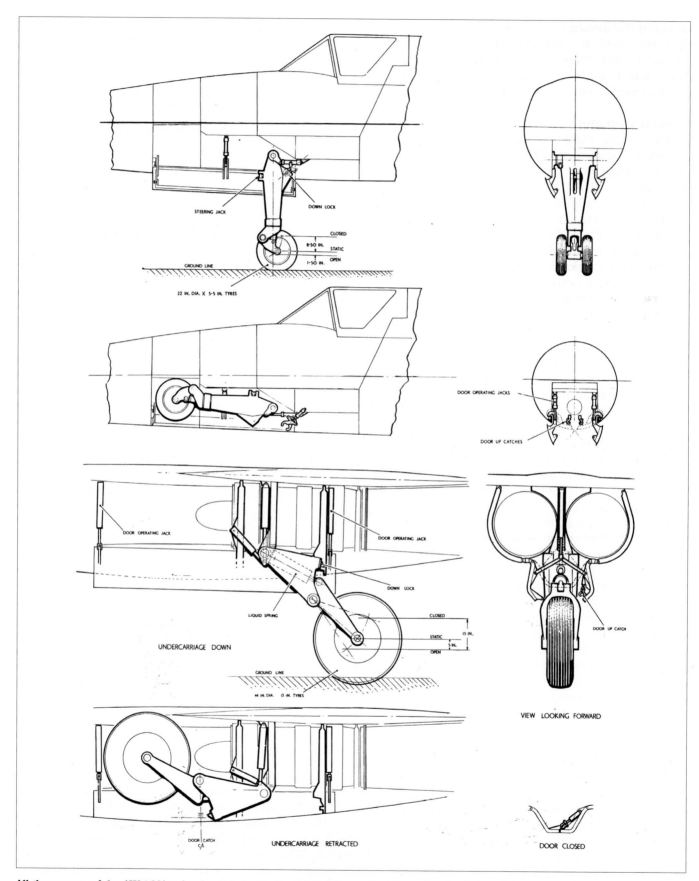

All three parts of the AW.169's tricycle undercarriage retracted forwards – the main wheels into the engine nacelles. *BAE Systems*

Making the attack

Having studied OR.329 very carefully and read between the lines, Armstrong Whitworth came to the realisation that the requirement had actually been drafted with a pursuit course attack in mind, which it had, but had later been hurriedly changed to a collision course requirement.

According to the brochure: "In OR.329 some guidance is given as to the order of performance necessary if the fighter is to be capable of satisfactorily intercepting the targets for which it is intended, namely, raiders capable of low supersonic speeds at heights in the stratosphere of up to about 60,000ft.

"These requirements have been based on the pursuit course type of interception since it is in this case that the need for high performance is the greatest. This is clearly true in view of the time and distance wasted in flying out to the target before turning through up to 180° to complete the interception with a stern chase.

"However the basic requirement is for a collision course weapon system and, particularly since the passive homing weapon also is now thought to be capable of nearly all round collision attack, the greater emphasis should be on this system. This is particularly important if we envisage, as we must, operation in

the face of enemy radar counter measures when, in the absence of range information at the Ground Control Station, a ground controlled turn leading to a stern chase is no longer possible."

In short, as originally envisioned, the pursuit version of the F.155T fighter needed to have tremendous power if it was going to get up, round and behind its target before shooting it down. With collision course, all that was needed was a missile platform that could climb fast enough to get in front of the target before it flew past. The missiles, it was hoped, would do the rest.

Armstrong Whitworth felt the need to work all this through in

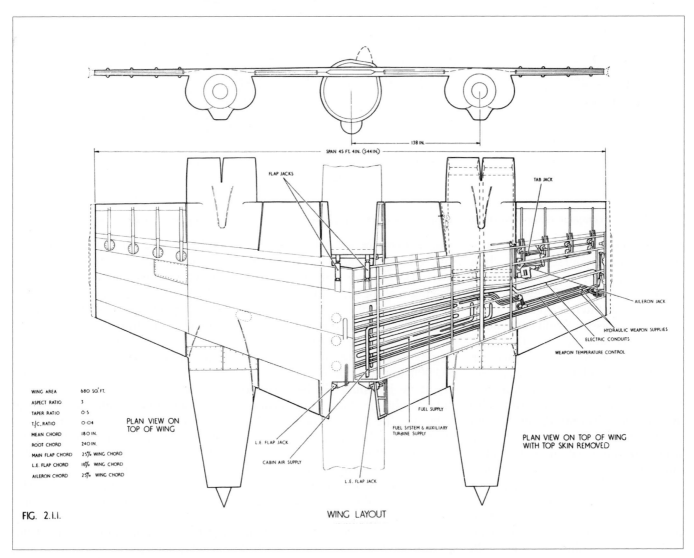

FIG. 2.1.1.   WING LAYOUT

WING AREA	680 SQ.FT.
ASPECT RATIO	3
TAPER RATIO	0.5
T/C.RATIO	0.04
MEAN CHORD	180 IN.
ROOT CHORD	240 IN.
MAIN FLAP CHORD	25% WING CHORD
L.E. FLAP CHORD	18% WING CHORD
AILERON CHORD	25% WING CHORD

The thinness of the AW.169's wings is evident from this structural layout drawing. *BAE Systems*

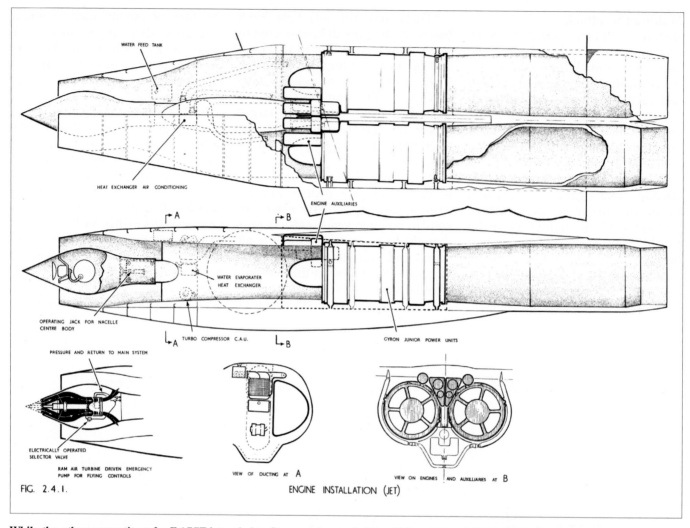

WATER FEED TANK

HEAT EXCHANGER AIR CONDITIONING

ENGINE AUXILIARIES

A

B

OPERATING JACK FOR NACELLE
CENTRE BODY

WATER EVAPORATER
HEAT EXCHANGER

A   TURBO COMPRESSOR C.A.U.   B

GYRON JUNIOR POWER UNITS

PRESSURE AND RETURN TO MAIN SYSTEM

ELECTRICALLY OPERATED
SELECTOR VALVE

RAM AIR TURBINE DRIVEN EMERGENCY
PUMP FOR FLYING CONTROLS

VIEW OF DUCTING AT A

VIEW ON ENGINES AND AUXILIARIES AT B

FIG. 2.4.1.   ENGINE INSTALLATION (JET)

While the other competitors for F.155T intended to fit one or two turbojets, AWA was the only company to specify four. *BAE Systems*

the brochure, with examples of first a pursuit course attack, then a collision course attack, to see whether the AW.169 would be effective for either or both: "A study of the ideal case of a collision course from the fighter base has therefore been made, together with possible operations involving flying along, or nearly along, the continuously rotating line of sight from the appropriate Ground Radar Station to the target. These studies have provided information concerning suitable fuel allowances, endurance, etc. for dealing with other than pursuit course interception."

For the studies, it was assumed that an early warning was given with the incoming bomber 220 nautical miles away, and that there

was a five-minute delay between the warning being given and the AW.169's engines being started. The interceptor's base was assumed to be 20 nautical miles inland, with the ground radar station on the coastline. The incoming target was doing Mach 1.3 at 60,000ft and its counter measures might be jamming British ground radar only or both the ground radar and the interceptor's AI. This jamming might be continuous or only intermittent.

For the pursuit course attack only, it was also assumed that the interceptor had to be doing Mach 2 at the same altitude as the target for at least 45 seconds before making a controlled turn to come around behind it; that once the turn was

made a chase of not less than 90 seconds would be needed before the bomber was destroyed; that the fighter had to be "drawn in from at least 50 nautical miles from bomber landfall"; and that the bomber had to be destroyed at least 30 nautical miles out to sea.

With these in mind, running the pursuit course scenario showed that "an appreciable increase of time of climb above six minutes is intolerable, and, in addition, the optimum distance covered towards the target during the climb is of the order of 65 nautical miles. The reason for this is that for smaller climb distances the fighter must fly out for a longer period to meet the target to achieve the desired kill line, whereas for longer climb distances the 45-second control period means that the fighter has flown too far before making its turn and the ensuing chase is lengthened.

"This aircraft, carrying pursuit course weapons, climbs to 60,000ft in about five minutes 30 seconds from start-up, covering about 58 nautical miles, or to 50,000ft in about four minutes 54 seconds, covering nearly 47 nautical miles, the times including engine starting. In either case, some 70 nautical miles of lateral cover on each side of the fighter base can be provided by this aircraft."

The pursuit course case wasn't an entirely rosy picture however: "Where the target is being tracked continuously during the organisational delay period prior to fighter take-off, no penalty should be incurred as a result of the target speed being less than Mach 1.3 since the fighter can delay starting accordingly. Should the target speed be appreciably in excess of Mach 1.3, or should early warning range or delay time not come up to expectations, it is highly improbable that a 30 nautical mile offshore kill line could be defended using pursuit course tactics, whatever the performance of the fighter."

If the Soviet bomber could sprint above Mach 1.3, if the warning came too late or if the delay getting off the ground was too long, the 'chase' would fail.

The other option was what Armstrong Whitworth called 'all-round attack interceptions': "Provided that the fighter establishes AI contact with its target in such a way that, within reasonable known limits, it is on an aircraft collision course with the target, the weapon system is capable of completing the interception on a collision course basis.

"It is anticipated that this will be possible equally well whether the enemy is jamming the fighter AI or not. The problem here is one of finding range for weapon launch in the face of RCM (radar counter measures). The present feeling is that under the circumstances sufficient range information is obtainable by means of an additional range finding dish working on Q-band and mounted in one of the engine centrebodies."

If the enemy bomber took absolutely no evasive action after the missiles were launched, it was almost certain that they would destroy it. And if there was no jamming, all the guidance calculations could be

made on the ground. If the target attempted to evade or manoeuvre, the fighter would have to make corresponding changes of course and if there were delays in getting aloft, this would also have an impact but "the results indicate that these parameters are not nearly so critical as in the pursuit case, although it is clearly important to keep the average speed in the climb as high as possible to achieve the maximum kill range."

Things got trickier when the enemy used radar jamming to prevent the ground station from establishing exactly how far away it was, in which case "the only hope of making an interception is to climb and navigate the fighter into a position on the same bearing from the GCI station as the target. The fighter then maintains its position on this slowly rotating imaginary beam as it flies towards the target. When the AI contact is made the interception is completed by flying a proportional navigation course up to the point of weapon launch."

If the enemy was jamming the waveband used by the interceptor's AI radar too, "difficulty would be experienced in obtaining range information for launching the weapons. It is hoped that this range

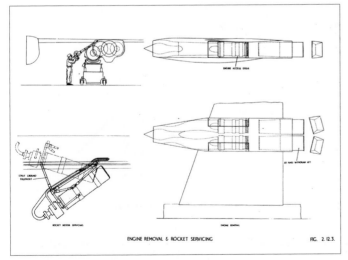

One of the main reasons for fitting turbojets into underwing nacelles rather than within the fuselage was ease of access. This brochure drawing shows how two men could extract a Gyron Junior using a simple hand-operated pulley. *BAE Systems*

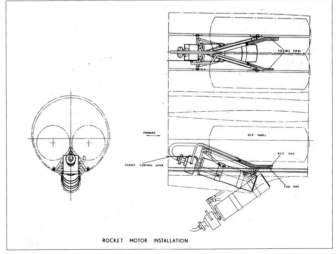

The precise model of rocket motor AWA intended to install in the AW.169 is unclear but whatever it was it would have been neatly housed within a fairing on the underside of the central fuselage section. *BAE Systems*

would be provided by means of the auxiliary range finder mentioned earlier".

In the event that the bomber attack warning came so late that the enemy were already less than 220 nautical miles away, or if pre-takeoff delays amounted to as much as nine minutes, Armstrong Whitworth believed that the AW.169 might still be able to stave off disaster through sheer high performance: "The only hope of dealing with such a case at all using pursuit course tactics is to accept a kill line nearer to the coastline and for the fighter to climb in the shortest possible time and distance.

"By using full reheat from the start of take-off to the top of the climb this aircraft can achieve

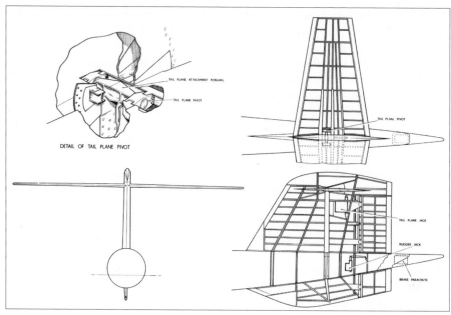

The simple and reliable nature of AWA's design is showcased in this drawing for the tail section. *BAE Systems*

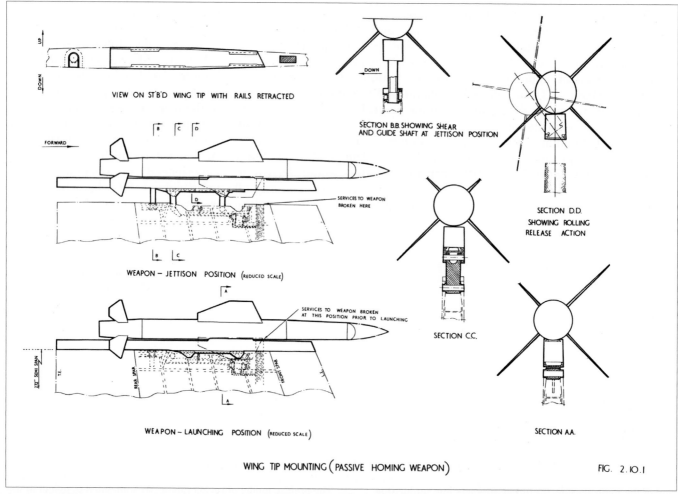

Armstrong Whitworth was unusual among the competitors for F.155T in having no real complaint about the requirement to fit either the Blue Jay, as shown here, or the Red Hebe. But the company did object to the Blue Jay Mk.4's blunt nose – hence the fairing shown sitting over it in this drawing. *BAE Systems*

Mach 2 at 60,000ft in three minutes 30 seconds from wheels rolling, whilst covering a distance of 44 nautical miles and using slightly under 6300lb of kerosene. The rocket is not required for such a climb so that the full rocket fuel load is available for the combat period at high altitude."

Future developments

AWA suggested six possible avenues of development for the AW.169 design: deliberately making it longitudinally unstable, making it out of steel instead of light alloy, fitting it with Bristol BE.30 engines, installing a full escape capsule for the crew, increasing the cabin pressurisation and fitting it out for long-range operations.

Creating the 'unstable aircraft', as AWA called it, involved shifting the centre of gravity by moving the wings forward on the fuselage by 4ft. The wing nacelles were also brought forward an additional 1ft 6in relative to the wing. In order to provide the correct centre of gravity position for the fuel load, the radio bay would be moved back to the rear of the main fuel tanks. Doing this would apparently reduce induced supersonic drag, meaning less fuel would be burned at all supersonic speeds. Tighter turns in flight would be possible and acceleration would be improved.

Building the AW.169 from strong, thin, heat-resistant steel was

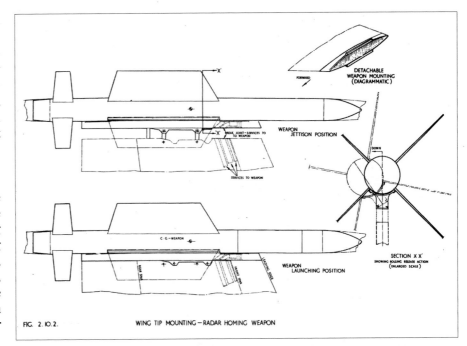

FIG. 2.10.2.   WING TIP MOUNTING – RADAR HOMING WEAPON

Substantial fairings would be needed for both the nose and tail of the Red Hebe, according to AWA. But otherwise the size and weight of the missile could be accommodated by the AW.169. *BAE Systems*

expected to offer all sorts of benefits – much higher diving speed and full manoeuvrability, from a structural standpoint, up to at least Mach 3 at 40,000ft. The downside was the time it would take to develop the necessary manufacturing and production techniques to make it happen.

Bristol's BE.30 Series 2 engine was said to have "a significantly greater thrust potential than the Gyron Junior". It was longer in body than the de Havilland power plant but had a shorter reheat nozzle, making it about the same length

overall so that it could fit into the AW.169's nacelles with a minimum of redesign work. According to AWA's brochure: "From a simple performance standpoint, rate of climb and take-off in particular, the Bristol engine aircraft shows up very favourably in relation to that powered by the Gyron Juniors.

"With some adjustment to the fuel loadings we can meet all specification requirements and achieve a satisfactory solution to the interception problem generally, the latter being in certain respects more dependent upon endurance

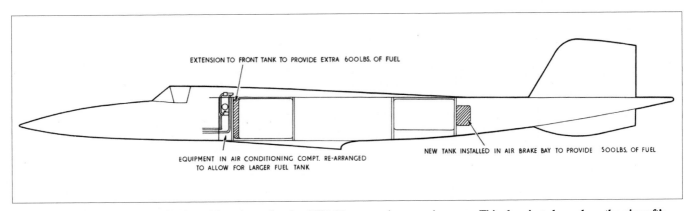

EXTENSION TO FRONT TANK TO PROVIDE EXTRA 600LBS. OF FUEL

EQUIPMENT IN AIR CONDITIONING COMPT. RE-ARRANGED TO ALLOW FOR LARGER FUEL TANK

NEW TANK INSTALLED IN AIR BRAKE BAY TO PROVIDE 500LBS. OF FUEL

The most useful development AWA could envisage for the AW.169 was an increase in range. This drawing shows how the aircraft's internal structure would be slightly rearranged to allow for greater internal fuel capacity. *BAE Systems*

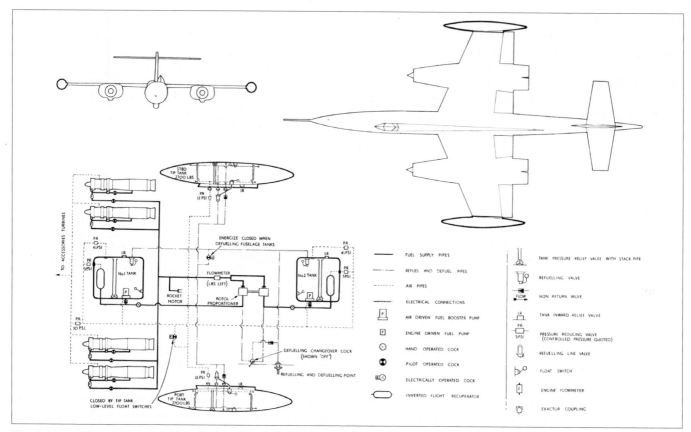

Tip tanks could be fitted to the AW.169 for ferrying but not combat operations, since the wingtips were the only mounting points available for missiles. *BAE Systems*

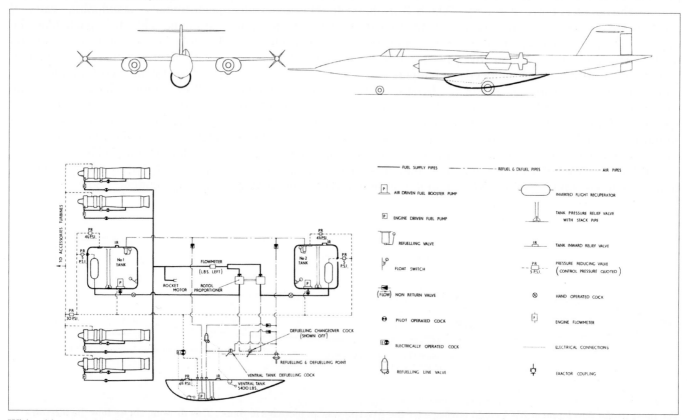

With a big ventral tank fitted, the AW.169 could carry another 5400lb of fuel – good for a patrol time of 71 minutes. *BAE Systems*

Armstrong Whitworth AW.169 with ventral fuel tank. *Art by Daniel Uhr*

than absolute performance. The slightly greater take-off weight and small reduction in flight load factors can be easily accepted."

Adding an escape capsule for the AW.169's crew was another option: "Some preliminary work has been carried out on this subject for a previous design study and applying the same principles to this aircraft would entail lengthening the fuselage by a foot between the cockpit and the aft radio bay. This would accommodate the severing system for the fuselage attachments and aircraft services, the stabilising fins for the capsule and a parachute for controlling its final descent.

"The system would be arranged so that for an escape at supersonic speed the capsule is jettisoned, the fins extended and, on reduction of speed to less than Mach 0.9, the crew ejected on their normal ejection seats. The capsule would remain pressurised for a considerable period in the descent for, although the pressurising air supply is lost, the cabin can be protected by an automatic coupling between the jettison control and the isolating valves." At low speeds the crew would eject as normal.

Increased cabin pressurisation would improve cooling for sustained flight at Mach 2 and 60,000ft and would be achieved by using a turbo-compressor or 'bootstrap system' with a secondary water evaporator between the compressor and turbine.

Finally, AWA hoped to win over the adjudicators by showing that the AW.169 could carry much larger

fuel loads if required. If the rocket motor and its fuel were deleted, the space could be used to carry an additional 1100lb of kerosene and a 5400lb ventral fuel tank could be installed too. In addition, yet another 4500lb could be carried in wingtip drop tanks if missiles were not required.

With its standard fuel tanks, plus the extra internal fuel, plus the ventral tank, the aircraft's combat radius could be improved from 190 nautical miles to 440 nautical miles – taking potential standing patrol time from 20 minutes to 71 minutes. For ferrying purposes, with the tip tanks, range increased to 1890 nautical miles.

Considering the company had little experience in the field of designing supersonic combat aircraft, Armstrong Whitworth put forward a highly detailed and

compelling case. The fact that the AW.169 was fundamentally based on the creaky 1952 RAE 'basic design' did not stand in its favour however, and the adjudicators remained wary about taking the word of such an inexperienced design team at face value.

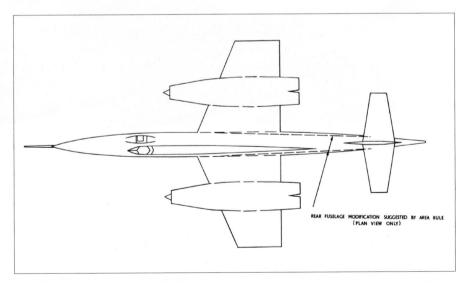

Among the numerous suggestions made by AWA for ways in which the AW.169 might be improved given more time was a narrowing of the rear fuselage to take advantage of area rule at higher Mach numbers. *BAE Systems*

SIR W G ARMSTRONG WHITWORTH AIRCRAFT AW.169

October 1955

Artwork by Luca Landino

— *Specification* —

Crew: Two   **Length:** 84ft   **Wingspan:** 51ft 8in   **Height:** 16ft 10½in
Wing area: 680sq ft   **Empty weight:** 36,600lb   **Loaded weight:** 53,520lb
Powerplant: 4 x de Havilland Gyron Junior with reheat plus 1 x Armstrong
Siddeley rocket motor
Maximum speed: Mach 2.25   **Service ceiling:** 65,000ft   **Armament:** 2 x Vickers Red Hebe

12

NO COMPROMISE

Saunders-Roe P.187

F.155T Issue 2 relaxed the specification significantly –
requiring submitted designs to carry Blue Jay and Red
Hebe missiles as alternative loads, rather than both at the
same time. Saunders-Roe, however, saw no reason why
the original F.155T could not be met in full. The resulting
P.187 was a truly awesome design.

With the first prototype of its mixed-propulsion experimental single-seater, the SR.53, nearing completion and its P.177 mixed-propulsion fighter looking almost certain to enter full production for both the RAF and the Navy, Saunders-Roe was in a bullish mood when it came to F.155T.

The brochure it submitted outlined a design that was bigger, heavier, more expensive and more powerful than any of its competitors. The P.187 embodied a refusal to accept anything that might be regarded as second best and the brochure was unambiguous in pointing this out right at the beginning: "The proposed design meets the specification in its entirety. No compromise has been admitted. The original weapon load required in Issue 1 of the Specification consisting of two developed Blue Jays and two developed Red Deans is carried.

"It is shown that the specification can be met by an aircraft having a take-off weight of 97,000lb and a dry weight of 54,700lb. This aircraft is powered by two de Havilland Gyron turbojet engines and two Double Spectre rocket engines. The proposed aircraft follows very closely the engineering and aerodynamic layout of the Saunders-Roe F.138D (SR.53) and its development, the F.177T (P.177).

"Attention is drawn to the following particular features of the design: a first-class view from the cockpit is provided for the two crew members, who are seated side-by-side. This has been achieved without supersonic drag penalty. Particular attention has been directed to providing independent survival arrangements for each of the crew. In an emergency, they have the choice of escaping simultaneously or independently."

In terms of performance, a light alloy structure restricted speed to a maximum of Mach 2.2 but

"the aircraft is aerodynamically capable of a top speed of Mach 3.5 at 70,000ft" which it was suggested might be approached using different materials for the P.187's construction, such as titanium. And the titanium P.187 would be

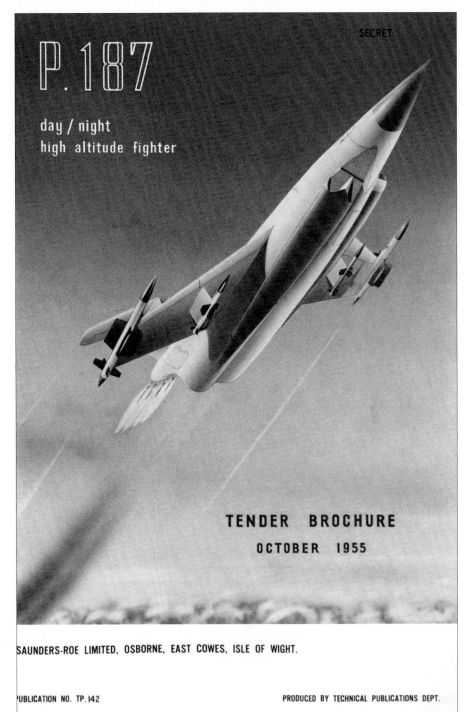

The enormous futuristic-looking Saunders-Roe P.187. This brochure concept art shows the design's key feature – its ability to carry both Blue Jay and Red Hebe missiles at the same time. *GKN*

"capable of intercepting a Mach 3 target flying at 70,000ft over a front of 80 miles".

Under a heading of 'design policy', Saunders-Roe outlined its thinking behind the decision to ignore Specification F.155T Issue 2:

"In view of the uncertainties at present attending missile and AI development and performance, particularly in the presence of jamming, this company agrees with the requirement put forward in Issue 1 of Specification F.155T. This calls for an aircraft capable of supersonic turns through large angles while carrying simultaneously high performance radar and infrared weapons. Such an aircraft, carrying the officially recommended armament and equipment, is presented in this brochure.

"In formulating the design the company was aware that a much reduced all-up weight could have been obtained by challenging the weapon and/or sortie assumptions of the F.155T specification, and by accepting the concession in Issue 2 of the specification that the radar and infrared weapons need only be carried as alternative loads."

The company claimed to have made its choice with its eyes wide open, even if it was a choice it might later have real cause to regret. However, despite the hard line there was still an attempt to leave the door open for compromise if that proved to be the only way forward: "Should the armament and equipment requirements of the F.155T Specification be alleviated, the experience gained from … the tender design would enable the company to prepare an alternative design for a smaller aircraft at very short notice.

"The possibility of using combinations of developed Gyron and developed Gyron Junior engines is of interest in this connection. In particular, the company considers that the Saunders-Roe P.177 design, to Ministry of Supply contract 6/Acft/12284/C.B.7(b) offers a realistic alternative to the present requirement, in so far as the carriage of missiles of Blue Jay size is concerned."

In effect, Saunders-Roe was attempting to take the same approach as Fairey – a large all-out design to meet or even beat the spec, with the option of a more lightly developed version of an existing design as an alternative. But where Fairey went ahead and offered that with a separate brochure, accepted as a tender in its own right within the competition rules, Saunders-Roe withheld its second brochure and concentrated on the P.187 in the first instance.

The 12 points

When the P.187 was designed, Saunders-Roe stressed, "great emphasis" had been placed on a dozen key design features: it would carry four missiles – two Blue Jays and two Red Hebes – because "this increases to a maximum the

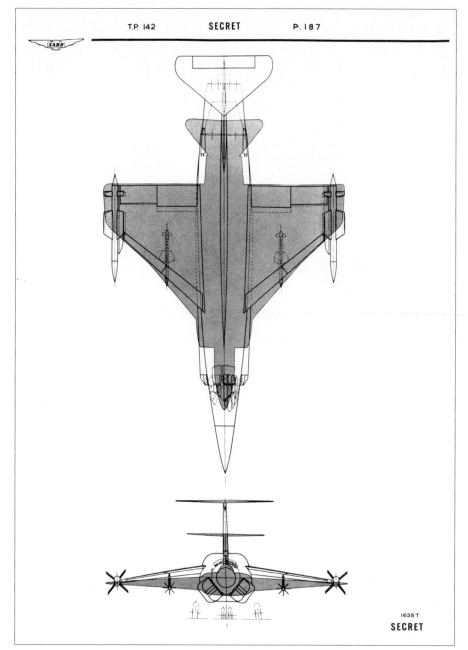

From the outset, Saunders-Roe had no qualms about pointing out just how huge the P.187 would be. This shows its outline overlaid on the silhouette of a Gloster Javelin. *GKN*

SECRET

A second piece of concept art from the P.187 brochure shows the type's sliding nose for better visibility when landing. *GKN*

likelihood of a kill, even in the presence of jamming. The under-wing location of the infrared weapon has been recommended by the weapon design firm, de Havilland Propellers".

It would have enough fuel to allow a choice between pursuit or collision course attack "as the tactical situation demands" and its nose would slide down so both crew members would have a good view during approach and landing. Somewhat incredibly, it had to have enough power to attack the target from above no matter how high it was flying, even if this meant flying on rocket power alone at super-high altitude, finish the interception even if one turbojet should fail and "cruise economically at Mach 2, on turbo-jets alone, up to at least 56,000ft".

The fuselage was wide enough to house the turbojets, allow easy access to them for maintenance and carry all the fuel needed. The jet engines were positioned in the lower fuselage so they could have 'two shock' intakes, minimal intake length and enough room for undercarriage retraction.

Putting the twin rocket engines at the extreme rear of the aircraft would prevent "difficulties arising from the large efflux expansions which occur at low ambient pressures". And "recent advances in undercarriage design have been incorporated to provide alighting gear of competitive size, which meets runway and braking requirements without the need for thrust reversal or braking parachutes. The main units retract into the turbo-jet engine air intake

fairings in a manner which provides minimum fuselage cross-sectional areas and fairing coning angles. Blow-down flaps are employed to hold down the approach speed to an acceptable value."

The P.187 was to have overload fuel tanks for the 'extended warning sortie' and these would be positioned between the main undercarriage fairings "with minimum disturbance to the clean lines of the fuselage". Since it was uncertain what level of flight system might be available, the P.187 was designed to accommodate "existing, interim, and fully developed installations".

Saunders-Roe was at pains to point out that "the design innovations introduced have been fully investigated as to their practicability. Proven techniques

The sheer bulk of the P.187's fuselage is clear from this three-view drawing, as is the design's oddly framed windscreen arrangement. *GKN*

and equipment have been employed, wherever it has been possible to do so efficiently.

"The extensive design work undertaken in connection with our F.138D and P.177 contracts has been fully drawn upon and, in principle, the present design is a scaled version of these earlier aircraft. In particular the company's experience in the design of fuel systems involving segregation of HTP and kerosene has been utilised with advantage."

Unsurprisingly, however, there were a few niggling features of the design which would be "subject to modification in detail, as the result of further investigation". In particular, wind tunnel tests would be needed for the sliding nose, the fairing housing the main undercarriage

and the arrangement of the rocket engines – "as tendered, these are side-by-side, giving an almost flat-topped fuselage which provides the fin with end plate effect".

Finally, and perhaps hardest of all to swallow: "The proposed aircraft has been designed to allow the detailed engineering and construction to be undertaken in the shortest possible time, while having the developmental potential necessary fully to exploit the equipment and weapons that will be available during its operational life."

Structure and layout

The P.187's layout was, according to Saunders-Roe "a development of that proposed for the P.177 aircraft". The wings were thin – too thin to house the undercarriage or

any fuel – and this had "resulted in a relatively simple structure" made largely of aluminium alloy. However, "the design of this aircraft will permit it to be developed to fly at speeds between Mach 2.5 and Mach 3.5. At these speeds the use of aluminium alloy for the wing structure not be practicable. Investigations have shown that for this wing, the structural box strength requirements over-ride the stiffness requirements with the result that a titanium alloy box is lighter than one in steel". The titanium alloy chosen for this future development was ICI titanium 314A, a high aluminium-manganese alloy.

The brochure stated that: "The wing planform and the relative position of the wing and tailplane

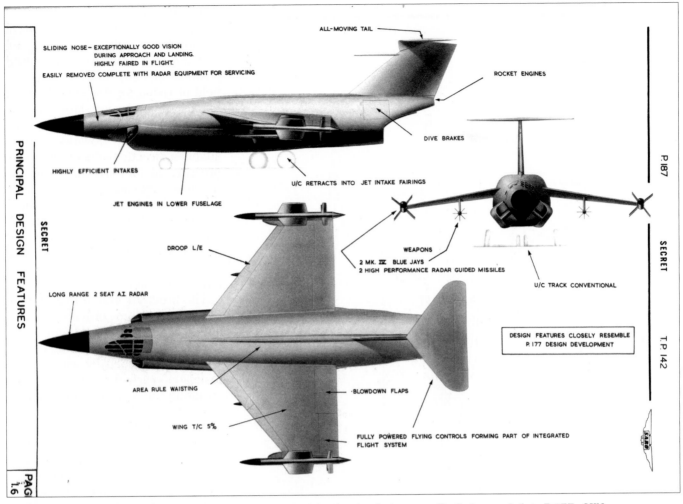

The following annotations appear on the drawing:

ALL-MOVING TAIL

SLIDING NOSE – EXCEPTIONALLY GOOD VISION
DURING APPROACH AND LANDING.
HIGHLY FAIRED IN FLIGHT.
EASILY REMOVED COMPLETE WITH RADAR EQUIPMENT FOR SERVICING

ROCKET ENGINES

DIVE BRAKES

HIGHLY EFFICIENT INTAKES

U/C RETRACTS INTO JET INTAKE FAIRINGS

JET ENGINES IN LOWER FUSELAGE

DROOP L/E

WEAPONS
2 MK. IV BLUE JAYS
2 HIGH PERFORMANCE RADAR GUIDED MISSILES

U/C TRACK CONVENTIONAL

LONG RANGE 2 SEAT A.I. RADAR

DESIGN FEATURES CLOSELY RESEMBLE
P.177 DESIGN DEVELOPMENT

AREA RULE WAISTING

BLOWDOWN FLAPS

WING T/C 5%

FULLY POWERED FLYING CONTROLS FORMING PART OF INTEGRATED
FLIGHT SYSTEM

PRINCIPAL DESIGN FEATURES

SECRET

PAGE 16

P.187

SECRET

T.P. 142

The P.187 three-view drawing with annotations, making it plain that the design was effectively a scaled-up P.177. *GKN*

are based directly on wind tunnel information obtained on the SR.53 and P.177. A previous investigation on these aircraft has shown that unless a variable incidence wing is used a tailplane positioned in the wing chordal plane is not practicable." So a low tailplane position was ruled out, meaning "a very high tailplane position is the logical choice".

The P.187's wide fuselage carried both turbojets and rocket engines, most of the fuel, the entire undercarriage, the pressurised crew compartment and most of the electronic equipment. The HTP was kept in tanks positioned directly above the turbojets but the lower tank structure had evidently been carefully designed "against seepage of HTP on to the jet engines".

The engine intake was to be a two-shock wedge type with complete boundary layer removal. The intake's frontal area had been "designed to avoid choking in the transonic region. At supersonic speeds there can be a large spillage drag because the engine does not require all the air that the intake is capable of supplying. To reduce the spillage drag a bypass operating above Mach 1.6 has been incorporated within the centrebody.

"The bypass is in the form of a flush grille on the centrebody just aft of the first enclosed section and is covered by a sliding plate when not in operation. This after-spillage system reduces the spillage drag of the intake by about 40% at Mach 2 at 60,000ft and saves approximately 2200lb of rocket fuel."

Most of the fuselage would be made from aluminium alloys except for the nose radar housing, which would consist of polyester glass cloth laminates. And for the future: "Development of the aircraft to Mach numbers higher than the design value of 2 will be accompanied by the same changes in material as those indicated for the wing, but only for the structure adjacent to the skin." This also applied to the tail unit.

The moving nose mentioned in the 12 points was intended to combine a smoothly streamlined aerodynamic form in flight with clear visibility during landing. Unlike the 'droop nose' proposed by Fairey and already in use on its Delta 2, Saunders-Roe put forward a design where the whole nose slid vertically

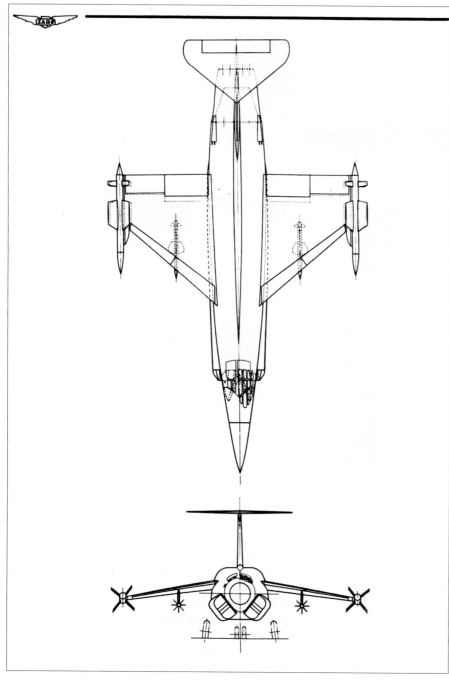

Line drawing from the brochure showing the P.187's unusual mass and features. *GKN*

Saunders-Roe also studied the design with a normal single-seat canopy for the pilot but concluded that the view from the submerged position actually offered a better field of vision for not only the pilot but also the radar operator.

The hydraulic mechanism for sliding the nose downwards was attached directly to the crew cabin's pressurised forward bulkhead. As the nose came down, it would bring down with it a fairing which would otherwise remain hidden beneath the crew cabin floor. This would help to smooth the flow of air into the engine intakes and prevent any disturbance.

The brochure stated that "it may be necessary to provide venting and blow at the forward end of the fairing. Details of the fairing design will be determined by wind tunnel tests at an early date. A scheme for swinging the rear end of the fairing down, to permit access to the crew station from below, is also under development. Alternative access is via a ladder to the pilot's escape hatch". In other words, none of this had yet been designed in detail.

The pilot would use a single lever to control both jet engines, with it being "advanced linearly in the normal way and taken through a gate to bring in the engine reheat. To obtain differential thrust a handle forming an 'L' with the head of the lever is rotated about the lever vertical axis". A similar single throttle was intended to control the two Double Spectre rocket engines. However, any of the six power plants could be controlled separately if necessary. Alternatively, the brochure offered the opportunity to control all jets and rockets from a single throttle control, with the rockets igniting if the lever was moved beyond reheat and "in this way the complete power unit operating pattern could be set in motion by one continuous movement of the throttle. Electronic relays would provide the required

downwards to expose a V-shaped windscreen which extended for the full width of the fuselage. With the nose in the 'up' position, the crew were to be completely submerged within the fully faired forward fuselage.

While the aircraft was flying, "glazing in the upper rear portion of the sliding nose permits some view oblique to the fuselage surface, even when the nose is fully retracted. If direct vision is required at high speed, the sliding nose can be designed permanently to leave exposed a narrow upper segment of the windscreen. Small faired blisters in the escape hatches would then allow the crew to position themselves at heights providing direct forward vision".

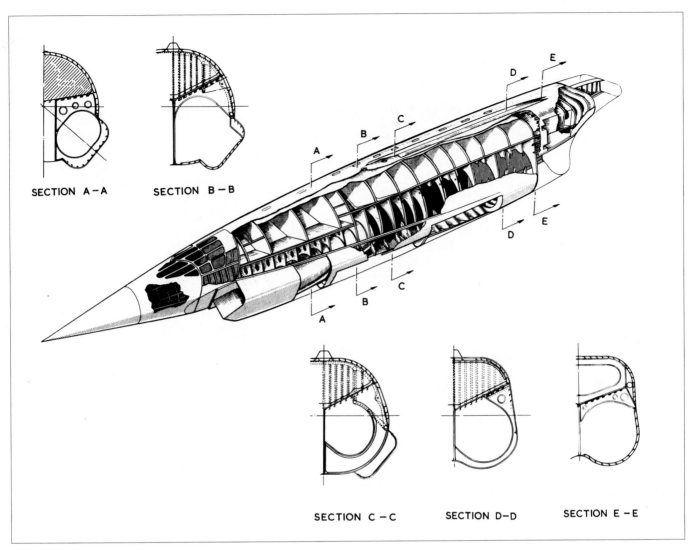

SECTION A – A

SECTION B – B

SECTION C – C

SECTION D–D

SECTION E – E

Internal structure of the P.187's fuselage. *GKN*

time lags for development of the jet and rocket engine cycles".

When it came to escaping from the P.187 in an emergency, the company had at one point studied downward ejection through the nose fairing but the scheme chosen for the brochure was mercifully simpler: "The interim scheme shown employs current stabilised ejection seats in an arrangement especially suitable for a twin-seat cabin.

"Separate escape hatches, each of which jettisons by hinging on its rear edge and moving rearwards and outboard, are employed. The radar operator can escape independently of the pilot, or both crew members can eject together without danger of interference.

Wind tunnel tests to optimise trajectories will be necessary, and it should be possible to make sure that jettison of the radar operator's canopy will not cause undue turbulence in the cockpit which would interfere with the pilot during his subsequent escape."

Weapon options

The P.187 was to carry its two Vickers Red Hebes/Red Deans on its wingtips where they would enjoy "an uninterrupted view". Another reason for putting them there was in order to effect a slight centre of gravity shift towards the rear of the aircraft which, along with other factors, would eliminate "trim effects".

The Blue Jays were carried on underwing pylons not only because that is evidently where de Havilland felt they would be at their most effective, but also because this put them laterally in line with the aircraft's centre of gravity and "sufficiently inboard of the aileron flap junction to minimise aerodynamic interference".

Putting the pylons closer to the fuselage provided a "stiff platform while being sufficiently far from the engine intakes to avoid engine flame out when the weapon is fired. It is known that positions still further inboard, close to the fuselage, would give lower supersonic drag interference and this would be a matter of further study.

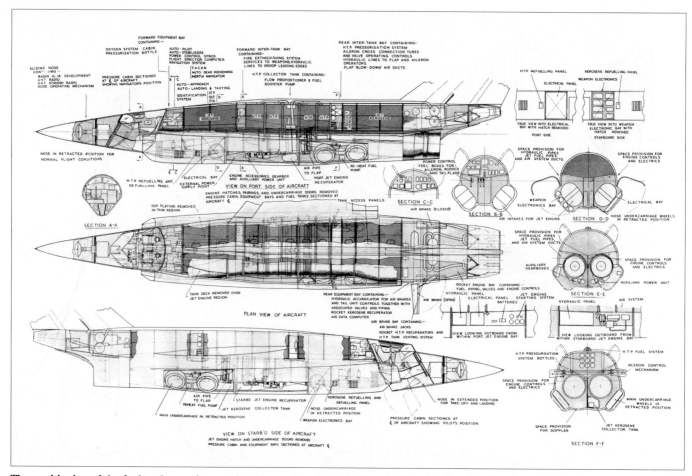

The positioning of the fuel tanks, engines and undercarriage is made clear in this drawing. Putting the rocket fuel tanks above the hot jet engine would have required very careful insulation and sealing to avoid even the slightest chance of seepage. *GKN*

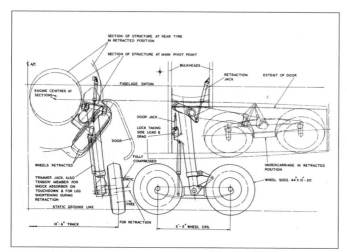

Suitably large wheels and thick legs were necessary for the P.187's main undercarriage. *GKN*

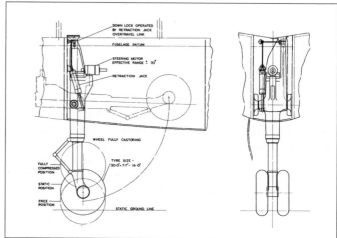

The P.187's jet engines were positioned centrally but with easy access from beneath via large hatches. *GKN*

"It would necessitate some signalling from the radar nose to the Blue Jay head to cover the period between initial launch and the attainment of full vision".

The Blue Jays would be cooled using a system within the fuselage but it was thought the Red Hebes might need cold air units installing in the wingtips. Unusually, owing to "the close tolerances between the weapon and the rails carrying it", the missiles would be attached to their pylons first, then the pylon/missile combination would be loaded on to the aircraft.

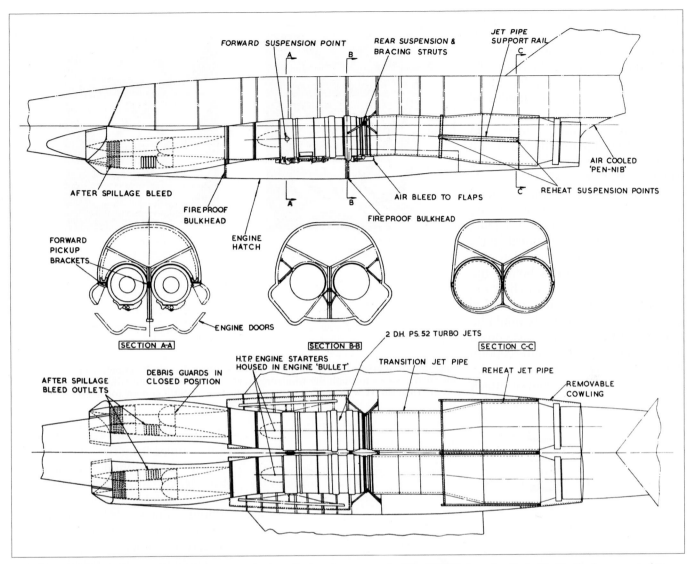

A pair of Double Spectre rocket motors were to be installed at the very end of the P.187's long fuselage. It effectively amounted to provision of four hugely powerful rockets. *GKN*

Saunders-Roe accepted that radar-guided missiles were always likely to be larger than those using infrared guidance but "on the other hand, US experience with the MX.1179 (Hughes) project, and Falcon missiles, admittedly under less stringent conditions, suggests that actual strikes occur considerably more frequently than 'miss distance' calculations might suggest".

Part of the reason for the radar missile being larger was due to its larger warhead – a compensation for the likelihood of a greater 'miss distance'. But if the calculations proved to be inaccurate then the radar missile could accept a smaller warhead and the overall size of the weapon could be reduced.

"Thus," the brochure went on, "the development of weapons, having the two types of homing, but more equally matched in size and weight may be practical. Alternatively two types of guidance might be provided in one, rather large, missile. The serious problem of reliability at present demands the carriage of two weapons of the same type. Here again the situation should improve. The Saunders-Roe Company, believing that air-to-air weapons may get larger, is here proposing an aircraft that has the

development capacity necessary to take maximum advantage of this."

The P.187 was designed to carry a substantial military load, the size of the aircraft having been increased to allow this, and there were certainly indications at the time that air-to-air missiles might increase in size – the faster aircraft could fly, the more propellant missiles might need to carry in order to catch up with them. But set against the designs submitted by the other F.155T competitors, Saunders-Roe was clearly following a different path.

The double attack
Carrying two infrared and two radar

guided missiles, in theory, gave the P.187 more tactical potential during an interception than its single-missile-type competitors. As other firms had done, Saunders-Roe presented some examples of how the aircraft might be operated in practice. These were an interception against a Mach 1.3 target at 60,000ft, and against a Mach 3 target at 70,000ft.

For the former, it was assumed that the enemy bomber was flying directly towards Britain's coastline, it was detected 200 nautical miles out and there was an administrative delay of three minutes before the P.187's engines were switched on. For a pursuit course attack with Blue Jays, a total of 45 seconds would be needed for the P.187 to chase down its quarry and the interception would be made 53 miles from the coast. In a collision course attack with radar weapons, "developed

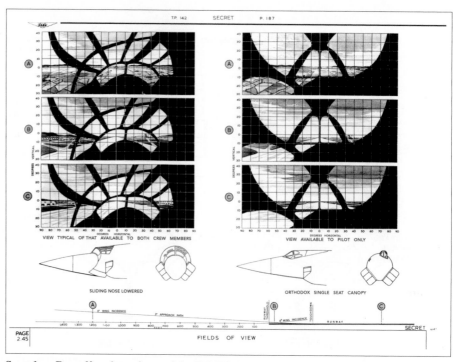

Saunders-Roe offered no views of the P.187's internal cockpit arrangement, only alternative views through the windscreen. On the left is the view with the nose lowered, on the right the view through a conventional static cockpit canopy for the pilot only. *GKN*

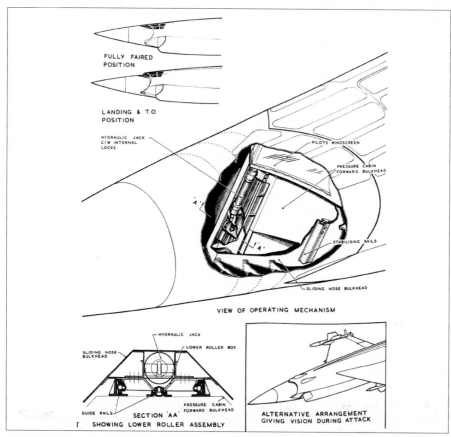

A third cockpit arrangement is shown to the bottom right of this brochure drawing – a thin slit windscreen with a couple of Perspex blisters on the top of the fuselage for when better visibility was necessary. *GKN*

Red Dean" missiles could make the kill 73 miles from the coast.

The third option presented for the Mach 1.3/60,000ft case was described by Saunders-Roe as the 'double attack': "After completing a beam attack with collision course weapons enough fuel remains to continue a turn parallel to the target course and complete another 45 second level flight at Mach 20. However, at the end of the second 90° turn the fighter is on a parallel course to the target, 11 nautical miles on the beam and slightly ahead. At this point the fighter is out of AI contact and any continuation of the manoeuvre at Mach 2 places it ahead of the target.

"It is therefore suggested that during the first turn on to a beam attack, the fighter should decelerate to near target speed which will allow the interceptions to be made further out, and in the second turn will place the fighter on a parallel track near, and to the rear of, the target, and in a position to make a second attack with pursuit course weapons. Detailed investigations of this manoeuvre show that the first attack can be made 70 miles from the coast and the second 50 miles from the coast."

No other company offered the opportunity to attack more than one target during an interception – in fact several of them believed such a thing was impossible.

The other thought-to-be-impossible task Saunders-Roe believed to be possible was the Mach 3 target interception. The brochure said: "The aircraft presented in this brochure has been specifically designed to the very stringent requirements of Appendix 8 of Specification F.155.

"These requirements are so well matched that it has been possible to design a near optimum aircraft that will only just fall within their boundaries. However one of the particular advantages of a mixed unit aircraft is the versatility afforded by varying the HTP to kerosene ratio."

Saunders-Roe suggested that an HTP to kerosene ratio of 2:1 would allow maximum performance – Mach 3.5 at 70,000ft – during severe short warning interceptions: "Assuming the development of a head-on collision course weapon, and an extension of the early warning range to 230 nautical miles such an aircraft could defend an 80 mile front against a Mach 3 target at 70,000ft, given a three minute administration delay time, and would be capable of intercepting it at about 42 miles from the coastline. It is worth noting that the entire interception performance must not take longer than five minutes."

In effect, the P.187 would become more rocket interceptor than jet fighter. It was heady stuff but assumed that the aircraft could handle speeds up to Mach 3.5, which it couldn't, even if the whole "interception performance" took less than five minutes.

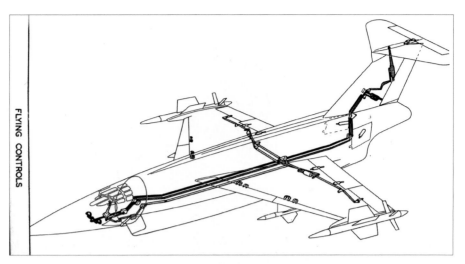

Arrangement of the P.187's flight controls. *GKN*

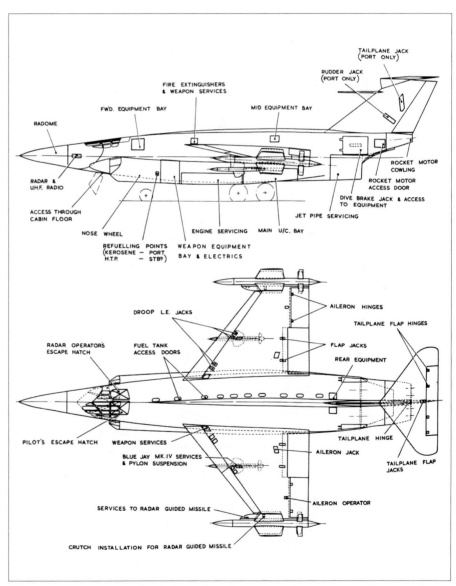

With so much housed in the fuselage, Saunders-Roe was keen to show that everything could be accessed as required without undue difficulty. *GKN*

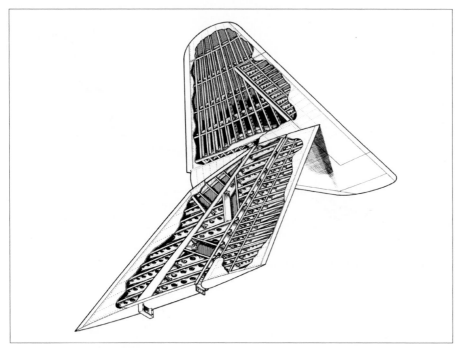

Structure of the P.187's tail unit, its design based on wind tunnel experience gleaned from the SR.53 and P.177 programmes. *GKN*

Production schedule
Unlike most of its competitors, Saunders-Roe declined to offer any actual dates for the detailed design and production of its tendered project. Instead, it calculated the number of hours everything was expected to take: "The work estimated to be necessary for draughtsmen and loftsmen, up to the completion of the prototype design, together with allowances for mock-ups, models, tests, leave and sickness, amounts to 29,700 gross man/weeks.

"The standard of drawing allowed for in the design estimate would be suitable generally for the manufacture of both prototype and production aircraft. An additional allowance to make all the drawings suitable for production purposes is, therefore, only necessary for detail

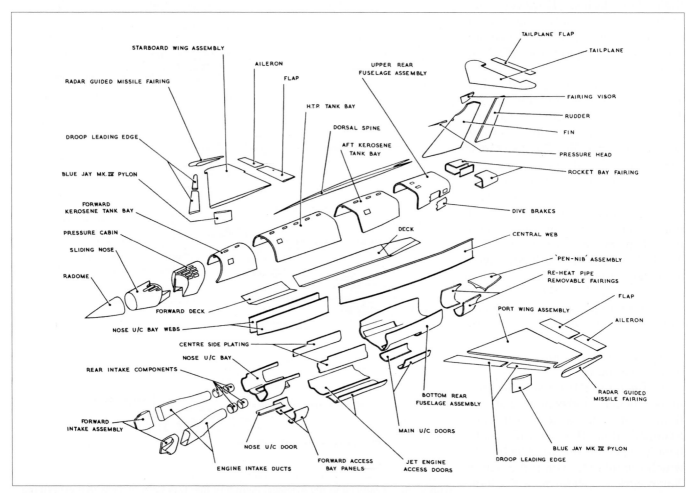

A remarkable number of subassemblies and structures were necessary for the P.187. *GKN*

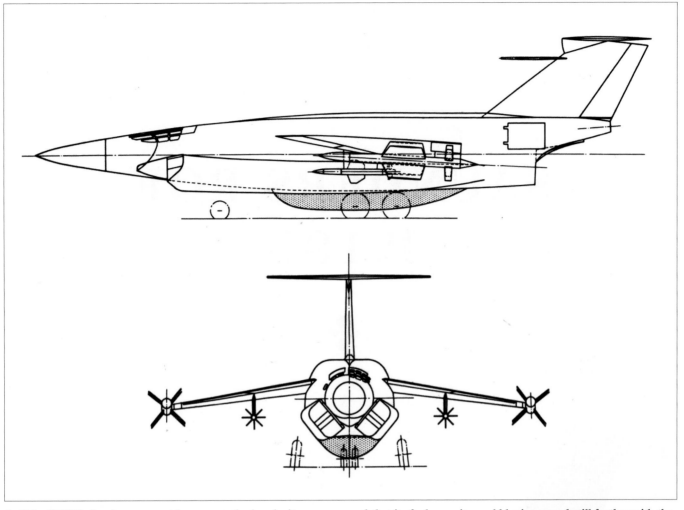

As if the P.187's fuselage was not large enough already, it was proposed that its fuel capacity could be increased still further with the addition of a large belly tank. *GKN*

changes and is estimated to be 6000 man weeks. The estimated time from the receipt of the Indication To Proceed to a) the completion of the design is 260 weeks. b) The first flight of the prototype is 200 weeks.

"Depending on the date of receipt of Indication To Proceed and in accordance with our present programme, additional drawing office staff to the extent of some 30 men will be needed to meet the estimates given. The estimated work necessary to design the prototype jigs and tools, which will be qualitatively suitable for production orders amounts to 60,000 man hours. The estimated work necessary to design the additional jigs and tools required for manufacture under a reasonable

production order amounts to 75,000 man hours."

For an order of 50 aircraft, it was estimated that on average each aircraft would take 253,000 man hours to build. An order of 100 would equate to 205,000 hours per aircraft, 250 would be 167,000 and 750 would be 106,500.

Taken as a whole, the P.187 could be seen as the ultimate answer to the problem of providing the ultimate interceptor. Alternatively, it could just as easily be seen as a giant leap into the unknown, given the technological problems that would need to be overcome if it was to enter service with the RAF by 1962. There was a third way of looking at it: as an expensive disaster waiting to happen. It was physically huge,

with the potential for devastating performance, but it was based on the SR.53 and its larger sibling the P.177. And not even the SR.53's first prototype had yet taken flight.

Choosing the P.187 over the other designs would have been a monumental risk and perhaps Saunders-Roe had some inkling that this was the case, therefore taking the design as far as possible in order to demonstrate a capacity for innovation and a desire for boundary-pushing performance. However it might have been viewed, there can be no doubt that the P.187 represented a dramatic gesture on Saunders-Roe's part.

SAUNDERS-ROE
P.187

October 1955

Artwork by Luca Landino

— *Specification* —

Crew: Two **Length:** 83ft 6in
Wingspan: 51ft 7in **Height:** 24.66ft
Wing area: 860sq ft **Empty weight:** 54,700lb
Loaded weight: 97,000lb
Powerplant: 2 x de Havilland Gyron plus 4 x
de Havilland Double Spectre rocket motors
Maximum speed: Mach 3.5 (structural limit
Mach 2.5, fuel limit Mach 3)
Service ceiling: 76,000ft
Armament: 2 x Vickers Red Dean
(capability to also carry 2 x Blue Jay)

13

SOUND EFFECTS

Vickers-Armstrongs (Supermarine) Type 559

A high-performance interceptor was going to need rocket
motors and advanced turbojets – but firing both together
was likely to create severe noise and vibration. Vickers
believed that this might result in a serious risk to the
aircraft and tried to design accordingly. The result was
unconventional to say the least.

Unlike its competitors, Vickers used a photograph of a model as its opening illustration. Just barely visible on the side of the fuselage is its fictitious and never-allocated serial: VA559. *BAE Systems*

After years of prototype development, Vickers-Armstrongs' Supermarine Works was preparing for the first flight of its prototype Type 544 as the finishing touches were being applied to its F.155T submission. The company had been working on jet fighter designs since the end of the Second World War and felt by 1955 that it was uniquely qualified to meet the necessary requirements.

However, during the design process the Vickers team identified what they believed to be a worrying problem – the effect of the soundwaves produced by high-powered engines. The company designers were so concerned about noise vibrations that they specifically gave the aircraft a highly unusual layout to mitigate the damage which, they thought, might otherwise be caused.

The firm's brochure stated: "The aircraft performance requirements have demanded a mixed power plant of large size, the thrust of the jet engines being augmented at high speed by reheat and at high altitude by rocket motors. These high thrusts have influenced the form of the aircraft.

"Recent experience has already suggested that airframe structure and equipment adjacent to jet nozzles may suffer damage from noise and other high frequency vibrations. The noise level has been estimated to be very much higher with these later and more powerful engines, particularly with reheat, and there appears to be a serious danger that structure in the sound wake of the jets of both turbine and rocket would suffer serious damage.

"This view has the unqualified support of the engine manufacturers.

If it is accepted, there can be only one possible position for propelling nozzles, namely, at the extreme aft end of the aeroplane. Several alternative layouts have been examined with this feature in common. It was found that layouts of orthodox form tended to be tail-heavy unless the engines themselves were separated from the nozzle and reheat sections and moved forward to about amidships, in which case the whole afterbody of the fuselage became 'hot' and practically useless for the accommodation of fuel and/or equipment. Estimates indicated that such arrangements would be very heavy."

Vickers thought the best way around this was to adopt a 'canard' layout, effectively putting foreplanes ahead of the main wing rather than tailplanes behind it. This resulted "in a compact power plant installation free from noise troubles and well-placed from the point of view of the fire risk. Being a compact arrangement it is also light. The 'canard' arrangement has the further merit that the foreplane contributes substantially to the lift of the aircraft, whereas the tailplane of the more orthodox form does the reverse.

"Thus less load is carried by the wing and fuselage, and the wing is smaller. The resultant total weight saving on power plant, fuel and structure is large compared with the Military Load carried. By implication, a conventional aeroplane, if feasible at all, would need to be several times as large as a 'canard' for the same performance."

With a starting point of the canard layout, Vickers then had to decide which engines to fit, how many engines to fit, how to fit them, and how to split the thrust output needed between turbojets and rocket motors. According to the brochure: "Design studies have been made with a large number of different power plant arrangements, including non-reheat engines and

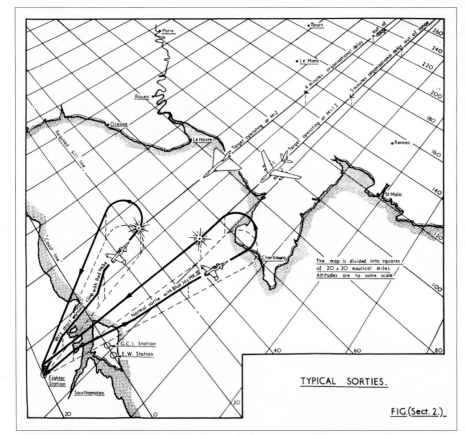

This drawing graphically shows how the Type 559, armed with either the Red Hebe or Blue Jay, would have tackled approaching supersonic raiders – head-on with the former and chasing with the latter. *BAE Systems*

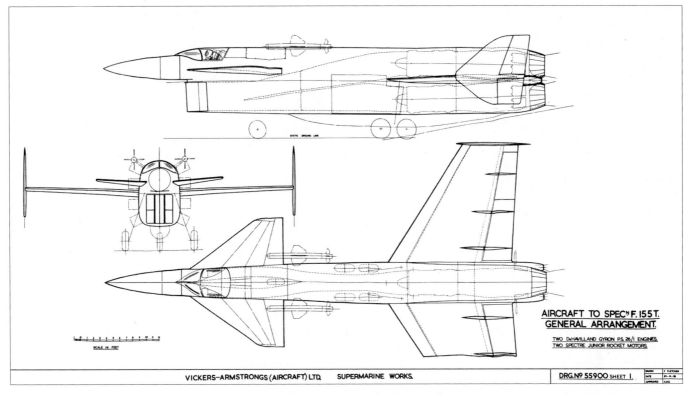

AIRCRAFT TO SPEC° F.155 T.
GENERAL ARRANGEMENT.

TWO DeHAVILLAND GYRON PS.26/1 ENGINES.
TWO SPECTRE JUNIOR ROCKET MOTORS.

SCALE IN FEET

VICKERS-ARMSTRONGS (AIRCRAFT) LTD.   SUPERMARINE WORKS.   DRG. N° 55900 SHEET 1.

The Vickers-Armstrongs Type 559's radical form appears less strange to modern eyes than it must have done in 1955 – apart from the lack of a central fin and stacked engines its layout is not too dissimilar from that of the Eurofighter Typhoon. *BAE Systems*

multiple small engines, but it has been found that two large reheated engines of approximately 27,000lb sea level static thrust each (reheat on), and rockers giving a total thrust of 10,000lb at sea level, provide the optimum arrangement for this project."

The selection was narrowed down to three likely candidates: "The de Havilland Gyron PS.26-1, the Rolls-Royce RB.122 and an Armstrong-Siddeley 172F uprated by about 15% would all be suitable for this application. When considered on an installed thrust-drag basis over the whole sortie, the differences between them are not large.

"Since the Gyron is in a more advanced state, and has the greatest development potential, it has been chosen as the basic engine for the purpose of this tender. The de Havilland Spectre Junior rocket motor will be uprated to 5000lb sea level thrust before 1962, and two of these rockets have been assumed. Two Napier N. R. E. 20 rockets also

uprated to 5000lb sea level thrust, could be fitted as an alternative with little change in the quoted figures." With two Gyrons in mind, Vickers had assessed both fuselage and wing-mounting. The wing-mounted layout apparently had "some very attractive features" but the intakes would not be clear of the foreplane wake and a single-engine failure on take-off would result in uncontrollable swing. As a result, the engines went into the fuselage. But should they be fitted side-by-side or one on top of the other? The latter resulted in "a more efficient intake position for a given frontal area" so the Type 559 ended up with canards and a tall narrow fuselage to boot.

Structure

The Type 559 had thin wings which were a compromise "between aerodynamic and structural requirements. The structure is of the type commonly described as 'lobster-claw' and contains a

large proportion of the fuel. They would be made mostly from light alloy but "the drooped leading edge nose box will be subject to rain erosion in addition to a fairly high temperature. It is proposed, therefore, that this part should be constructed in titanium alloy". The foreplanes would also be light alloy but with a titanium skin on the leading edge.

Rather than a single central fin, the Type 559 had a pair of wingtip fins. According to Vickers: "Investigations have suggested that fins and rudders in the normal position on the fuselage would be unsatisfactory and in some circumstances actually destabilising."

The undercarriage was housed in the fuselage on either side of the engines' air intake ducting and the main wheels arrangement gave a track of 10ft 8in. The conventional nosewheel simply retracted straight back without twisting. All three parts of the tricycle undercarriage

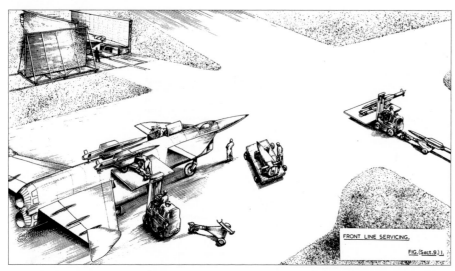

Type 559s being serviced on the front line. The nose cone was designed to be easily removed and replaced. *BAE Systems*

would have brakes since "trials with a Swift aircraft have shown that this system is 25% more effective than main wheels alone".

The fuselage would be made in four sections, the largest bit being a semi-monocoque structure 35ft long which contained half the kerosene and all the HTP fuel, the main undercarriage and the Gyrons. The forward section was 16ft long and contained the cockpit, most of the equipment, the foreplane actuating gear and the nose undercarriage. The other two pieces were the radar nose unit, and a tail fairing for the reheat units and rocket motors. Both of these last two parts could be taken off quickly for access or replacement.

The nose unit was to be made of neoprene coated fibreglass laminate, about 0.4in thick. Within it, the AI radar was packaged into a cooled and pressurised unit. Inside the crew compartment, the pilot and radar operator sat next to one another, with the latter's seat set 9in further back to "ensure shoulder clearance within a minimum enclosed width". Each had a normal ejection seat and wore a pressure jerkin. Vickers' own pilots had said that a sliding canopy was "of no value on an aircraft of this type. They would prefer to depend on 100% reliability of the demisting, anti-icing, and rain clearance systems. A clamshell canopy is considered to provide the maximum reliability in jettisoning".

The forward section of the fuselage was also home to one of the Type 559's most advanced features – its variable geometry wedge intake: "The wedge itself

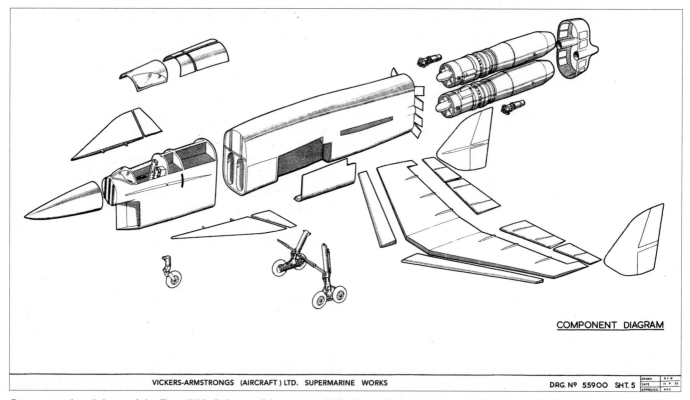

COMPONENT DIAGRAM

VICKERS-ARMSTRONGS (AIRCRAFT) LTD. SUPERMARINE WORKS   DRG. No 55900 SHT. 5

Component breakdown of the Type 559. It is possible to see, within the cockpit, how the pilot's seat on the left is set slightly further forward than that of the radar operator to provide additional shoulder room. *BAE Systems*

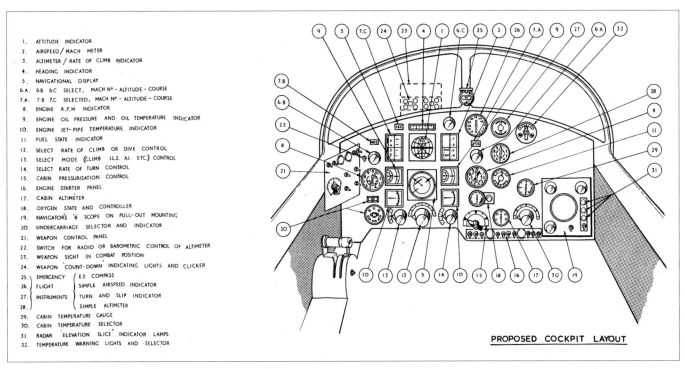

1. ATTITUDE INDICATOR
2. AIRSPEED / MACH METER
3. ALTIMETER / RATE OF CLIMB INDICATOR
4. HEADING INDICATOR
5. NAVIGATIONAL DISPLAY
6.A. 6B 6C SELECT, MACH Nº - ALTITUDE - COURSE
7.A. 7.B 7.C SELECTED, MACH Nº - ALTITUDE - COURSE
8. ENGINE R.P.M INDICATOR
9. ENGINE OIL PRESSURE AND OIL TEMPERATURE INDICATOR
10. ENGINE JET-PIPE TEMPERATURE INDICATOR
11. FUEL STATE INDICATOR
12. SELECT RATE OF CLIMB OR DIVE CONTROL
13. SELECT MODE (CLIMB I.L.S. A.I. ETC.) CONTROL
14. SELECT RATE OF TURN CONTROL
15. CABIN PRESSURISATION CONTROL
16. ENGINE STARTER PANEL
17. CABIN ALTIMETER
18. OXYGEN STATE AND CONTROLLER
19. NAVIGATOR'S 'b' SCOPE ON PULL-OUT MOUNTING
20. UNDERCARRIAGE SELECTOR AND INDICATOR
21. WEAPON CONTROL PANEL
22. SWITCH FOR RADIO OR BAROMETRIC CONTROL OF ALTIMETER
23. WEAPON SIGHT IN COMBAT POSITION
24. WEAPON 'COUNT-DOWN' INDICATING LIGHTS AND CLICKER
25. EMERGENCY   E2 COMPASS
26. FLIGHT   SIMPLE AIRSPEED INDICATOR
27. INSTRUMENTS   TURN AND SLIP INDICATOR
28.   SIMPLE ALTIMETER
29. CABIN TEMPERATURE GAUGE
30. CABIN TEMPERATURE SELECTOR
31. RADAR ELEVATION SLICE INDICATOR LAMPS
32. TEMPERATURE WARNING LIGHTS AND ·SELECTOR

PROPOSED COCKPIT LAYOUT

Arrangement of the Type 559's instrument panel. *BAE Systems*

comprises two portions. The forward portion is fixed while the second consists of hinged plates which are automatically adjusted to give the optimum ramp angle as determined by flight and engine conditions.

"These plates are faired into the nose undercarriage housing by means of flexible walls, the mechanism being operated hydraulically. Auxiliary intakes will be positioned immediately aft of the intake lips for use during ground running and take-off."

The weapon system

Like Fairey and Armstrong-Whitworth, Vickers offered a weapons system which could accommodate either Blue Jay Mk.4 or Vickers' own Red Hebe. But as might be expected, where most of the other companies believed that Blue Jay was the weapon of choice, Vickers had only good things to say about Red Hebe.

The brochure said: "When carrying two Blue Jay Mk.4 weapons, the aircraft achieves the specified performance and the kill is made at more than 40 nautical miles from the coast line, even after a stern chase. When two Red Hebe are carried, the higher weapon performance more than compensates for the reduction in aircraft performance due to the increased weapon size. A target operating at Mach 2 at 60,000ft can be intercepted effectively at more than 30 nautical miles out to sea. A change of weapon type can be completed in two hours."

Armed with Blue Jays and about to face a Mach 1.3 target at 60,000ft, the Type 559 would already be "at an operational readiness platform at the end of the runway (assumed to be 20 nautical miles inland). Some equipment will have to be operated continually while at readiness, so as to be immediately available for take-off. Ground power services, e.g. electrical and air conditioning, will be required at the platform. The aircraft will be carrying an auxiliary tank in the ventral position, filled with turbine fuel or HTP."

When the order to scramble was given, if the situation gave 'normal warning' the auxiliary tank would be "dropped into a cradle immediately after pressing the engine starter buttons". Five minutes was allowed for the order being given and the tank being sorted. As the engines fired up, the target would be just 158 nautical miles off the coast.

At five minutes 20 seconds, the Type 559 would be wheels rolling, reheat lit and taking off. Thirty seconds later it would be wheels up, turning, climbing and accelerating to Mach 0.9 at about 1000ft. In another 30 seconds, the aircraft would be pulling 3g, holding Mach 0.9 and climbing initially at a rate of more than 50,000ft per minute.

One minute and 14 seconds later, at 36,000ft, the pilot would begin accelerating up to Mach 2. At 45,000ft the aircraft would "zoom climb to reach Mach 2.2 at 60,000ft" – but the pilot was no longer in control. Ten minutes and 25 seconds from the warning being given, the aircraft was 35 nautical miles out over the sea and being guided by ground control intercept (GCI) radar.

The target was 91 nautical miles away from the coast and the Type 559 was about to give chase. At 11 minutes 40 seconds GCI would begin a 180° turn at Mach 2.2, pulling 2.25g. One minute and 25 seconds later, the enemy bomber was 58 nautical miles from the coast with the Type 559 five miles behind and closing, its AI now locked on target.

Thirty-four seconds later and two miles behind the target, the pilot would fire his two Blue Jays. Eight seconds later: "Kill. Target is now 49 nautical miles from the coast and the interceptor will have opened the air-brakes or broken off the attack, losing speed to Mach 1.5. With the above pessimistic assumptions it will be noted that a kill can be achieved at more than 40 miles out to sea over more than 180 miles of coastline." Thirty minutes and 16 seconds after take-off, the interceptor was back on the ground.

Operating with Red Hebe, however, offered a number of benefits: "The Red Hebe can be used in a similar manner to the Blue Jay weapon, but has the advantage of allowing attack anywhere in the target's forward hemisphere. Under these conditions the speed of the bomber becomes of less importance, since the fighter does not need to turn through 180° or undertake a stern chase. Further, the effectiveness of jamming by the target is reduced, since no difficult choice of the fighter's time-to-turn has to be made."

Using a collision course attack would mean that the Type 559 would need an improved guidance system: "At this stage the use of Lock Follow Ground Radars appears more attractive. The aircraft then becomes a beam rider; the equipment carried in the aircraft becomes simpler and is reduced in weight.

For Red Hebe, seemingly, there would only be an administrative delay of four minutes to engine start. But that wasn't the only way in which Vickers moved the goalposts. The interceptor was now up against a Soviet bomber doing Mach 2 at 60,000ft – just to really show what the big radar-guided weapon could do. Wheels up was at four minutes 55 seconds, the start of acceleration to Mach 2 at 36,000ft began at six minutes 34 seconds. Two minutes and seven seconds later, the Type 559 was at 60,000ft doing Mach 2 with GCI in control. The target was 54 miles from the coast and about to be picked up by the interceptor's AI – 75% chance of a lock-on at 23 miles away.

Fifty-six seconds later, with the two aircraft heading directly towards one another on full power at Mach 2: "Weapons launched. The target is now at 36 nautical miles from the coast, six nautical miles ahead of the interceptor. The weapon will have locked on to the target prior to release." Eight seconds later: "Kill. Target is now 34 nautical miles from the coast and the interceptor will have opened the air-brakes and broken off the attack. Note that the angular deviation achieved will be small and there is no fear of the AI failing to illuminate the target for the semi-active weapon up to the kill." The interceptor was back on the ground just 25 minutes and 44 seconds after the warning was given.

Vickers noted: "It will be seen that the above sortie is well within the capabilities of the aircraft." And: "As would be expected, interception with Red Hebe against targets operating at Mach 1.3 at 60,000ft gives considerable improvement in kill distance from the coast even with five minutes organisational delay. It is still necessary to increase the radar range or to reduce the delay time in order to exploit the interceptor's range fully."

However, each weapon – Red Hebe or Blue Jay – had only a 50% probability of making a kill "including the probability of remaining serviceable from ground check until firing of warhead". Vickers gave the 'possible' probability of achieving a kill, not allowing for pilot and radar operator errors, as a slightly unnerving 51%. The pessimistic probability of achieving a kill was just 19%.

Building the 559

Vickers set out a very detailed timetable for designing, building, testing and finally bringing the Type 559 to full production. It was also careful to add a few caveats along the way: "When considering the production of aircraft in quantity it should be borne in mind that instructions a) to purchase difficult materials and b) to proceed with the manufacturing of tools would be required at least three and a half years ahead of the date of commencement of deliveries. This should be followed up after not more than six months with the complete instruction to proceed with the manufacture of the aircraft."

Assuming the go-ahead was given, Vickers had planned a programme of physical equipment testing using existing types while the Type 559 was being worked on: "The firm is approved by Ministry of Supply for flight testing and a number of aspects of clearance for service use are delegated to us by A&AEE. In order to reduce the time of clearance of other items – particularly the missile and radar systems – to a minimum, combined programmes would be arranged with the interested parties e.g. A&AEE, RAE, missile firms etc. as is being done in the case of the Swift, to avoid duplication of tests.

"Preliminary work on the radar systems and on the missiles themselves would be carried out on test bed aircraft such as Canberra, Valiant, Javelin or P.1, as soon as the equipment is available for flight testing."

According to the timetable summary: "The following dates for this programme should be achieved assuming that a contract is received in March 1956 and that the large amount of design work by

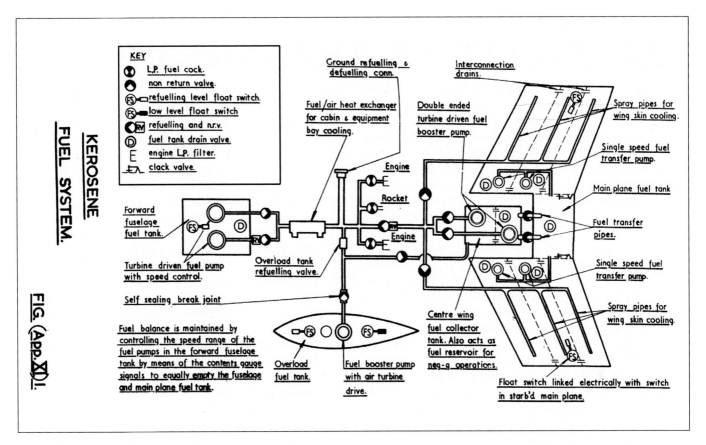

KEY

- L.P. fuel cock.
- non return valve.
- refuelling level float switch.
- low level float switch.
- refuelling and n.r.v.
- fuel tank drain valve.
- E engine L.P. filter.
- clack valve.

KEROSENE FUEL SYSTEM.

FIG (App. XI) 1.

Forward fuselage fuel tank.

Turbine driven fuel pump with speed control.

Self sealing break joint

Fuel balance is maintained by controlling the speed range of the fuel pumps in the forward fuselage tank by means of the contents gauge signals to equally empty the fuselage and main plane fuel tank.

Overload fuel tank.

Fuel booster pump with air turbine drive.

Ground refuelling & defuelling conn.

Fuel/air heat exchanger for cabin & equipment bay cooling.

Engine

Rocket

Engine

Overload tank refuelling valve.

Double ended turbine driven fuel booster pump.

Centre wing fuel collector tank. Also acts as fuel reservoir for neg-g operations.

Interconnection drains.

Spray pipes for wing skin cooling.

Single speed fuel transfer pump.

Main plane fuel tank

Fuel transfer pipes.

Single speed fuel transfer pump.

Spray pipes for wing skin cooling.

Float switch linked electrically with switch in starb'd main plane.

then completed will not be negated by changes in the specification for the aircraft or other major weapon system components.

"If a firm contract for development aircraft is not placed until later than March 1956, all dates will be later by about the same amount. The necessity of ordering materials and tools at least three and a half years before aircraft delivery is also emphasised.

"A partially equipped shell will fly in March 1959 and some evaluation by visiting A&AEE pilots should occur before the end of that year. During 1960 handling trials with and without missiles will be completed and by December 1960 two aircraft will be flying in Australia on combined aircraft and missile development trials. Service personnel will have been trained by Vickers-Armstrongs (Aircraft) Ltd in order to take part in these trials. This will facilitate the rapid achievement of an operational standard by squadrons engaged on

ABOVE and BELOW: Charts showing details of the aircraft's fuel system. *BAE Systems*

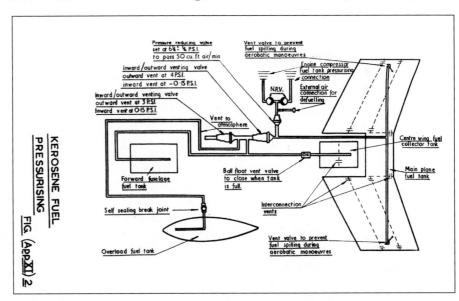

KEROSENE FUEL PRESSURISING FIG (App XI) 2

weapon system acceptance trials during 1962."

Vickers followed a risky strategy with the Type 559. It pointed out a problem that none of the other manufacturers had felt would pose any serious difficulty – at least one of them had investigated it

and dismissed it after consulting American sources – and then proposed a radical solution involving unusual aerodynamic features. As with Saunders-Roe and its massive P.187, it is hard to know whether Vickers genuinely felt that it had a reasonable chance of success.

ALTERNATIVE ARRANGEMENTS

Aware of how unusual the Type 559 looked, Vickers explained in detail how it had come to decide on that particular layout. It gave 15 examples of layouts that had been studied in some detail, dividing them up into three groups: Group A were 'conventional', Group B were 'canard' and Group C were 'tailless', although there was only one design given in the latter. All were examined with the following in mind: "It is considered that the noise associated with the required engine powers would seriously damage any structure lying within a 120° included angle rear cone from the reheat nozzles. Damage could also be expected anywhere behind the plane of the nozzles and they must therefore be placed well aft."

In Group A, layout A2 was preferred to A1 because its undercarriage was mounted in the forward end of the nacelle, resulting in lower weight and drag. But then A2 was dropped because "the high tailplane was expected to give unacceptable pitch-up characteristics unless wing leading-edge sweep became very small" and the jet noise would damage the rear fuselage and tail unit.

Regarding layouts A3, A4, A5 and A6: "These double or triple boom layouts attempted to solve

the noise problem by moving the reheat units aft while retaining a nacelle type engine mounting. In general, their weight and drag were excessive, even when the effects of airframe flexibility were neglected and calculations based on optimistic assumptions showed that up to 30% increase in structure weight would be required.

"When allowing for engines and fuel suitable for the A2 layout at 55,000lb, but not allowing for stiffening, the weight of A4 was estimated at 65,000lb. The structure accounted for nearly 40% of the all-up weight, although the stressing conditions adopted were expected to make this figure about 30% (and have done so on the layout finally chosen).

"The profile drag of these layouts varied between 40% and 50% in excess of that for the chosen design B6 and the engine power considered in the above weight estimates was therefore insufficient. In consequence it proved impossible to approach the specified performance with this type of layout."

Layouts A7 and A8 were also rejected as too heavy and too draggy. In general: "After A1 and A2 had been discarded, (mainly because of jet noise considerations) none of the remaining conventional layouts had a satisfactory tail volume coefficient

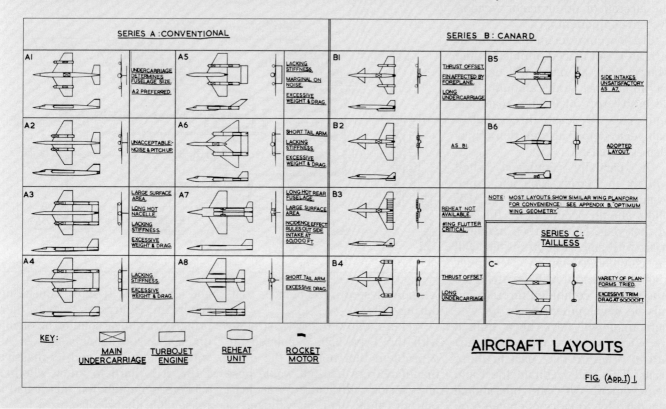

while at the same time avoiding the penalties of a long hot rear fuselage or nacelle."

The company evidently began studying the canard layout "for its low drag at supersonic speeds, but it was found later that this type of aircraft avoided noise and balance problems". B1 and B2 were rejected mainly due to thrust offset problems connected to the wake effects of the foreplanes.

B3 was to be powered by 12 Rolls-Royce RB.121 engines but these "would be unsatisfactory without reheat, which would cause considerable extra complication. The amount of stiffening required to clear wing flutter is large, due to the aft position of the engines. These considerations led to layout B4".

Vickers liked B4 and pitted it directly against layout B6 – the eventual winner. According to the brochure: "Both this layout and B6 were studied using an analogue computer to predict roll yaw instability. Although both layouts could be made satisfactory, B4 would have to be stressed for considerably larger angles of yaw during rolls. The rolling control was also expected to be touchy on B4 and artificial damping in roll would most likely be required.

"The four wheeled undercarriage necessary on B4 is not favoured as it requires either long undercarriage legs or heavy outriggers." And the foreplane wake would interfere with the engines too – but there was no real difference in performance between B4 and B6. It was the combination of niggling small difficulties which finished off the B4.

B5 – featuring side-by-side fuselage-mounted engines – was likewise compared against B6 but the latter's under-fuselage intake "with sharp intake lips, required for good supersonic performance" would apparently have given better performance at high angles of incidence.

Lastly, the single tailless layout shown was just one of a number of tailless layouts "studied in varying amounts of detail". However, none of them lived up to expectations due to high trim drag at high altitude. In conclusion, B6 won and Vickers noted: "The canard layout is shown to offer the best compromise and has therefore been adopted."

VICKERS-ARMSTRONGS SUPERMARINE WORKS TYPE 559

October 1955

Artwork by Luca Landino

— *Specification* —

Crew: Two **Length:** 68ft 3in **Wingspan:** 42ft **Height:** 15ft 6in
Wing area: 615sq ft **Empty weight:** 41,485lb **Loaded weight:** 59,765lb
Powerplant: 2 x de Havilland Gyron plus 2 x de Havilland Spectre Junior rocket motors
Maximum speed: Mach 2.5 **Service ceiling:** 65,000ft
Armament: 2 x de Havilland Blue Jay Mk.4

14

ALL-WEATHER OUTSIDER

Avro CF-105

The Hawker Siddeley Group owned two of the seven
companies competing directly for F.155T – Hawker and
Armstrong Whitworth – but A V Roe Canada, a third HSG
firm, was also working on an aircraft which it was thought
might just meet the specification: the Avro CF-105.

Immediately after the Second World War, the Canadian government decided that a two-seater twin-jet all-weather fighter was needed which was suitable for operations in the harsh conditions it was likely to encounter in service with the Royal Canadian Air Force.

A V Roe Canada (Avro) was given a contract to build the straight-winged CF-100, powered by engines made by the same company's gas turbine division. But even before this aircraft's first flight, the company's design team began to look at ways of improving it. A swept wing configuration was studied in July 1948 and the following year efforts commenced to design a supersonic version of the CF-100. The CF-100D of July 1949 was in fact a design for a completely different aircraft – its two engines were to be stacked one on top of the other within the rear fuselage, fed by side intakes, and it had larger, broader wings.

The first straight-wing CF-100 prototype made its flight debut on January 19, 1950, and before the year was out Avro felt it had carried out sufficient research to be able to offer the government the swept wing version – redesignated the CF-103 in January 1951. It was believed that this re-winged design, retaining most of the original fuselage, would be capable of supersonic flight during a shallow dive. For Avro, the CF-103 would only ever be an interim measure, however. The company had ambitious plans to develop a new advanced fighter with a nose intake and the same stacked engine configuration from 1949 – the CF-104. Over a two-year period, the CF-104 project grew to encompass numerous different fighter designs and configurations. The delta wing layout came to be a common theme.

Meanwhile, the Canadian government had ordered two CF-103 prototypes and a static test aircraft. Wind tunnel testing and tool design was under way by February 1951 – aiming for a first flight date of July 1952. By June 1951, jigs and tools were being made but a new first flight date was set for July 1953 to allow more time for analysis of test data. At this point, work on

Arrow in flight – Avro Canada CF-105 Arrow RL201 undergoing tests. It was not named 'Arrow' until 1957, after it had been dismissed as a possible purchase for the RAF. *via author*

CF-105 RL201 during its official roll-out on October 4, 1957, at Avro's factory at Malton, Ontario. *via author*

Mk.3 and Mk.4 of the CF-100 was given greater priority and the CF-103 project work slowed. When the wind tunnel data was finally given a thorough analysis, however, it was found to be very disappointing – the aircraft was unlikely ever to reach Mach 1, even in a dive. It was cancelled the following month, though work on the delta-wing CF-104 continued unabated.

The month after the abject failure of the CF-103 design, January 1952, a new All-Weather Requirements Team was set up by the RCAF to work out exactly what the Canadian military actually wanted from a CF-100 replacement. Its findings were reported to Avro two months later and three months after that, in June 1952, Avro responded with two new brochures for single-seat delta-wing combat aircraft based on the long-running CF-104 programme.

The CF-104/1 was the single-engine day fighter while the CF-104/2 was a twin-engine all-weather fighter. The second design better suited the RCAF's requirements

so Avro dropped the CF-104/1 and continued to develop the CF-104/2.

A specification for a new all-weather fighter was issued to Avro Canada in April 1953. This would have to be capable of Mach 1.5 and a ceiling of 50,000ft – both fairly modest compared to the all-weather Mach 2 fighter requirement then being worked on in Britain. What was less modest, however, was a requirement that Canada's new fighter should be able to carry its missiles internally – primarily to protect them from the nation's harsh climate.

By now, the CF-104/2 had been redesigned as a two-seater and given the new designation CF-105. This was duly presented to the RCAF in May 1953 and two months after that the Canadian government's Department of Defence Production gave Avro the go-ahead to produce a full design study on the type. Wind tunnel testing commenced in September 1953 and preliminary design work was completed by early 1954.

By the summer of 1955 work was progressing well but Avro's original plan to fit the CF-105 with Rolls-Royce RB.106 engines had fallen by the wayside when the company announced that their development had been discontinued in late 1954. The chosen replacement, Curtiss-Wright's J67, was then also cancelled in early 1955 – leaving the CF-105 without an engine. Avro next turned to Pratt & Whitney's J75 as a temporary measure while its own Orenda PS13 engine was developed.

At the point when the Canadian government revealed to the press that it was planning to place an order for the CF-105, on August 1, 1955, the project was at a relatively advanced stage. The prototype design had been finalised and component and tooling manufacture had already begun.

When Avro Canada was sent copies of OR.329 and F.155T, on August 17, 1955, the firm was heavily invested in the CF-105 and responded simply by presenting the Ministry of Supply with its latest brochure for the type – which would not be given the name 'Arrow' until 1957, long after the British dismissed any idea of buying it. And as it stood, the anticipated performance of the CF-105 was a long way short of meeting British requirements at this point.

According to the brochure, the Canadian fighter would take seven minutes to climb to 60,000ft, by which time it would be travelling at only Mach 1.6. The worst performing British design in this scenario, de Havilland's DH.117, would take six minutes to reach 60,000ft and Mach 2. This was down to the CF-105's lack of rocket power.

In addition, and for the same reason, the CF-105's top speed at that altitude was Mach 1.77, and its overall maximum speed was Mach 1.94 at 50,000ft. The slowest British design was English Electric's P.8, which would achieve

Mach 2 at 46,000ft without reheat. Furthermore, at 60,000ft the CF-105 would take 6.4 minutes to accelerate from Mach 1.3 to Mach 1.7.

By comparison, Fairey's Large design was expected to take less than one minute to go from Mach 1.3 to Mach 2 at the same altitude. In fact, Vickers' Type 559 was expected to go from Mach 1.55 to Mach 2 in an incredible 4.5 seconds at 60,000ft. Even the worst performer, de Havilland again, would only take 1.3 minutes for a Mach 1.3 to Mach 2 dash at 60,000ft. All the British designs had a ceiling of at least 65,000ft, whereas the CF-105 topped out at 55,200ft, by which point its performance was severely tailing off.

And there was more. The CF-105's tandem seating arrangement was frowned upon and its much-vaunted internal payload bay was designed to carry American missiles – the AIM-4 Falcon and the AIM-7 Sparrow – and was ill-suited to the de Havilland Blue Jay. The Vickers Red Hebe, which came increasingly to be regarded as essential to the F.155T aircraft, would not fit in it at all. The intended radar unit was the American Hughes MX.1179,

Another view of RL201, this time from the factory roof, showing its distinctive delta-wing form. *via author*

which would undoubtedly result in contractual and supply difficulties, even assuming it was not decided to simply have it built with a British system installed instead.

Nevertheless, the CF-105 was seen to be already approaching production readiness – offering the significant benefit of early availability. It was light too, at 55,000lb fully loaded, which meant there was likely to be significant potential for further development. Avro Canada was part of the Hawker Siddeley Group, making it technically a British company, with huge resources to draw upon should significant modifications to the design prove necessary.

It was therefore on the basis of the CF-105's future potential, more than its then-current design, that it was considered as a contender for the OR.329/F.155T interceptor requirement. If it failed to meet this, its performance was still potent enough to outmatch the RAF's intended interim interceptor, the F.153D Thin Wing Javelin.

RL201 banks away from the camera high above the Avro factory. *via author*

AVRO CANADA
CF-105

❖

February 1956

Artwork by Luca Landino

— *Specification* —

Crew: Two **Length:** 77ft 9in
Wingspan: 50ft **Height:** 21ft 2in
Wing area: 1225sq ft
Empty weight: 47,000lb
Loaded weight: 55,000lb
Powerplant: 2 x Pratt & Whitney
J75-P-3 turbojets
Maximum speed: Mach 1.94
Service ceiling: 55,200ft
Armament: 8 x Hughes AIM-4 Falcon
carried internally

15

FINAL DECISION

The future of fighters

With the detailed interceptor brochures now in hand,
the Ministry of Supply, the Air Staff and the technical
specialists began their assessment to determine which
company would be declared the winner and offered a
contract to build its design. The contest did not end quite
as expected, however.

Alongside a highly detailed design brochure, each company tendering for F.155T had to supply a letter outlining the costs associated with its aircraft. Particularly illuminating were the figures given for designing and supplying it in quantities of 12, 18 and 24 aircraft.

The most expensive by a considerable margin was de Havilland's DH.117 – a hefty £937,000 per aircraft (£22.5m in today's money – still peanuts compared to the £125m cost of a single Eurofighter Typhoon) if 24 were ordered. Next most expensive was Saunders-Roe's P.187 at £718,715 each for 24, followed by Vickers-Armstrongs' Type 559 at £565,000 apiece for two dozen.

Just behind this was Fairey's Large design at £557,000 each and £343,000 each for its Small design. English Electric declined to offer three prices on a sliding scale, asking instead for a lump sum up front of £7,366,682 for 24 examples, valuing each aircraft at £306,945 – less than a third of the cost of a DH.117.

Right at the bottom end of the scale were the Hawker and Armstrong Whitworth designs. Hawker wanted just £285,000 per aircraft in a batch of 24, while AWA's AW.169 was positively bargain basement at just £270,000 (£6.5m in today's money) each for an order of 24.

With all of the brochures in hand by October 8 – Fairey's two having apparently been received late – and having quickly skimmed through them, project officer Ian Otto Hockmeyer wrote a memo headed 'Notes on Firms' Philosophy'. For Fairey he wrote: "Choice of delta planform: gives excellent manoeuvrability at high altitude, best landing and take-off characteristics and lightest structure, suitable for engines in fuselage. Can draw on experience of ER.103. Choice of two engines

and steel and titanium construction provides scope for development up to Mach 3.

"English Electric: The only certainty of meeting service date will result from a 'short step' development of the existing F.23/49, AI23 and IR weapon combination. This excludes a large and complex radar collision system and leads to the adoption of the two-stage concept based on the claims made for an all round IR weapon: it entails height differential and three-dimensional interception with beam riding information from a single ground station.

"Hawker: The objective is to submit the smallest possible aircraft to meet the requirement of the specification. Blue Vesta or small Vickers radar weapon is offered since the Red Hebe is completely out of harmony with an aircraft of this type. Swept wing chosen for favourable transonic characteristics, load relieving ability and structural suitability for the single engine arrangement. Advantages of detachable rocket motor.

"De Havilland: To meet service date of January 1962 some pruning of equipment and weapon system is thought to be necessary. Doubt about availability of Red Hebe, therefore, initially designing for Blue Vesta and relying on its all round capabilities. Expect to be able to develop the equipment systems; particularly towards increased automaticity, with time. Importance of twin engines. Straight wing chosen to obtain: high lift at low speed (hence smaller area and lower weight), reduces stability and handling difficulties, less tendency for pitching troubles near the stall (at high subsonic speeds), better directional stability above Mach 1.5. DH.110 experience.

"Armstrong Whitworth: Service date precludes unconventional design. No alternative configuration offers significant advantage (except

similar rear-tailed aircraft with negative longitudinal stability). Scope for development in steel. Unswept wing allows engines to be in underslung nacelles and facilitates change of type (as well as accessibility). Advantages also in landing attitude and in weapon positioning.

"Vickers-Armstrongs (Supermarine): Belief that structure and equipment adjacent to jet nozzles may suffer damage from high frequency vibrations (noise) – hence nozzles must be extreme aft. To avoid tail heaviness and to avoid long portion of 'hot' fuselage led to canard layout. Further merit that foreplane contributes to lift, reduces wing size and weight. Weapon change in two hours. Consider that group organisation of interceptors will be extremely limited are due to aircraft's relatively short endurance. Hence Intermittent Proportional Navigation or Intermittent beam riding do not appear attractive. Suggest use of EW and GCI in close association with a small number of interceptor bases. GCI would employ a number of ground mounted AI sets each locking on to its individual target. Interceptor would pick up beam at 26,000ft. Saving of aircraft nav equipment and reduce organisational delay time.

"Saunders-Roe: Belief that Issue 2 of the specification is regarded as a concession and that Air Staff really want Issue 1 to be met: this the firm claims to have done in full and produced an aircraft with development capacity to Mach 3 and truly all weather (the special sliding nose ensures excellent landing vision). The aircraft follows the design of current designs (F.138D and P.177) and this limits the development required and new problems to be solved.

"Avro Canada: The firm were asked to comment on Specification F.155T and have submitted the CF-105 brochure and a statement of its capability relative to F.155T. This they have done. A further stage of study, to examine what might be done to approach the F.155T requirement by increasing engine thrust, will be undertaken if the Ministry of Supply (MoS) requests."

Three days later, a meeting was held to discuss the tenders. The chairman was MoS Director General of Technical Development (Air) George Gardner and in attendance were 10 Air Ministry representatives, four men from the RAE, two from the RRE and another 10 from the Ministry of Supply, plus Hockmeyer as secretary.

Gardner began by stating that the Deputy Chief of the Air Staff, Sir Thomas Pike, had asked whether the F.155T should be made a pursuit course interceptor only due to "the difficulty of reconciling performance, equipment and all-up-weight". Gardner said this needed to be considered and that the meeting was to "decide how further work should be steered to try and arrive at a sane and wise design when the choice of weapon system was made".

Air Ministry Assistant Chief of the Air Staff (Operational Requirements) Air Vice-Marshall Harold Vivian Satterly then "explained that the Air Staff had become alarmed, as the requirement crystallised, at the weight of the fighter". He said Pike thought the RAF might get a bigger fighter force if Red Hebe was ditched and only Blue Vesta (Blue Jay Mk.4) missiles were specified.

At this point the MoS's Director General of Guided Weapons, John Edward Serby, interjected to say he could not accept the suggestion that Red Hebe "could not be developed and produced in seven years and stated that it was a matter for Air Ministry to arrange appropriate priority".

The RAE had estimated that removing Red Hebe from the spec would lighten those aircraft designed for both types of missiles by 10,000lb and it was noted at this point that both the Hawker and small Fairey submissions had not met the F.155T performance requirements. It was also noted that Saunders-Roe's design, able to carry both missiles, had an all-up-weight of nearly 100,000lb and it was agreed that the firm should be given the opportunity to put forward the smaller design it had mentioned in its brochure.

Further discussions then ensued about the relative effectiveness of Blue Vesta versus Red Hebe against targets at various altitudes and speeds. This debate went round in circles until it was finally agreed that "for the time being, precedence should be given to those designs which catered for the carriage of both Blue Vesta and Red Hebe".

There was then a long discussion about the various airborne intercept (AI) radars available and whether the F.155T should be ground-controlled for part of its mission. It was decided that a second meeting should be held in a month's time when it might be possible to eliminate "those designs which were clearly unacceptable, and subsequently to concentrate on those which offer the full collision course facility". The date was set for November 28 at 3.30pm.

No second chance for Saro

On October 13, 1955, Hockmeyer wrote: "Saunders-Roe assumed that the Air Staff still really wanted the original concept and regarded Issue 2 as of the nature of a concession. They made this assumption despite the information they received when representatives of Air Staff visited them on June 14: my notes of this visit indicate that Air Staff said that the change from Issue 1 to Issue 2 was a deliberate change of policy and not a concession. Initially Saunders-Roe appeared to take advantage of what, on April 5, was a concession, in their design work, but some three months ago decided to try and meet the full original requirements and this is what has been submitted in their design brochure.

"At a meeting held by Gardner on October 11, Satterly stated that they were not interested in this larger Saunders-Roe offer, the meeting felt, however, that the firm should be invited to complete and submit their design for a smaller aircraft. In their brochure they state that they can do this very quickly. It is for consideration as to whether such action would be equitable in relation to the other firms in the competition.

"One offer at least falls short of the requirements, namely that of Hawkers. My view is that such firms should not be given the chance of submitting another design. The Hawker design in particular has been offered in the teeth of the specification 'as their view of the next logical step in fighter development'.

"On the other hand it should be recalled that I was instructed to impress upon the firms informally that if they thought the present specification (i.e. Issue 1) too ambitious to be met within a reasonable time they should not hesitate to bring this up at the April meeting. It could be said that Issue 2 was in fact a recognition of an opinion that the specification was too ambitious."

Hockmeyer asked whether Saunders-Roe should be allowed to submit a design for a smaller aircraft. His superior, George Leitch, stated that he had no objection to this on October 14, 1955.

However, three days later the Air Ministry's Director of Contracts (Air), A W Isherwood, wrote: "We spoke about this i.e. the invitation to tender for the F.155T. The proposal to invite Saunders-Roe only to submit an alternative tender would be quite contrary to the normal principles of competitive tendering.

"In my view, it is necessary either to extend the time and give all the firms a chance to think again or to consider only the tenders already submitted. I gather that you propose to adopt the second course."

Isherwood's decision, to prevent Saunders-Roe from submitting a smaller design, had the effect of freezing the other firms' designs too. Only the brochure designs submitted would be considered – although further explanation of these designs' features was allowable.

On October 28, Air Ministry Deputy Director of Operational Requirements 1, Group Captain Neil Wheeler, wrote a memo stating: "I am at a loss to understand how we can ever legislate for a firm that is determined to be kind to us. The requirement is quite clearly stated in the issue of OR.329 that is current and I do not believe we should take any further action to explain the background to the deletion of the necessity to carry a mixed weapon load.

"Moreover, if Saunders-Roe get an order for the P.177, which I believe must go through, we cannot possibly tie up the whole of our future fighter development with Saunders-Roe. Rather, therefore, than worry unduly over persuading Saunders-Roe not to tell us what we think we want, can we not concentrate on the other aircraft."

Eliminations

Between November 5 and November 9, the Air Ministry carried out its own quick assessment of Avro Canada's CF-105 brochure against the requirements of OR.329. The following day, Satterly wrote a summary: "The CF-105 as planned for introduction into the Royal Canadian Air Force will be equipped with a US fire control system and US guided missiles stowed internally. In this form the

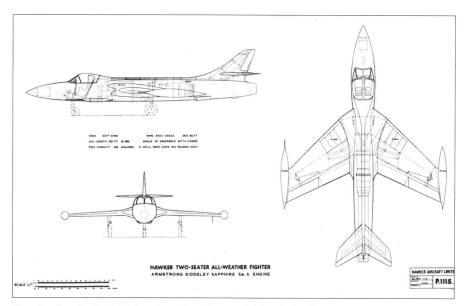

Shortly after its P.1103 brochure had been submitted, Hawker produced the P.1115 – one of many interim interceptor designs of the period. It had wingtip tanks for extended patrol, two seats and radar, but two Aden cannon rather than guided weapons. *BAE Systems*

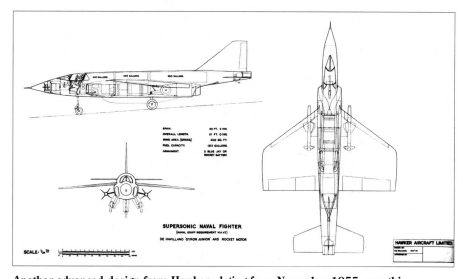

Another advanced design from Hawker, dating from November 1955, was this supersonic fighter for the Navy – to Naval Staff Requirement NA.47. It serves to indicate the direction of Hawker's thinking on supersonic guided weapon-equipped fighter design – with options of a ventral fuel tank and rocket motor in the extreme end of the fuselage. *BAE Systems*

aircraft could be made available to the RAF in about 1960.

"The aircraft does not meet the requirements of OR.329. Using the Falcon missile (astern attack) the aircraft would be capable of destroying its target at a range of 17½ miles from the coast. Provision has also been made for the carriage of the Sparrow 2 which was designed to be capable of front hemisphere collision course attacks.

"Using this weapon the aircraft could theoretically deal with the Mach 1.3 threat at a distance of 64 miles from coast. Unfortunately, I understand that many problems have been encountered in the development of this weapon and it is now unlikely this or any other suitable collision course weapon will be available in time."

He said it might be possible to fit the CF-105 with a British radar

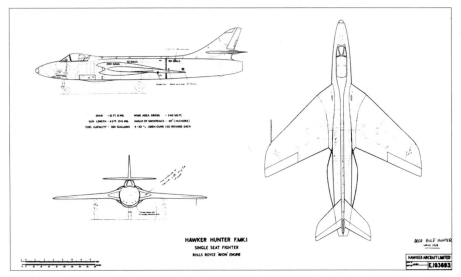

As the F.155T competition continued, Hawker worked on ways of improving the performance of its Hunter fighter, the troubled development of which had served to damage the company's reputation in the eyes of the Air Staff. *BAE Systems*

and missiles but this would delay its introduction until about 1962: "Blue Vesta is the only suitable weapon which could be stowed internally. The aircraft so equipped would not be capable of meeting the requirements of OR.329, the performance being similar to that of the RCAF Falcon missile. Red Hebe could only be carried externally and I believe that the decrease in aircraft performance caused by the carriage of this weapon would be considerable."

If a rocket motor could be fitted to the CF-105, "in this configuration it is probable that the aircraft would meet the requirement of OR.329" but even greater delays would ensue.

"At first glance the CF-105 offers a performance less than OR.329 but at an earlier date. It would appear that to achieve a comparable performance to OR.329 we will forfeit the advantage in time. Nevertheless I consider that we should continue more detailed study of this aircraft as a possible contender for OR.320. This is being done."

The meeting on November 28 was chaired by Arthur Edgar Woodward-Nutt, who was now acting DGTD (A), Gardner having left the MoS to become director of

the RAE in the meantime, but most of the other attendees returned. This time the meeting opened with a heated debate about Red Hebe and Blue Vesta, then the AI systems.

Regarding Vickers' worries about extreme noise causing damage, the RAE agreed that "the risk of structural damage due to vibration set up by the jets was a real one and that both de Havilland's and AWA's designs might be affected. They did not consider, however, that this was any justification for eliminating them from the competition and were satisfied that if such effects did occur they could be cured by design, e.g. by reasonable changes in material."

On Avro Canada's CF-105, "it was agreed that this aircraft in its present form falls short of OR.329 (it is designed to meet a threat of Mach 0.9 at 50,000ft). As a short step, however, we were bound to give the aircraft consideration." Three options were discussed – firstly, buying the aircraft from Canada in standard form, which was "unlikely to be financially feasible except under some 'aid' programme, and date-wise might not be so attractive as it seemed. Reports suggested that the Canadian delivery date was slipping".

Secondly, the CF-105 could be built in the UK under licence. This would be cheaper, it was said, but

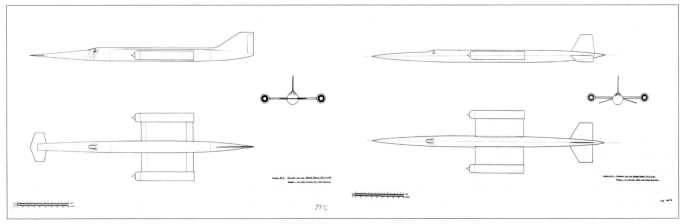

Even as its designers worked on a multitude of different designs and concepts for fighters that could break the sound barrier, Hawker continued to push at the boundaries of the possible with designs such as these Armstrong Siddeley turborocket-powered experimental aircraft – intended for flight at speeds of up to Mach 3-4. *BAE Systems*

would lead to further delay. Finally, was "Anglicise and bring up to OR.329 standard. This proposal envisages the use of British engines, weapons and radar. A preliminary investigation had already shown that it would not be possible to carry Red Hebe internally in the present fuselage on account of its size. Wing tip mounting would involve complete redesign of the wings." It was agreed the MoS would provide the Air Ministry with more details of each option and put them to Avro Canada's UK representative. Now came "elimination of unsuitable tender designs" and it was noted that the ability to carry both Red Hebe and Blue Vesta, though not at the same time, was regarded as essential. The meeting first looked at Fairey's OR.103 design: "It was agreed to recommend that this should be deleted, in favour of Fairey's larger submission, since it will not carry Red Hebe."

Then English Electric's P.8: "It was agreed to recommend that this should be eliminated from this competition because it would not carry Red Hebe, because it did not provide all-round collision course facilities and because it was a single seater. Since the Air Staff might possibly ask for the continuation of this design as a P.1 development, MoS would not terminate the wind tunnel model contract."

Hawker's P.1103 squeaked through: "Hawkers claim, in their brochure, to be able to carry Red Hebe, although at the expense of performance. Pending clarification of this statement it was agreed that Hawkers should not be eliminated." De Havilland's somewhat ambiguous stance on Red Hebe was to be clarified: "Although this design is larger than the larger Fairey one, the ability to carry Red Hebe is not claimed. It was agreed that de Havilland's should be invited to state what the performance would be when carrying Red Hebe."

And finally the Saunders-Roe P.187: "Air Staff considered this aircraft to be too large, too heavy and too expensive: it was agreed to recommend elimination. It was noted that Saunders-Roe had been clearly informed that the change from Issue 1 to Issue 2 of the OR (changing from the carriage of both types of weapon together to carriage as alternative loads) was a change of Air Staff policy rather than a concession."

No case was made to eliminate the Fairey large design, AWA AW.169 or Vickers Type 559. The date for the next tender design conference was to be February 6, 1956.

Air Ministry Director of Operational Requirements (Air), Herbert James 'Jimmy' Kirkpatrick, came away from the meeting believing that English Electric, Saunders-Roe and Fairey's small design had now definitely been eliminated from the competition – and wrote a note to that effect on December 5, 1955, but he was mistaken. Hockmeyer wrote a more qualified note on December 9 to state that while it had been recommended to the Ministry of Supply's Controller of Aircraft that those three firms' designs should be dropped, they had not yet actually been eliminated. It was decided that the firms should be kept in the dark about these recommendations.

Meanwhile, on December 8, the Air Ministry's science department delivered its views on the 'surviving' five tenders and found the DH.117's cruising altitude was too low at 55,000ft, the P.1103's performance at altitude was poor and the Fairey Large relied too heavily on an engine which was largely undeveloped, the RB.122, for its on-paper performance advantage. In conclusion: "Final views, of course, may be influenced considerably by MoS assessment, but if the firms' claims are nearly correct, then the choice appears

to lie between the Vickers and Armstrong-Whitworth designs."

Following on from this, the Air Staff were becoming increasingly concerned about the short-range nature of the F.155T interceptor. On January 12, Kirkpatrick wrote: "The Air Staff now place much emphasis on the long range capabilities of OR.329. It is in fact our intention to issue an appropriate amendment to the OR as soon as the tender design conference has been held."

Hawker and EECo reprieved

Regardless of the supposed secrecy surrounding the outcome of the November meeting, Fairey soon discovered its 'small' ER.103 design was being rejected and on January 18, Hockmeyer wrote: "The Fairey Aviation Co, gleaning the information that their smaller submission was to be dropped as the Air Staff were only interested in aircraft which would carry alternative loads of both types of weapons, have now submitted an appendix to their brochure showing how this smaller aircraft would perform when altered so that it could carry Red Hebe." He duly circulated the appendix.

E T Jones, the new DGTD (A), wrote a memo on January 19, 1956, noting it was recommended that the small Fairey, Saunders-Roe and English Electric designs should be eliminated from the competition but that MoS Controller of Aircraft, Sir John Baker (CA), had subsequently "decided not to write to these latter firms, and so we find that they are incurring expense to MoS in continuing the manufacture of models of their designs for wind tunnel tests".

In the meantime, the next meeting date had slipped to March 27. Jones said he intended to get Baker to write to the firms as soon as possible but was offering the opportunity of further comments from the Air Ministry before January 27. He also wrote: "You will recall that the meeting on November 28 was inclined to recommend the elimination of the Hawker submission too, but decided not to do so pending receipt of information on its performance when armed with Red Hebe. This has now been received and a preliminary examination shows that the project falls short of the performance required when carrying this weapon. I therefore think that we can now eliminate Hawkers also, if you have no objection."

At the last minute, Satterly wrote back: "I am in full agreement that the Fairey Small, the Saunders-Roe and, from an administrative point of view, the English Electric submissions can be finally eliminated at this stage as competitors for OR.329. I understand, however, that English Electric have prepared, and will shortly be submitting, an addendum to their brochure giving details of a two-seat version of their aircraft.

"In view of this addendum, and the Air Staff view that the English Electric P.8 should be regarded as a development of the P.1, I recommend that the English Electric model should not be cancelled. I think that the elimination of the Hawker design may be premature. This is mainly based on my apprehension regarding the Red Hebe weapon. I believe it is far too big and the Hawker aircraft might be much more satisfactory when carrying four smaller weapons.

"However, I understand that DGGW will be holding a meeting at the end of January to re-examine the weapon requirements and I suggest that the Hawker proposal remains pending the outcome of this meeting."

The Air Staff view
A detailed assessment of the tendered designs by the Air Staff had been under way since their submission in October 1955 and the first draft was ready by January 31, 1956. This indicated that Fairey's new Red Hebe appendix for its 'small' design was not eligible for consideration but English Electric's P.8 with two seats was allowable since the design as a whole was a development of the F.23 (Lightning). Saunders-Roe's P.187, it reiterated, was too large, too heavy and too expensive.

Regarding the crucial matter of weapon load, "it is now considered that the speed of the threat in the time scale of OR.329 is likely to be increased to between Mach 1.5 and Mach 2". The ability to carry either radar or infrared missiles "was confirmed" and Hawker and de Havilland were to be asked to clarify their position on Red Hebe.

In assessing performance, the draft assessment restated the views of the ministry's science department over a month earlier but with a

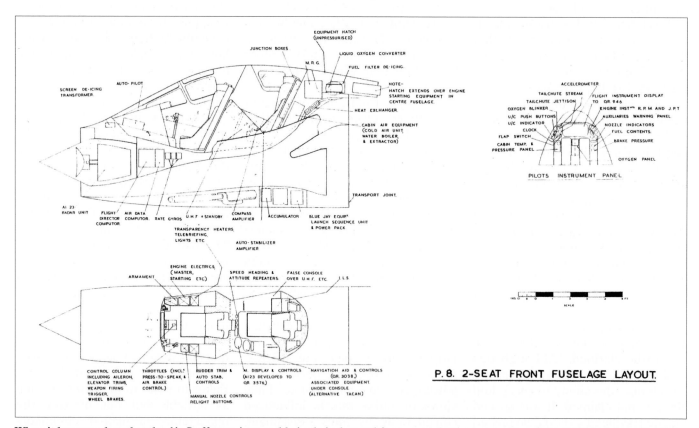

When it became clear that the Air Staff were immovable in their demand for a second crewman on board the F.155T fighter, English Electric swiftly drafted an addendum to their brochure – allowable under the competition rules – showing the P.8 with a radar operator's position directly behind the pilot. *BAE Systems*

slight twist: de Havilland's cruise altitude was too low, Hawker's altitude performance was weak, the Vickers and AWA designs offered similar performance but "the Fairey design appears to be slightly better than either of these aircraft, but it is to be remembered that this aircraft incorporates the more developed engine, the RB.122."

Given the new importance being placed on range, both the Fairey and Vickers designs had a 'radius of action' 20% smaller than that of the AW.169 – although Vickers could carry more fuel to compensate as an overload. De Havilland and Hawker were the worst of the five. Concern was also expressed about the very high tyre pressures de Havilland intended to use – 300psi.

It was considered that the Hawker design could be in service before any of the others, de Havilland "place much stress on the impossibility of meeting the service date of 1962 if the electronics and weapons requirements are to be fully met", AWA said the service date precluded unconventional design, Vickers with its unusual canard layout was likely to take longest to get into service and the steel construction of Fairey's aircraft was also likely to delay it – although "flight experience on the ER.103 may well offset any delays so caused".

And in conclusion: "There seems to be little to choose between the Armstrong Whitworth, Vickers and Fairey designs. The climb performance of the Fairey is superior but the long range patrol performance is likely to be markedly inferior in comparison with the other two. The choice appears to lie between the Armstrong Whitworth and Vickers designs."

A second draft was produced on February 17 which clarified that Air Staff might support the development of English Electric's P.8 "but not in the context of OR.329". A new section was inserted concerning

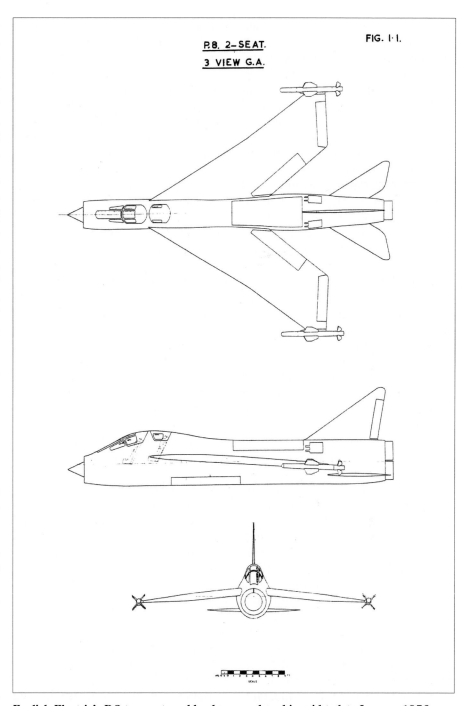

English Electric's P.8 two-seater addendum, produced in mid to late January 1956, retained the clean lines and coke bottle shape of the single seater. It was enough to keep the company in the running beyond the initial round of eliminations. *BAE Systems*

acceleration too: "Assuming the firms' claims are substantially correct, the acceleration and manoeuvrability of the AWA aircraft without rocket at high altitude is likely to be somewhat inferior to those of the Vickers and Fairey aircraft." It was now noted also that Vickers' worries about noise were

something no one else seemed concerned about.

A section absent from the first draft was 'weapons'. This noted that Hawker and de Havilland had designed for Blue Vesta only but later supplied an addendum concerning carriage of Red Hebe – but only with big performance penalties.

And: "The position of the missile installation on the Vickers aircraft may well give rise to damage of the windscreen canopy or radio when the missile is fired, and to screening of the target from the missiles' homing heads when allowing for aim off for collision course launch during a head-on climbing attack." Vickers had provided the best set-up for mid-course ground-based radar guidance, although not on early production aircraft.

Escape was also now considered: "With the exception of Faireys, all tenders propose ejection seats as the only means of escape from the aircraft. This is not really acceptable in aircraft of the proposed performance."

And the thorny issue of production capacity was addressed in detail. The assessment now began to read like a list of complaints, starting with Hawker: "This firm has a traditional reputation as an excellent fighter firm and their design experience of fighters must clearly be taken into account. However, up to now the firm appear to have taken few steps to equip themselves for handling a 'weapons system' and, of late, have fallen down seriously in their ability to produce the Hunter in quantity as an 'effective operational aircraft'.

"Vickers Supermarine. While this firm has in the past built up a fine reputation for the design and production of fighters, its ability to stand the pace in the design of future fighters is questionable. One cannot disregard the failure of the Swift, and, even more important, the slowness with which the firm met the shortcomings of the aircraft after they had been brought to light.

"De Havilland. Although this firm has a long and fine record in the aircraft industry its design team have clearly received a considerable jolt from the Comet disaster, although it is fair to say that military aircraft are handled by a separate design team. Nevertheless, this is a strong firm and with its associated

divisions, particularly for guided weapons, clearly capable of tackling a weapon system in its entirety.

"Armstrong Whitworth. This firm has not produced a fighter type of aircraft (except for the NF Meteor) since the early 1930s. Moreover, in view of the lack of experience of this firm in original designs and high speed aircraft, their ability to handle this very complex weapons system is debatable. It is backed by the resources of the Hawker Siddeley Group but this firm may well be required to contribute to other military designs which have already been awarded to the group.

"Fairey. While this firm has had very little association with fighters, they have flying at the moment a very successful research aircraft (on which their tender is based) which has already achieved Mach 1.73. Despite their limited experience of fighter design, one cannot deny the obvious ability that has gone into the design of the ER.103. In addition most of the chief engineer's experience was at Hawkers, a leading fighter firm. Despite the relatively small size of the firm, they have a specialist interest in guided weapons and power controls and should be able to handle a complete weapon system."

Finally the firms were ranked according to their capacity to "handle successfully this very complex weapons system": De Havilland first, then Fairey, then Hawker, then Armstrong Whitworth and finally, dead last, Vickers.

Baker duly confirmed, on February 20, 1956, that the small Fairey and Saunders-Roe designs had been eliminated – but English Electric and Hawker were still in the race. Letters informing the firms of the decision went out on February 23, the same day that English Electric's brochure addendum, showing the two-seat P.8, was delivered.

The next day Kirkpatrick commented: "At first glance this

addendum seems to be very thin on performance information, and I fear that the assessment of it both in the Ministry of Supply and here in Air Staff, is bound to be very much less thorough than that which has been carried out over the past months on the designs submitted by the other firms."

E T Jones, of the MoS, arranged a meeting on February 28 to discuss cancelling both the Hawker and English Electric tenders ahead of the tender design conference. Satterly went along and reported back that: "The MoS, supported by RAE, say that the Hawker design does not and cannot meet OR.329, the de Havilland design is doubtful and the latest English Electric two-seat proposal is also a non-runner." He was asked to support the elimination of both Hawker and English Electric and while he "could not contest" the former, he fought hard to retain the latter.

The deadline for submission of the Air Staff's official view was March 6 and a third draft was completed on March 2. This confirmed that the Avro Canada CF-105 "cannot in its present form be considered as a competitor for the F.155 tender" because it was designed to meet much slower threat at a much lower altitude than the other designs.

English Electric was now back in the picture: "In view of the obvious lead which the firm has in the design and development of supersonic aircraft and the overall reputation of the firm, this new proposal (the two-seater P.8) has, despite its apparent limitations, been considered in this paper." But the P.8 was deemed to lack sufficient ceiling to tackle threats at 70,000ft, with or without two seats, its range was severely limited and its radio bay was too cramped. It would easily meet the 1962 in-service date though. The summary ranked the firms first according to potential, with English Electric at the top and Vickers at the bottom, then according to

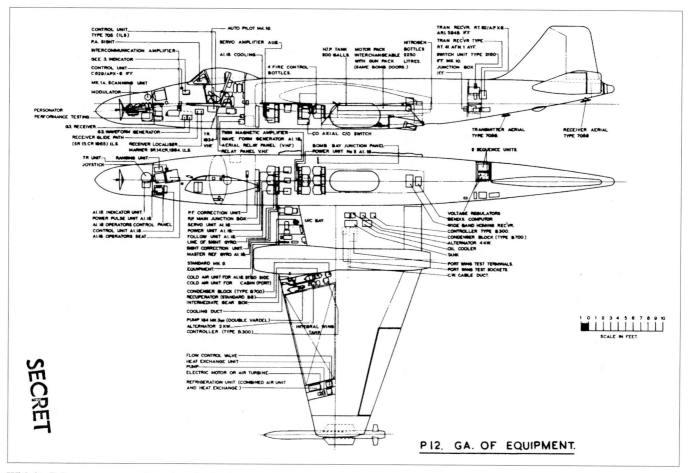

With its P.8 two-seater on the point of rejection, English Electric got on with the business of developing its Canberra jet bomber to provide another all-weather interceptor option. The P.12, proposed in March 1956, was a two-seat fighter equipped with AI radar and guided weapons. *BAE Systems*

specific tender order with Fairey at the top and Hawker at the bottom, with English Electric second from bottom.

Canberra all-weather fighter

Even as English Electric was in the process of being eliminated from F.155T behind closed doors, the company was preparing another option for the Ministry of Supply and Air Staff to consider – an all-weather fighter version of the Canberra.

On March 7, 1956, the firm's chief designer Freddie Page wrote to Gardner in his new position at the RAE: "From time to time various people in the Ministry of Supply, Air Ministry and Commands have made suggestions that the Canberra might be developed as an all-weather fighter. Hitherto pressure of work on other Canberra developments, and the fact that with conventional

weapons the advantages of such a development were not clear cut, have combined to discourage us from proceeding further with the idea.

"However, studies of the AI 18-Red Dean type of airborne missile system in relation to new projects have made it clear that the carriage of such a large and bulky system on a subsonic fighter of conventional size or on a supersonic fighter,

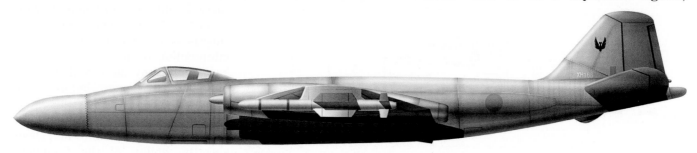

English Electric P.12 fighter. *Art by Daniel Uhr*

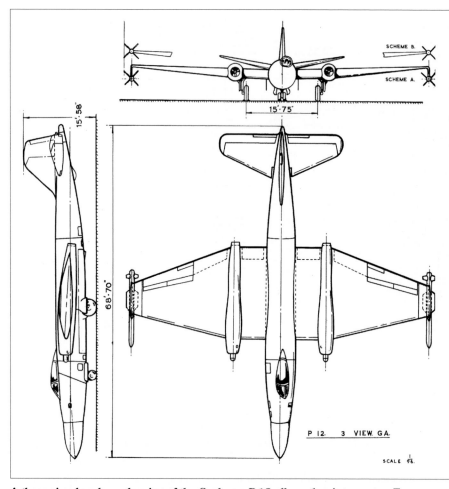

A three-view brochure drawing of the Canberra P.12 all-weather interceptor. Two different options were presented for the wingtip mounting points of its missiles. *BAE Systems*

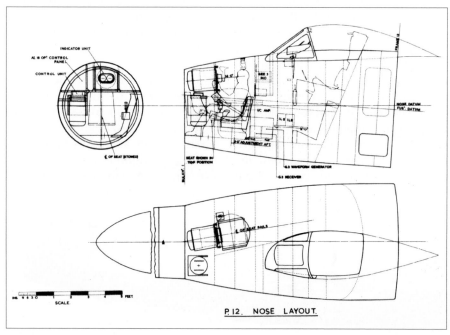

Drawing showing the internal layout of the P.12's nose section with pilot and radar operator positions. *BAE Systems*

present considerable difficulties. Nevertheless all the essential elements of this system have been, or are being, developed on Canberra aircraft and will have to be brought together on an aircraft of this type for final proving."

English Electric had worked closely with Vickers-Armstrongs' guided weapons division to fit the large AI 18 and enormous radar-guided Red Dean missiles on to a modified Canberra on the basis that collision course weapons did not require a high-performance aircraft – they simply needed to be taken aloft and put into a position ahead of the incoming enemy bomber. Assuming the missiles' homing heads could lock on in time, the missiles would be able to hit their targets.

Page stated that, while English Electric itself was working flat out on other projects, if a Canberra fighter was of interest it could be developed using Boulton Paul as a subcontractor. English Electric designated the project P.12 and the project brochure stated that a fully equipped prototype could be ready in just two years – by March 1958 – with a complete operational squadron of Canberra fighters becoming operational during 1959.

The brochure further stated: "To obtain an effective operational aircraft it is proposed to install this equipment in the latest Canberra Mk.8 Interdictor. Boulton Paul Aircraft have been made responsible for this installation, due to their special experience in this connection. Studies of the resulting operational performance have been carried out in conjunction with Vickers Armstrongs. Somewhat surprisingly, these have shown an interception performance equal or superior to any aircraft that could operate this system before it is superseded.

"This is due to the high performance intended for Red Dean and the ability of the Canberra to carry the complete system to

A Canberra test aircraft carrying prototype Red Dean missiles. *BAE Systems*

Canberra VN828 fitted with the single-seat bubble canopy and new nose cone to test the AI18 radar installation which would have been part of the P.12 modifications carried out by Boulton Paul. *BAE Systems*

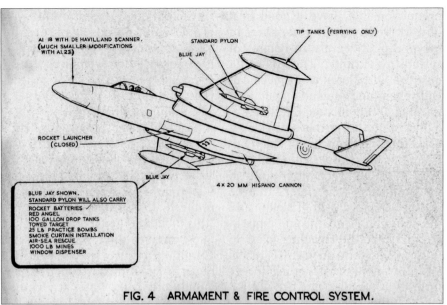

Although the P.12 brochure mainly discusses its performance when equipped with Vickers' Red Dean radar homing missile, most of the accompanying drawings show it fitted with Blue Jay infrared heat seekers. In this drawing, it also carried a quartet of 20mm Hispano cannon. *BAE Systems*

adequate speed, just short of buffet and other transonic problems, without suffering the endurance, stowage or other limitations of a supersonic aircraft. More important for a fighter that may have to attack targets faster than itself, the radar collision weapons have adequate all round scan due to their situation on the tips of an unswept wing.

"Furthermore, the Canberra has sufficient endurance for a standing patrol, or to take full advantage of Advanced Early Warning. Operational flexibility is far greater than on other fighters, due to the ability to operate off small airstrips and to disperse rapidly to different parts of the world. Much higher interceptions can be made, particularly with the Napier rocket motor installation and the later marks of Avon engine.

"It is therefore suggested that this may be the only way to get sufficient aircraft fully cleared into operational service with this system within the time and expenditure available. This is due to the main components of the aircraft being already in large-scale production."

The P.12 fighter retained the Canberra Mk.8 pilot canopy with accommodation being provided for a radar operator within the fuselage. The AI.18 scanner was carried in a de Havilland modification kit and the Mk.8 cannon installation could be removed and replaced with Red Dean or a Napier rocket motor installation although "this is not recommended for intercepting targets well below 50,000ft".

The Mk.9 high-altitude wing and power control ailerons fitted and large access doors would be placed in the trailing portion of the centre section for the installation of a 4kW generator. The leading edge centre section would be modified to accommodate an additional cold air unit. The Red Deans would be carried on modified wingtips.

Ten different Canberra airframes were listed as already being involved in trials of various components and one of them, WD956, was used for firing trials using Red Dean prototypes. However, English Electric's proposal never resulted in a Canberra missile platform and the company remained busy with other work.

Maudling's five-year plan

The last draft of the Air Staff view on OR.329 was finally submitted on March 8, 1956. The following day the Minister of Supply, Reginald Maudling, completed a five-year plan for the future of Britain's aircraft industry, which was then sent to the Minister of Defence, Sir Walter Monckton, on March 14.

Firms were to be "given a reasonable balance between development work and production work" to help them work more efficiently. However, its true focus was not on efficiency but rather on preserving and protecting the status quo. Every company was to be given enough work to keep it ticking over but not so much that it would become overburdened.

Regarding the Hawker Siddeley Group, the note says: "We have Hawkers with production shortly to tail off, but with their development resources still heavily committed to continuing work on the Hunter. Glosters have plenty in hand with the Javelin, and will become seriously overloaded if the thin-winged Javelin continues. Armstrong Whitworths, who are a sound design and production unit, have a good deal of work to do for other members of the group. Avros are in danger of serious overloading. They have not only the Shackleton and the Vulcan with their developments, but also the stand-off bomb and OR.330".

In light of the group's workload, Maudling recommended the Thin Wing Javelin should be cancelled "and we should reduce their future commitments on later marks of the thick-winged Javelin and the Hunter. The group should be told that the existing load on Avros plus work on the CF-105 is all the work they are going to get from us in the course of the next 10 years. If they are given this amount of work and no more, I should judge that the technical resources of the group as a whole should be adequate, but only just adequate, to meet what we want".

De Havilland needed to be given more military work "to enable them to carry the burden of the Comet development". At this point the Comet had been withdrawn from service for over a year while de

Havilland redesigned it in the wake of a series of fatal crashes – resulting from stress cracks forming around its square windows. Options were to order more Sea Vixens or rope de Havilland in to help Saunders-Roe with P.177 development.

Vickers had "about the right amount of work in hand" but it was hoped that development of the "pretty unattractive" N.113 – the Supermarine Scimitar – could be reduced to a minimum because "this should enable effort at Supermarines to be put behind the 'Swallow' project which we want Supermarines to develop from the initial work by Dr Wallis at Vickers".

Bristol had too much work on, with the 188 research aircraft, helicopters and a replacement for the Britannia. Short and Harland was to be tasked with sharing this load. English Electric was to be aided with the P.1 to help speed up its development and "we should then have them in mind, perhaps with Faireys collaborating, as the firm most likely to be selected for an all-weather fighter to follow

the CF-105". In addition, Fairey was to continue work on its Rotodyne helicopter and its guided missile work. Handley Page was to keep working on the Victor and Herald, while Blackburn kept on with its naval strike fighter, the soon-to-be Buccaneer. Westland was to keep working on the S.58 (Wessex) while Folland was likely to be "quite a problem" as the Gnat "may well have to drop out of the picture unless the firm have some export success". Boulton and Paul was to continue working on power controls and Percivals, Scottish Aviation and the other small firms were to have "sub-contract work and possibly trainers".

Based on all this, Maudling then looked at what the future RAF was expected to look like. In short, its bomber force would soon be receiving Victors and Vulcans with the OR.330 bomber following on their heels. The "only danger being that even now, after cancelling a certain amount of Avro's work, we are leaving a very large proportion of the deterrent force in the hands of this firm".

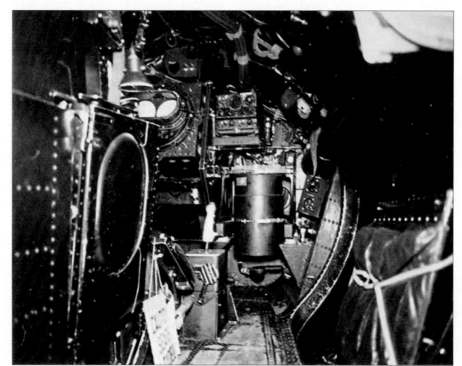

Looking down the nose of the AI18-fitted Canberra at the radar operator's station. His seat is on the left. *BAE Systems*

The AI18 scanner, as fitted to a Canberra and seen with the nose cone removed. *BAE Systems*

AI18 radar equipment was fitted inside the Canberra's bomb bay. *BAE Systems*

In terms of fighters, "once the Venom/Hunter/Swift/Javelin congestion is overcome" the P.1 would replace the Hunter to then be joined by the P.177. The latter "is very important since it will be the first operational truly mixed power plant aircraft, a technique which may be vital in the ultimate all-weather fighter. For all-weather fighters the programme offers, after the present Javelin, the CF-105 with collision course guided weapons in place of the thin-winged Javelin, as previously proposed and it should admit a further aircraft in this class being developed whose deferment for a time should enable a still more advanced specification to be conceived than the present OR.329".

Summing up, Maudling proposed postponement of OR.329 and wrote: "We shall order the CF-105 from the Hawker Siddeley Group and the Swallow project from Vickers Supermarine, in addition to our present research programme."

The decider

The winner of F.155T/OR.329 was to be decided at the tender design conference on March 27. It took place in two parts – a morning session to rank the submission in order of technical merit, and an afternoon session to which fewer people were invited to consider whether firms were actually capable of producing the aircraft designs they had pitched.

But the first order of business was to address the Hawker and English Electric designs. According to the minutes of the meeting, "it had been agreed at a meeting on February 28, 1956, that the English Electric and Hawker submissions had no chance of meeting the specification but since they had not been officially discarded they were, in theory, still in the competition. The chairman (Jones) continuing said that the basis of comparison adopted at this conference must be that laid out in

OR.329. This decision in itself did not rule out further consideration of the English Electric and/or Hawker designs though any such later discussion of them would need to be concluded in a different context to OR.329. This was accepted by all present."

Then Armstrong Whitworth and Fairey were chosen as equal first, Vickers as third and de Havilland as fourth.

The AW.169 was "an attractive design which generally met the performance and handling requirements, had engines in the wing which is convenient for servicing or fitting larger engines subsequently and had provision for all the main components of the weapon system". The Fairey Large "had shortcomings in relation to high altitude manoeuvrability and endurance but it was believed that these could be overcome by detail design changes". It also had good development potential and the firm could draw on its ER.103 experience.

Vickers' Type 559 suffered from complicated lateral control and "there were serious doubts about the wisdom of adopting the aerodynamic unknowns of the canard layout when there did not appear to be compensating advantages in an aircraft of this type". Finally, de Havilland's DH.117 simply did not meet the performance requirements, its wing was too thick and inadequate provision had been made for carrying Red Hebe.

The afternoon session, however, was where the real decision on F.155T was made. Each company was assessed in turn, starting with Vickers-Armstrongs: "The chairman said that it was probable that the department would decide to proceed with an aircraft to the Wallis conception (Vickers Swallow bomber) and it was quite clear that no other firm could be given this project. Thus, since the Vickers F.155T submission was a poor third in order of technical merit, it should

be considered unsuccessful. This was agreed."

For Armstrong Whitworth: "The chairman drew attention to the fact that the Hawker Siddeley Group were already committed to building the RB.156D (Avro 730) and its three research models, all of which were different. They were designing the engines for this bomber and were also undertaking the guided bomb project. In addition they were responsible for Vulcan development, the thin wing Javelin (which might be replaced by the CF-105) and they would probably be asked to undertake the design of the two narrow delta research aircraft.

"This accordingly raised two questions. Would the group have sufficient overall capacity and secondly would it be wise to place a further major project in this group?" Woodward-Nutt, also at the meeting, pointed out that the engines and equipment for F.155T would be developed outside Hawker Siddeley. The deputy director of the RAE, Morien Morgan, "considered that the team at Armstrong Whitworth was rather small and he questioned the wisdom of encouraging the firm to enlarge it to a fully fledged design team for fighters, particularly as the Hawker Siddeley group already had a large number of projects." However, it was recognised that Hawker Siddley had ample facilities available for AWA to call upon if necessary.

Where de Havilland was concerned, it was considered that the company ought to be concentrating on its Blue Streak ballistic missile, although it did have good experience in designing all-weather fighters. Woodward-Nutt added that "the contract should only be placed with de Havillands if there were overwhelming policy reasons for doing so as they were a bad fourth in order of technical merit". It was agreed that the de Havilland submission should not be considered further.

A prototype Vickers Red Dean missile being fired from Canberra WD956 during trials. *BAE Systems*

Jones pointed out that Fairey Aviation "had few up to date facilities and not a particularly strong design team in respect of well known persons. They have, however, built up a guided weapon element at Heston and part of the Green Cheese (missile) team had become available as a result of cancellation of this project. Robert Lickley would be chief executive of the F.155T project and would be able to call upon help from the Heston organisation." It was considered that the firm could handle the F.155T "on the assumption that the AEW Gannet would go ahead but that the Rotodyne would peter out and would not go ahead as either a civil or military type".

The Air Staff felt three designs should be ordered since they were nervous about Fairey handling the project if, for any reason, Lickley became unavailable. AWA would be the 'reserve' choice and it was felt that one of the other two should also go ahead simply because they were both experienced fighter firms.

Wheeler "drew attention to the striking fact that the submissions by those firms who had most experience showed the least probability of meeting the specification whilst those with least knowledge were the most optimistic". Air Ministry science advisor Handel Davies "supported this and said the Air Staff view was that one firm rather

than one project should be chosen and that English Electric had shown a far better approach than any of the others.

Morgan agreed "on the merit of the English Electric team but emphasised that they had proposals for very much more advanced aircraft (likely referring to the ramjet-powered P.10) and that nationally it might be better to encourage this rather than to ask them to reconsider the F.155T design".

After more discussion, Jones concluded there was little to choose between the Fairey Large and AW.169 on technical grounds but the Fairey design had the edge due to greater development potential and the benefit of research data and experience from the ER.103 (Delta 2). It was "agreed by the meeting that a recommendation should be made to the Controller of Aircraft that the Fairey project should be ordered". The next day Jones put on record the fact that "this recommendation is made despite the fact that the Fairey tender will cost more than AWA and that a new engine will be needed".

Hawker's parting shot

Maudling discussed the Fairey and AWA designs at a meeting with Monckton on April 9, 1956, and told him the Avro Canada CF-105 was unlikely to be needed. He is reported

as saying that "the British aircraft industry could cope with either the CF-105 to be made here or OR.329 but he did not believe that we had the resources to do both. There was a genuine possibility of an aircraft to OR.329 being available by 1963".

Another meeting took place on April 16, 1956, to decide what decision should be formally put before Maudling – even though he already knew the outcome of the March 27 meeting. MoS Controller of Aircraft, Sir John Baker, proposed that all the firms except Fairey and AWA should be told they had been unsuccessful, and interim development contracts should be placed with Fairey and AWA covering a period of six to 12 months.

This strategy was discussed at length before eventually being agreed. Morgan "expressed concern over the proposal to let two interim aircraft contracts, which would entail much profitless labour. He suggested that it would be far better to order only one or to go right through with two". But the Air Staff wanted at least two and Jones was inclined to take his lead from Baker. Maudling rubber-stamped the decision the following day – April 17, 1956.

Formal letters using the standard form of words for a rejection went out to de Havilland, English Electric, Hawker and Vickers-Armstrongs, on April 25: "I am directed to inform you that your tender for the design and supply of aircraft to specification F.155T has been fully considered, and is declined with thanks."

Somewhat unhelpfully, the Air Staff announced on May 2 that "in order to ensure that more than lip service is paid to the weapons systems concept, the Air Staff are re-writing OR.329 for an all-weather interceptor. Instead of issuing a detailed requirement for part of an aircraft and attempting to complete the weapons system by the addition of a family of associated requirements, the intention is to produce one document which will describe in full what the Air Staff require."

Around a fortnight later, shortly after a meeting on May 16, Jones wrote that he had received a revamped brochure for F.155T from Hawker, a new proposal from Gloster to redesign its F.153D (Thin

Wing Javelin) and had discussed the possibilities of the CF-105 with a representative of Avro Canada.

He wrote: "I do not think any of these later matters are of importance in respect of the major decision on OR.329 but if the Olympus 21R is to proceed in any case for the V bomber programme then Gloster's proposals to redesign the F.153D might well influence the decision on the CF-105.

"Hawker P.1116. Sir Sydney Camm has revamped P.1103 into a 'single-seat long range interceptor and ground-attack fighter with all-weather facilities'. I understand he has had some encouragement from Air Staff to do this and though his proposition has merit it cannot be considered in relation to OR.329 or CF-105 capability. I do not propose, at this stage at any rate, to have this brochure examined in detail because I see no good reason in using the

staff's time except when something outstanding is presented."

Following the rejection of the P.1116, Camm had his team revise the design again, this time into the P.1121, which would be worked on throughout the remainder of 1956, and into 1957, being remodelled into a potential contender for the OR.339 requirement. In this contest, the P.1121 was defeated by Vickers and English Electric, working together on a design which eventually became the TSR.2.

Thin Wing Javelin redesign
The Gloster proposal to redesign the F.153D amounted to moving the Thin Wing Javelin's front fuselage and cockpit 6ft further forward, inserting a new fuselage section aft of the navigator's cockpit to house extra fuel tanks, extending the rear fuselage by 4ft, and redesigning the rear to accommodate full reheat jet

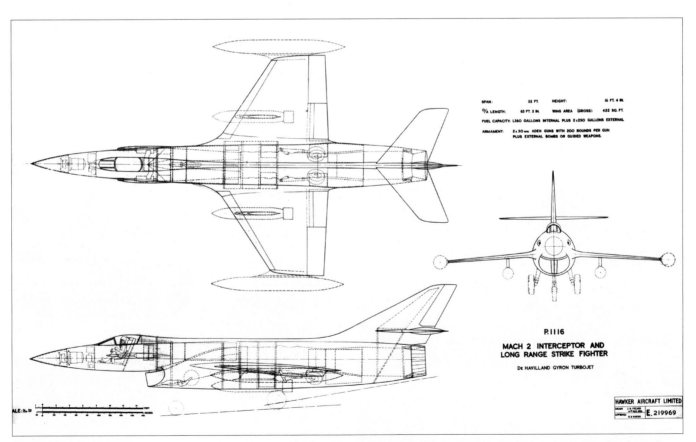

Hawker refused to give up on the basic design premise of its P.1103. Chief designer Sir Sydney Camm was encouraged to have the design altered for additional range and ground-attack capability and the result was the P.1116 – a design quickly dismissed by the Ministry of Supply. *BAE Systems*

pipes. The jet intakes would be swept to increase air flow and overall the new shape would allow area rule to be taken into account – upping the potential maximum speed to Mach 1.63 at 45,000ft with 1800°K reheat in level flight, or Mach 1.79 with reheat for 2000°K.

The company baseline for this design was drawing P.376, Issue 1 being drafted on January 27, 1956, with Issue 2 following on May 4, 1956.

The brochure received by Jones began: "The initial conception of the F.153D was that of a subsonic/transonic aircraft associated with a pursuit or collision course guided weapon system, AI.18, and with Aden guns as secondary armament. Speed has been accepted as secondary to altitude performance. Emphasis latterly has been on the Red Dean combination with which the existing aircraft speed has been judged adequate for action against targets with speeds up to Mach 1.3 on ahead collision course interception."

Gloster was already gearing up to build the Thin Wing Javelin at this point as the RAF's interim all-weather interceptor missile platform similar to that latterly proposed by English Electric with its P.12 and Avro Canada's CF-105.

The brochure continued: "Within the time scale in view for introduction into service, and against the prospect of further advance in target speeds it has been recently suggested that the F.153D in its present form may fall short of future requirements.

"Consideration has, therefore, been given to further development of the F.153D with the objective of raising it to the category of a truly supersonic fighter, which would serve as a valuable interim type pending the introduction of the more advanced aircraft and equipment now being planned."

In addition to extending the aircraft's fuselage, consideration had been given to thinning the wings down still further – but this was ruled out because it would "severely reduce fuel capacity and would involve an extent of structural redesign resulting in what would be virtually a completely new aircraft".

The primary role envisaged for this lengthened and much faster Javelin would be "the interception of enemy bombers approaching our coastline, after receipt of the radar early warning. In arriving at a suitable fuel capacity to enable this role to be adequately fulfilled, it has been necessary to cover a range of variables related to fighter

and bomber speeds and operating altitudes". Ventral drop tanks would increase total fuel capacity to 2960 gallons.

With this configuration, Gloster estimated that a first prototype could make its first flight by December 1958, with an in-service date of late 1960 or early 1961.

Around two weeks later, on May 31, 1956, the Thin Wing Javelin project as a whole was cancelled. The first prototype is believed to have been substantially complete. Plans to purchase the Avro Canada CF-105 appear to have been dropped altogether at the same meeting – ending any hope of an interim all-weather interceptor for the RAF.

Macmillan's manifesto

It seemed as though Fairey's Large design, the Delta 3-in-waiting, had won the contest to become the RAF's ultimate Cold War interceptor. But the whole philosophy upon which the OR.329 interceptor concept was founded was about to face a challenge it could not overcome.

Harold Macmillan was Chancellor of the Exchequer from December 20, 1955, until January 10, 1957, when he became Prime Minister. On June 4, 1956, he asked that some notes he'd had prepared be circulated to Monckton, Secretary of State for

Gloster invested heavily in the F.153D Thin Wing Javelin project and was not far from completing the first prototype by May 1956. This photograph shows the fourth mock-up with normal Red Dean missile pylon. *Jet Age Museum*

Air Nigel Birch, Maudling and the Cabinet Office.

These notes encapsulated a growing feeling within government that fundamental change was needed in the way the RAF was supplied and, indeed, in what it might be required to do. Headed 'Military Aircraft Programme', their contents would have a profound effect on both the development of aircraft for the RAF and on the RAF itself. They began: "The crucial question is whether the UK can afford to maintain and arm Fighter Command unless the Command can be expected to provide effective defence against determined attacks with thermo-nuclear weapons. Can it prevent enough Russian bombers (and, later, guided weapons) from evading the defences and paralysing the country?

"Can it hope to do more than mitigate to a relatively small extent the full severity of the attack, whatever the target? If not, can the government justifiably spend up to £1000m on this sort of 'secondary deterrent' during the next 10 years, with all that means in the shape of continuing drain on the UK economy (brains, skill materials etc.)?

"As regards the protection of strategic bomber bases in the UK, in order to ensure retaliation if the deterrent policy fails, are not the chief safeguards (a) dispersion; (b) the early warning system?

"Assuming that (i) Fighter Command cannot achieve its real purpose in global war; (ii) it has no part to play in other types of war; (iii) that the advent of the ballistic missile must in any case set a term to all fighter effectiveness against long-range attack, is not the sensible, though difficult, decision for the government the abolition of Fighter Command?

"This need not, however, be done at once. Action to carry out so important a decision must be planned if too great a strain is not to be placed on the RAF, the aircraft industry and the public.

"And in any case the Americans are (we hope) to pay for most of the Hunters and Javelins now coming into service. We must, for this and wider reasons, try to carry the Americans with us.

"The Government should decide now, however, that the Hunters and Javelins, which are planned to continue until 1959-60 in any case (this period might be stretched somewhat), should be the last aircraft to enter into service with Fighter Command.

"The exact date for the abolition of Fighter Command can be set later after a decision in principle has been reached. In the meantime it could be reduced in size. A start should be made in the current year as a contribution to the £100m.

"The effect of the foregoing on the aircraft programme must be that none of the fighters proposed should be developed or produced unless there is an agreed (underlined) requirement for it for service in the RAF overseas or in the Navy. This probably means that, the thin-winged Javelin and the CF-105 having disappeared, the Government should not buy more than one of the P.1, P.177 and OR.329 – or perhaps some aircraft not now in the programme at all.

"The UK surface-to-air and air-to-air guided weapon programmes for the defence of the UK will also need review. As regards the deterrent, as the United Kingdom's main political and defence instrument, the Minister of Defence's proposals for the Victor and the Vulcan should be accepted. There should, however, be further study of the size of the deterrent force, which must be kept down to the minimum necessary for our purposes."

These notes make Macmillan's plans for the future of the RAF very clear – no more Fighter Command

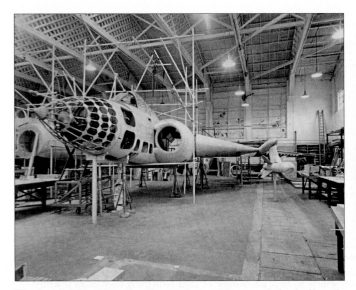

The fourth Thin Wing Javelin mock-up with extended missile pylon. *Jet Age Museum*

The starboard side of the cockpit inside the Thin Wing Javelin mock-up. *Jet Age Museum*

and only one future fighter. Monckton, Birch and Maudling, now burdened by this knowledge, had the difficult and unpleasant task of preparing their respective ministries for the increasingly likely event that it would become official government policy.

Defence review

The first draft of a new specification, F.155D, was completed during June 1956. This was largely a restatement of F.155T (Issue 2) but with additional procedural clauses added at the beginning to cover a chosen design, rather than a competition with an uncertain outcome. Point 1.4 began: "This specification is written to define the final development aircraft to be designed and constructed by", with a space left for whichever of AWA or Fairey was ultimately chosen to proceed, or both if that was going to be the case.

In July, British Prime Minister Anthony Eden ordered Field Marshal Sir Gerald Templer to begin preparations for an invasion of Egypt. At the end of the month, the Ministry of Defence's chief scientific advisor, Sir Frederick Brundrett, told the Deputy Chief of the Air Staff, Sir Geoffrey Tuttle, who had now replaced Sir Thomas Pike, that he

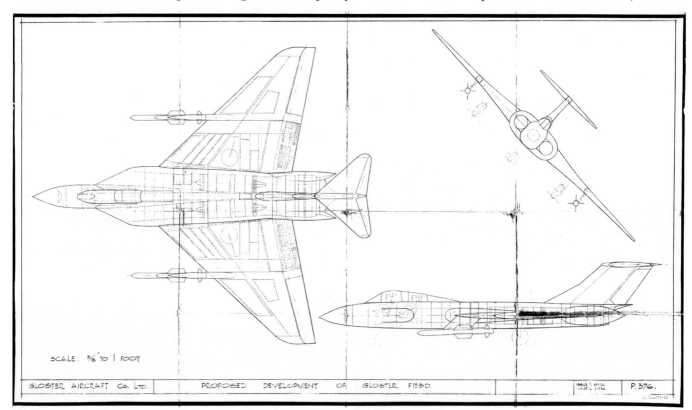

By early May 1956, Gloster was aware its F.153D Thin Wing Javelin project was in danger of cancellation. It responded with this proposal for a truly supersonic Javelin – created by lengthening the fuselage to take advantage of area rule for a maximum claimed top speed of Mach 1.79. *Jet Age Museum*

thought OR.329 would be cancelled. On August 1, 1956, Satterly wrote to Tuttle: "I understand that Sir Frederick Brundrett thinks OR.329 will not be allowed to go ahead in its present form but that a fighter will be allowed providing it has longer range."

He told Tuttle that by replacing most of its rocket fuel with kerosene and carrying a 10% fuel overload, the AWA design's interception sortie range could be increased to more than 400 miles. The Fairey design's could be increased to between 345 and 400 miles. Range for a patrol sortie would be 172 miles with the AWA aloft for an hour and the Fairey up for 45 minutes, flying at Mach 0.9, with five minutes' combat at Mach 2.

He finished the letter with: "We must realise that each month of delay in getting on with OR.329 will bring it later into service and make it more likely to be obsolescent when introduced. A new OR will put the whole thing back between one and two years.

"I most strongly recommend that we should be allowed to go ahead with the present selected designs and that the firms be given the minimum financial cover they need to do so. If the final decision is adverse, less damage will have been done than if we just do nothing."

Tuttle wrote to Baker at the MoS on August 9, saying the OR.329 project was on hold pending approval from the Chiefs of Staff, which had not yet been forthcoming. "Nevertheless," he wrote, "I would be glad to be assured that all preparatory paperwork is being carried out so that when final approval is given there will be no delay."

He wrote back to Satterly, thanking him for the range options, but also stating: "I think you will know that one of the cuts which the Controller of Aircraft thinks may be forced upon him, when the Ministry of Supply R&D budget is reduced

to £175m, is the removal of OR.329 from the programme. In addition to this there are others who feel it is not necessary, and I shall not have an easy time keeping it in the programme".

Wheeler wrote to Tuttle on August 27, 1956, outlining all the reasons why the ministry felt that the RAF needed the OR.329 fighter: "The intelligence staff have recently estimated that a manned supersonic threat will start to come into service in the early 1960s and that by about 1964/65 we can expect a threat of about Mach 2 at 60,000ft or greater. The most advanced fighter under development in this country, the F.177 due in service in late 1960/early 1961, is limited to meeting a maximum threat of Mach 1.5 up to 65,000ft.

"Even this threat can only be intercepted with continental early warning and considerable accuracy and control. The height performance of all other fighters, including F-102, is inadequate. In other words, the OR.329 fighter is the only fighter with a capability of meeting the threat of Mach 2 at 65,000ft."

In an unused draft version of this letter, Wheeler was slightly less definite in this last paragraph, stating instead: "The height performance of the F.23, the CF-105 and as at present designed the F-102B are of course quite inadequate. The only possible contender is the F-103 or a development of the CF-105."

The Republic F-103 was intended to replace the F-102 Delta Dagger, which itself had only just entered service in 1956, and reach speeds of up to Mach 3. It was cancelled in 1957.

Baker replied to Tuttle on August 30, saying: "I am sending you the following just to keep the record straight. The present position is that we are allowing both Faireys and AWA to continue with work on wind tunnel models but, in the present financial climate, we would not be

justified in authorising any further expenditure on the project.

"It would, I consider, be premature to come to any final decision about placing the contracts until we have a decision from Ministers about the future of OR.329."

He said no decision could be taken until the defence review was complete.

On September 25, 1956, Wheeler wrote a 'loose minute' for Satterly ahead of a meeting with the Secretary of State for Air, Nigel Birch, later that day. This looked at how well suited or otherwise the F.155T aircraft might be for taking on other roles, such as defence against fighters overseas, tactical strike with nuclear bombs or reconnaissance.

Wheeler wrote that Fairey had produced a supplement to its brochure, outlining how its F.155T design could be used in tactical strike and photo reconnaissance. It would be able to meet the necessary 690-mile radius of action requirement if it used Rolls-Royce Olympus engines and could have an all-up-weight increase to 85,000lb.

"The cruising speed of the Fairey aircraft is, in fact, Mach 0.94, slightly in excess of the requirement. In this configuration the aircraft would carry a ventral drop tank with a special weapon under one wing and an additional drop tank under the other wing.

"Nobody has yet carried out a detailed examination of the requirement for navigation but undoubtedly we would have to remove such features as the AI in order to get in the navigation equipment."

Under a heading of 'fighter operations in overseas theatres' however, Wheeler wrote: "As you are aware, I frankly cannot see a fighter of the OR.329 type being used in any role as a fighter other than as an interceptor in the straightforward air defence role. I cannot, for example, conceive how

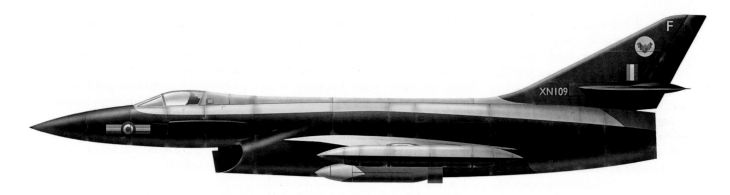

Hawker P.1116 long-range interceptor and ground-attack aircraft. *Art by Daniel Uhr*

this particular aircraft could fight against another fighter.

"I am therefore assuming that the use of this aircraft overseas would be limited to the defence of our bases and in this respect I do not believe that the problem would be basically dissimilar to that of UK defence. In the UK defence environment OR.329 can intercept a threat of about Mach 1.8 at 65,000ft with 220 nautical miles early warning and up to about Mach 2.5 at the same height with unlimited warning.

"Assuming that in a limited war we are almost certain to be up against a country with at least moral, and possibly material, support from the Soviet Union, I suggest that it would be unwise to assume a threat much less than we will expect in the UK. The Intelligence Staff have recently estimated that a manned supersonic threat will start to come into service in the early 1960s and that by 1964/65 we can expect a threat of about Mach 2 at 60,000ft or greater. By the time OR.329 is in service I therefore think it reasonable for us to expect to meet a supersonic threat in overseas theatres.

"My conclusion therefore is that the ground environment for the defence of overseas bases will be comparable with that in the UK if an aircraft of the OR.329 type is to be operated effectively against a supersonic threat."

OR.329 as a bomber
During the meeting itself, Birch

seems to have been preoccupied with the need for an aircraft that could perform tactical strike operations. According to the meeting notes, Satterly "confirmed that OR.329 could follow the present Air Staff policy of starting life as a pure fighter and later be downgraded to the fighter/bomber role, with the subsequent loss of operational performance". He also "emphasised that OR.329 could not be considered as the Canberra replacement". Birch then "enquired when the paper on the tactical bomber would be ready".

This theme was continued in a letter from Ewen Broadbent, Birch's private secretary, sent to Tuttle a week later. He stated that there were two points Birch wanted to raise with him, the first concerning the establishment of joint project teams and the second was: "How far have we got in precise evaluation from Faireys or indeed from any other firms about using OR.329 to carry one or two 1000 pounders. The Secretary of State believes that Faireys have produced a brochure on how their version of OR.329 could be used in various roles and he would like to know how realistic the firm's plans are and whether they have been examined carefully by specialists.

"The Secretary of State is wondering whether anything more should be done at this stage to examine this problem now that this bombing capability in limited

war has become so linked with an aircraft of the OR.329 type."

The next day, October 3, 1956, Tuttle's own private secretary Anthony Bennell wrote to Satterly asking him to urgently supply Tuttle with answers to Birch's questions. At the end of the latter, he wrote: "P.S. The Chief of Air Staff (Sir Dermot Boyle) has seen the minute from the private secretary to the Secretary of State which I have copied. He considers it as important to evaluate the practicability of carrying a ground attack rocket on the aircraft being developed to meet OR.329 as 1000 pounders."

Satterly's response of October 4 states: "Air Staff policy for fighter aircraft has always been to design for the primary role of interceptor fighter, and then to begin to adapt the aircraft to perform as well as possible in its secondary ground attack role after the first prototype has flown. To date this policy has proved successful, although the increasing performance of modern fighters has, of course, made it progressively more difficult to include an adequate ground attack capability."

He said Fairey had been asked to carry out a preliminary examination of their aircraft's ground attack potential and they had supplied some information: "Tactical atom bomb. The aircraft can be made to carry the tactical atom bomb and will have a usable range when this is fitted. However, the provision

Gloster F.153D Thin Wing Javelin. *Art by Daniel Uhr*

of the necessary sighting and navigation systems will lead to extensive aircraft modifications, and we are not able to comment in detail without further serious study of this problem.

"One thousand pound HE bombs and/or rocket projectiles. Provision for the carriage of these weapons can be made. It will be necessary for a pilot attack sight to be provided for the accurate aiming of the weapon, and we cannot estimate the extent of the aircraft modification needed without further study."

Satterly said the OR.329 could be made to carry bombs and rockets but said there would be limits to the aircraft's tactical capability since "it has no blind bombing capability and is incapable of navigation beyond the line of sight, and will have very restricted reconnaissance capability. It therefore does not meet our requirement for a tactical strike/reconnaissance aircraft, the details of which are in our paper and draft OR, which I shall be sending you very shortly.

"There are, therefore, two separate requirements: i) OR.329 as an interceptor fighter. ii) A tactical strike/reconnaissance aircraft for use in global and limited wars. As I have said, OR.329 cannot really meet our needs in the second case. On the other hand, there does not seem to be any insurmountable reason why OR.329 should not eventually be used in a limited ground attack role, although the limitations will

undoubtedly be much more severe than with previous fighters."

At this point, the Chief of Air Staff Sir Dermot Boyle appears to have intervened and asked Tuttle to approach Fairey with a proposal of his own – why not just build a new all-weather fighter based on a scaled-up version of the world record-breaking Fairey Delta 2?

Tuttle drafted a response on October 11, under the heading 'OR.329': "I have discussed the possibility of getting a blown-up version of the Fairey F.2D World Record breaker being made into an all-weather fighter with Mr Lickley, chief engineer of the Fairey Aviation Co. The situation would appear to be as follows. He considers that it is possible to produce such an aeroplane, but that it would only arrive in service one year sooner than the fighter properly designed and built to meet OR.329.

"His own view is that we should get that aeroplane in five years and the one to OR.329 in six years. My own view is that he is very optimistic on both, but that the difference in time is correct, i.e. one year. The aircraft would, however, not be made of steel and would be limited even in a dive to a Mach of 2.2 because of structural overheating problems. This would mean that it could never deal with a Mach 2 enemy bomber.

"Either aircraft would have to have a Mk.3 Blue Jay or a British-made Mk.3 Sparrow, under licence from USA or a new weapon which

might be Red Hebe because that is already partly designed. The blown-up version of the F.2D would be about 30,000lb all-up-weight and that to OR.329 about 46,000lb and the former will have to have a developed version of an existing engine i.e. the Olympus or Conway, giving another limitation to its further development.

"I feel very strongly that we would be most unwise to consider this makeshift aeroplane any further because it will only distract others, delay a decision on OR.329 and finally if it went ahead give something which is inadequate and incapable of development. I am certain that it would be wrong for a gain of one year in six to go in for such an aeroplane of marginal advantage."

The final version of his response to Boyle was toned down somewhat, omitting the mentions of world records and the design being a 'blown-up' version; it was instead couched as though Boyle had suggested a return to the Fairey Small of the original tender competition – which does not seem to have been quite what Boyle had been thinking of.

On October 18, Monckton was removed from office as Minister of Defence for opposing Eden's plans for Suez and replaced by Anthony Head.

Cancellation
On October 25, 1956, Satterly wrote

to Kirkpatrick, saying: "Lickley tells me that the Ministry of Supply are pressing him to concentrate more on the tactical bomber as a successor to the Canberra, and to relax his efforts on the OR.329. I have told him that we would much prefer him to press on with OR.329 in accordance with his contract because we ought to get a decision in the near future."

Satterly also wrote to Tuttle on the same day, telling him: "Mr Lickley of Fairey's rang this morning to tell me that they fired their first model of OR.329 yesterday on the Larkhill range. It was apparently successful, although the records have not yet been examined. It achieved a speed of between 1500 and 2000ft per second (I understand this is equivalent to between Mach 1.4 and Mach 1.8). Lickley says that Fairey's have a small contract to continue with their model work, but are themselves financing a great deal of the development project work.

"By about Christmas they will have to review this expenditure and will probably have to stop unless a decision is taken by that time to proceed with OR.329 on the normal basis."

Broadbent wrote a memo to Assistant Under-Secretary of State (Air), Ronald Henry Melville, also on October 25, stating that Secretary of State Birch had discussed OR.329 the day before with Tuttle and was now "greatly concerned that little, if any, development work is going on (he understands that the firm have financial authority to spend something like £300 a week) especially now that this aircraft is considered capable of fulfilling the other role of the Canberra replacement". Birch agreed with Tuttle "that it would be desirable to send a minute to the Minister of Defence drawing his attention to the serious effects of having no decision as yet on OR.329 and suggesting that some greater temporary cover should be given to the firm".

Melville wrote back five days later: "The Ministry of Supply tell me that Fairey's have been allotted £50,000 in all, which ought to keep them going up to the end of the year; Armstrong Whitworth's have been allotted between £20,000 and £30,000, and have not asked for more, and the Ministry of Supply believe they are going slow, since they have got wind that their version is not particularly favoured."

The invasion of Egypt initiated by Prime Minister Eden, the Suez Crisis, began at the end of October and ended in ignominy on November 7 thanks to pressure from the US to call a ceasefire before its objective, the capture of the Suez Canal, was achieved. Eden survived a vote of confidence to remain prime minister on November 8.

OR.329 was discussed by Birch, Minister of Supply Reginald Maudling, Ministry of Supply Controller of Aircraft Sir Claude Pelly and Tuttle at their regular progress meeting on November 13. Birch told Maudling about his "growing concern at the lack of decision on this project". Maudling said "Fairey's and Armstrong Whitworth's were keeping going only with difficulty and with insufficient money" and he "enquired whether there had been any recent changes in the RAF requirement". Tuttle then "explained that we wanted to go ahead with OR.329 as it was drawn up but that recent developments had led the Air Ministry to decide that they would also wish to use this fighter, suitably adapted, in other roles and especially those of ground attack and light bombing".

Pelly "confirmed that he was increasingly confident that the Fairey aircraft should be able to carry out these roles as much successful trial flying had been carried out on the Fairey Delta". At this, Maudling asked whether Fairey's aircraft could also carry out the role of the aircraft chosen to

fulfil OR.330 – the Avro 730. Tuttle patiently explained "that this aircraft could not be regarded in any way as an alternative to OR.330".

According to the minutes of the meeting, it was "then considered whether the selected version should be the Fairey or Armstrong-Whitworth design. It was pointed out that the Fairey version would need a new engine which might add £3-4m a year to the R&D programme. On the other hand it was argued that the Armstrong-Whitworth version would probably be obsolescent by the time it came into service and that the Germans were regarding the P.177 as a lead in to the Fairey version of the OR.329. It was confirmed that the Air Ministry requirement was for the Fairey version of OR.329".

Maudling "mentioned two other aircraft which might possibly carry out the OR.329 role i.e. NA.39 (Blackburn Buccaneer) and the private venture supersonic aircraft being designed by Hawkers (the already-rejected Hawker P.1103's advanced derivatives – the P.1116 and P.1121). It was stated that the Air Ministry could not at this stage give a final opinion on those aircraft although it was unlikely that they would find attractions in the Hawker aircraft which appeared to be an inferior version of the Fairey design for OR.329".

On the Buccaneer, Tuttle stated that "the Air Ministry might have a requirement if the department had no success over a special aircraft for the Canberra replacement".

A memo to Kirkpatrick dated November 30, 1956, stated that Pelly had "recently written to Armstrong Whitworth's saying that they have not been successful in the F.155 competition, this decision arising from discussions between our respective Ministers. This leaves only Fairey's in the field, so that we are now in a slightly less complicated position in that since we know who will do the job if it does go ahead we could, without committing the department, explore directly with Fairey's any possible changes in the concept. From the latest Fairey brochure, dated November 1956, you will see the direction in which their own thoughts are going, which, with the deletion of the rocket engine installation, is a very major change".

On December 12, 1956, Wing Commander Thomas Balmforth of operational requirements wrote to Wheeler, saying: "In view of OR.339 (this number seems to be an unfortunate choice and may lead to confusion), the tactical strike requirement, can we come out in the open and ask for a nuclear/LABS capability, or even a conventional ground attack capability, in OR.329? I think perhaps our tactic should be that OR.329 remains purely the interceptor, in which case there should be few, if any amendments to the OR. However, this may not be accepted. It is not difficult to foresee a situation where we have to choose between getting OR.329 or OR.339. Our line of action here is relevant because if 329 is chosen, we may well wish at a later date to increase the factors to give us an offensive capability as a secondary role."

Eden resigned on January 9, 1957, after doctors told him his life would be at risk if he continued in office. Harold Macmillan was appointed as his successor by the Queen the following day. He brought in Duncan Sandys as his Minister of Defence four days later, replacing Head – who had only held the post for just over two months. Two days after that, Reginald Maudling was removed as Minister of Supply and replaced by Aubrey Jones, the former Minister of Fuel and Power. On the same day, Nigel Birch lost his post as Secretary of State for Air and was replaced by George Ward.

A special meeting of the Air Council took place on February 21, 1957 – just under six weeks after Macmillan's appointment – at which it was agreed that OR.329, along with OR.330 and OR.337 (the RAF version of the Saunders-Roe P.177) should be cancelled. By early 1957, Kirkpatrick was gone too. His replacement as Director of Operational Requirements, Air Commodore Jack Fendick Roulston, drafted the announcement on March 11, 1957, headed 'Cancellation of ORs 337, 329 and 330, and their associated equipments'.

He wrote: "The Air Staff has recently carried out an examination of the contribution which manned fighter aircraft could make to the defence of the United Kingdom. In view of recent technological advances and the fact that the major threat to this country is changing fairly rapidly from aircraft carrying nuclear weapons to one of ballistic missiles with nuclear warheads, it has now been decided that the contribution which future manned fighters could make is insufficient to warrant their development.

"In place of manned fighters it has been decided that surface-to-air guided weapons should be introduced as soon as possible. It is also thought that by eliminating any further expenditure of effort on fighter systems a worthwhile release of technical effort, which could be diverted to surface-to-air guided weapons development, will be made.

"The developed F.23 is expected to be able to deal with the manned aircraft threat within its timescale and its development is therefore to be continued. The development of the aircraft to ORs 337 and 329, and any work on equipment peculiar to these aircraft is no longer required by the Air Staff. At the same time, the Air Staff has also examined the problem of maintaining deterrent. In view of the increasing capacity of the Russian defensive systems, it is now considered most unlikely that the aircraft to OR.330 could survive in the timescale when it would be operational.

"Since more certain methods of delivering nuclear weapons are expected to be available in the same timescale, the Air Staff now no longer require the development of the aircraft to OR.330 nor any equipment peculiar to this aircraft."

Defence White Paper 1957
By March 15, Sandys and the rest of the Cabinet, working closely together, were on to the third draft of a new statement on defence entitled 'Defence – Outline of Future Policy'. Fundamentally, it was a restating of Macmillan's 'Military Aircraft Programme' notes from nine months earlier. Under a heading of 'nuclear deterrent', the third draft stated: "Though the Hunters and Javelins of the Royal Air Force would, in the event of war with Russia, be able to take a substantial toll of Soviet bombers, a proportion would inevitably get through. Even if it were only a dozen, they could, with hydrogen bombs, inflict widespread devastation and might well blot out a large part of the population of the big cities.

"It must be frankly recognised that fighters cannot give the country as a whole any effective protection against the catastrophic consequences of nuclear attack. Clearly therefore the central aim of military policy must be to prevent war rather than prepare for it. In present circumstances the only way to deter nuclear aggression is to possess the means of retaliating in time."

The statement recognised that the free world "is almost wholly dependent for its protection upon the nuclear power of the United States", that Britain had a stock of atomic bombs, and a megaton weapon that had now been developed, and that the "means of delivering these weapons is provided by medium bombers of the V-class. These will in due course be supplemented and later replaced by ballistic rockets". This included American Thor missiles.

Though there was no way to protect cities against nuclear attack, "the defence of the very much smaller target presented by an airfield is an altogether more manageable task. There is every reason to believe that fighters would be able to interfere sufficiently with enemy bombers for the short time needed to enable the retaliatory force to take off.

"The Government have accordingly decided that air defence must be provided for the nuclear deterrent. A manned fighter force of adequate size for this purpose will be maintained. This will later be replaced by a ground-to-air guided missile system." The strength of the 2nd Tactical Air Force in Germany would be reduced by half within a year.

On March 25, 1957, Roulston ordered that 'histories' of the now-cancelled OR.329, 330 and 337 requirements should be written by the relevant project officers.

The fifth draft of the Cabinet statement was ready by March 26, with Sandys proposing to issue the White Paper on Monday, April 1. Now the Hunters and Javelins would take a "heavy" rather than "substantial" toll of Soviet bombers and for defending the airfields "a manned fighter force, smaller than at present but of adequate size for this limited purpose, will therefore be maintained". It would still be replaced by missiles later and the rest was much the same.

A sixth draft was published two days later – the sections referring to the RAF being much the same, although now the manned airfield defence fighters would "progressively be equipped with air-to-air guided missiles. These fighter aircraft will gradually be replaced by a ground-to-air guided missile system".

By the eighth draft, of April 1, the 'blotting out' of city populations had been removed and the manned fighter force with its guided missiles

would be replaced "in due course" by ground-to-air missiles, rather than "gradually".

Pelly personally wrote to Fairey director Geoffrey Hall on April 3 to say that "following the recent review of the defence programme, it has been decided not to proceed with the development of an aircraft to meet OR.329, and accordingly we shall, I regret to say, be unable to adopt the design which you tendered in the competition. Nevertheless, I would like you to know how much I appreciate the very great effort that went into your proposals for meeting this very difficult requirement, and I would ask you to convey my thanks to those of your staff who have contributed to the submission".

The final draft of the Cabinet statement, published on April 4, was much more specific than its predecessors. The original paragraphs on the Soviet bombers, the Hunters and the Javelins had changed to: "It must be frankly recognised that there is at present no means of providing adequate protection for the people of this country against the consequences of an attack with nuclear weapons.

"Though, in the event of war, the fighter aircraft of the Royal Air Force would unquestionably be able to take a heavy toll of enemy bombers, a proportion will inevitably get through. Even if it were only a dozen, they could with megaton bombs inflict widespread devastation. This makes it more than ever clear that the overriding consideration in all military planning must be to prevent war rather than prepare for it."

The manned fighter force, still smaller than at present, still with its missiles and its replacement in due course, then appears in the text much as it had before. But in the three days since the eighth draft, a new section had appeared which specifically addressed the future development of aircraft: "Having regard to the high performance

and potentialities of the Vulcan and Victor medium bombers and the likely progress of ballistic rockets and missile defence, the Government have decided not to go on with the development of a supersonic manned bomber, which could not be brought into service in much under 10 years.

"Work will proceed on the development of a ground-to-air missile defence system, which will in due course replace the manned aircraft of Fighter Command. In view of the good progress already made, the Government have come to the conclusion that the RAF are unlikely to have a requirement for fighter aircraft of types more advanced than the supersonic P.1, and work on such projects will stop."

This last-minute addition had very publicly ended all doubt about the Government's position on the types that had already been cancelled during the first weeks of Macmillan's new administration. However, it was not until April 15, 1957, that the Air Ministry's latest Director of Contracts, L Clifton, finally wrote to Fairey and informed them that "your tender for the design and supply of aircraft to Specification F.155T has been fully considered, and is declined with thanks".

Golden age no more

The defence spending boom brought on by the Korean War, coupled with American military aid for the war on communism, resulted in Britain's aviation industry being dramatically revived after its postwar slump.

By 1953 however, maintaining a vastly inflated defence budget was becoming difficult in the face of competing demands for funding from other economic sectors. The British government was also in the uncomfortable position of trying to find work for aircraft companies which otherwise would have gone out of business – despite growing unease about the number of projects begun during the panic of the early 1950s which were continuing to consume large sums of money.

Efforts to build a specialised high-performance interceptor to shoot down marauding Soviet bombers were regarded as critical – Britain's most important defence project – but were continually undermined by a lack of intelligence on the nature of the threat facing Britain. Fears about Soviet technological progress, apparently without basis in hard factual intelligence, resulted in changing demands particularly from the Air Staff for aircraft to meet ever more powerful enemy forces.

As the goalposts continued to shift, the numerous different aircraft companies involved were already beginning to feel the effects of defence spending being spread too thinly for so many different projects. Some, such as Armstrong Whitworth, had become primarily subcontractors – yet were still being invited to tender for major contracts alongside the much larger firms.

Tentative moves were being made to encourage closer collaboration between firms – but this had only limited results.

Meanwhile, guided missiles and nuclear weapons, another major consumer of defence funding, were making rapid technological progress and most believed that the Soviets would eventually switch to a policy of reliance on near-unstoppable ballistic weapons – the only defence against which would be to build up and maintain a rival stockpile of ballistic weapons.

This would quickly turn a large force of high-performance interceptors into a very expensive white elephant. Had the OR.329 aircraft been capable of conversion to a multi-role fighter-bomber, its chances of survival as a front line 2nd Tactical Air Force bomber, for example, might have improved – but it was too highly specialised to carry out any other role.

Harold Macmillan, Minister of Defence when critical decisions were being taken about guided weapons projects such as the Blue Streak ballistic missile, became Chancellor of the Exchequer at the end of 1955; he found himself in a better position to begin making moves towards changing government policy in favour of nuclear deterrent as Britain's primary means of defence. The Suez Crisis and Eden's subsequent fall from grace left the door wide open.

His appointment of Duncan Sandys as Minister of Defence ensured that his policy would meet with no resistance – Sandys had been instrumental in getting Blue Streak into development during his time as Minister of Supply between 1951 and 1954, shortly before Macmillan became Minister of Defence.

It was evident to both men that switching to a nuclear deterrent – a threat of attack – would be much cheaper than attempting to mount an effective defence. It is not clear whether they had extrapolated the full consequences of this move in the first instance, but it would later allow finances to be shifted away from defence and for the badly-needed reorganisation of the British aviation industry to begin.

Looking back from April 1957, it must have been abundantly clear to most observers that Maudling's five-year plan of March 9, 1956, to keep the entire industry – in some ways little changed since the closing days of the Second World War – ticking over with just enough work for everyone, was unsustainable. With the cancellation of the largest projects then occupying the industry, an opportunity had presented itself to solve the problem of too many firms competing for too little money. Whether the ensuing process of enforced mergers and acquisitions was then allowed to go too far is debatable, but it was the end of a golden age for Britain's aircraft manufacturing industry and the end too for the ultimate Cold War interceptor.

Sources

The content of this book is based almost entirely on primary sources – original period documents – with very little drawn from secondary or tertiary sources. While several of the sources used are currently held in private or company collections and are therefore inaccessible to the public, copies of most can be found at the National Archives at Kew in London, UK, under the following references:

AIR 2/13042 Examination of firms' tender designs
AIR 2/13059 All weather interceptor O.R. 329 policy
AIR 2/15106 Generation of fighters to succeed Swift, Javelin and F23/48 O.R. 329 part 1
AIR 2/15107 Generation of fighters to succeed Swift, Javelin and F23/48 O.R. 329 part 2
AIR 2/13418 Rocket fighter – development policy
AIR 6/110 Air Council conclusions of meeting 21st February 1957
AIR 19/670 Aircraft production and development: policy
AIR 19/937 Fighter aircraft: correspondence and brief
AIR 19/1099 Air defence of UK: policy
AIR 20/6749 RAF: Fighter Command (Code 67/12): Proposed development plans for years 1950-1957
AVIA 6/17937 Investigation into an aircraft to fly at Mach 2 (RAE STRUT 131)
AVIA 6/18867 Interim note on some characteristics of supersonic fighter defence based on O.R. 329
AVIA 6/19287 Defence against high altitude bombers by Mach 2 fighters
AVIA 15/3910 Aircraft: manufacture and production: general (code 7/1): Aircraft specification numbers
AVIA 53/501 Tender for design and supply of aircraft to Specification F.155T
AVIA 53/502 Sir W G Armstrong Whitworth Aircraft design brochures for Specification F.155T
AVIA 53/503 De Havilland Aircraft Co design brochures for Specification F.155T
AVIA 53/504 English Electric Co design brochures for Specification F.155T
AVIA 53/505 Fairey Aviation Co design brochures for Specification F.155T
AVIA 53/506 Hawker Aircraft design brochures for Specification F.155T
AVIA 53/507 Saunders-Roe design brochures for Specification F.155T
AVIA 53/508 Vickers-Armstrongs design brochures for Specification F.155T
AVIA 54/2305 Index of aircraft specifications 1950-1957
AVIA 65/92 All-weather interceptor aircraft F.155T: tender design competition
AVIA 65/93 All-weather interceptor aircraft F.155T: action on specification
AVIA 65/94 All-weather interceptor aircraft F.155T: technical policy
AVIA 65/95 All-weather interceptor aircraft F.155T: flight performance
AVIA 65/293 F.155 day/night high altitude fighter: tender assessment
AVIA 65/629 F.155 day/night high altitude fighter: tender assessment
AVIA 65/1407 Research aircraft to specification E.R. 134: finance and policy
CAB 21/3472 Aircraft industry working party
CAB 128/31 Cabinet: minutes
CAB 128/32 Cabinet: minutes
CAB 128/33 Cabinet: minutes
CAB 129/88 Cabinet: memoranda
CAB 129/92 Cabinet: memoranda
CAB 129/95 Cabinet: memoranda
CAB 129/99 Cabinet: memoranda
CAB 129/100 Cabinet: memoranda
CAB 129/106 Cabinet: memoranda
CAB 129/107 Cabinet: memoranda
CAB 129/109 Cabinet: memoranda
CAB 195/16 Cabinet: meetings on the aircraft industry

CAB 195/17 Cabinet: meetings on the aircraft industry
CAB 195/18 Cabinet: meetings on the aircraft industry
DEFE 7/970 Air defence of Great Britain
DEFE 7/1128 Review of aircraft development and production
DEFE 7/1815 Size and future of Fighter Command
PREM 11/1712 Prime Minister's Office: correspondence and papers on military aircraft production
PREM 11/2214 Future size and shape of UK aircraft industry

Bibliography

While this book was compiled using primary source material almost exclusively, the following list is offered as an opportunity for further reading on the subject of British aircraft projects during the postwar period.

Battle Flight: RAF Air Defence Projects and Weapons Since 1945 by Chris Gibson
Black Box Canberras: British Test and Trials Canberras Since 1951 by Dave Forster
British Experimental Jet Aircraft by Barrie Hygate
British Secret Projects 1: Jet Fighters Since 1950 by Tony Buttler
British Secret Projects 5: Britain's Space Shuttle by Dan Sharp
Hawker P.1103 and P.1121: Camm's Last Fighter Projects by Paul Martell-Mead and Barrie Hygate
Listening In: Electronic Intelligence Gathering Since 1945 by Dave Forster and Chris Gibson
Project Cancelled by Derek Wood
The Saga of SR.53 by Henry Matthew and Allan Wood
TSR2: Britain's Lost Bomber by Damien Burke
TSR2: Britain's Lost Cold War Strike Aircraft by Tim McLelland and Tony Buttler

Index